Saumya Roy is a journalist and s~~…~~
in Mumbai. In 2010, she co-foun~~…~~
to support the livelihoods of M~~…~~
entrepreneurs; through this she ~~…~~
depend on Deonar. Her writing has appeared in *Forbes*
India, wsj.com and *Bloomberg News* among others, and she
has contributed a chapter to *Dharavi: The Cities Within*
(HarperCollins, 2013), an anthology of essays on Asia's
largest slum.

Praise for *Mountain Tales*

'It is rare that a book is a deeply moving love story
with unforgettable characters while also illuminating a
country and a culture. Saumya Roy's book is a riveting
love story set in the harrowing world of life as a trash
picker on Mumbai's garbage mountain. Read it for a most
delicious story, read it to understand India, read it to
know what it is like to grow up in extreme poverty in the
shadow of enormous wealth. If you read one book about
India, read this one' Geeta Anand, Pulitzer Prize winner
and author of *The Cure*

'Roy writes ... with utmost care and empathy ... [a]
powerful book' *Times of India*

'A terrific and thrilling book about people who are
trapped in the gravitational force of a garbage mountain
in Mumbai. Delightful and powerful' Manu Joseph,
author of *Serious Men*

'Roy unravels the truth about overconsumption,
pollution, climate change and how the most vulnerable
people bear the brunt of it all' *Vogue India*

'Roy has a journalist's unflinching eye, a poet's talent for detail and a radical sense of empathy that illuminates this account of the people who live on the Deonar garbage mountains. Urgent as a thriller, yet lingering in its unforgettable portraits of life, love and death, *Mountain Tales* deserves every accolade. A stunning achievement' Kiran Desai, Booker Prize-winning author of *The Inheritance of Loss*

'Saumya Roy's gorgeous *Mountain Tales* is a remarkable feat of immersive reporting and storytelling, a deeply felt exploration of ideas and a gripping chronicle of the fates of the garbage-pickers of Mumbai; Roy immerses you so deeply in her characters' lives and physical environment that at times I felt I was experiencing them myself. I loved this book' Suzy Hansen, author of *Notes on a Foreign Country*

'A gut-wrenching story ... her lucid writing not only draws the reader but also helps to reflect upon how one person's trash impacts another's life' Soma Basu, *The Hindu*

'Gorgeous and heartbreaking ... Roy succeeds in humanising her subjects while emphasising the role that consumer culture plays in their degradation ... Readers of *Behind the Beautiful Forevers* will be drawn to this harrowing portrait' *Publishers Weekly*

'A story of selflessness and sacrifice, of acceptance and renewal. The goodness in people, both in the streets where the Shaikh family lives and beyond, comes to the fore ... A sense of mystery and wonderment gives Roy's tale a special edge' Mustansir Dalvi, *Wire India*

MOUNTAIN TALES

Love and Loss in the Municipality of Castaway Belongings

SAUMYA ROY

P

PROFILE BOOKS

This paperback edition first published in 2022

First published in Great Britain in 2021 by
Profile Books Ltd
29 Cloth Fair
London
ECIA 7JQ

www.profilebooks.com

1 3 5 7 9 10 8 6 4 2

Typeset in Berling Nova Text by MacGuru Ltd
Printed and bound in Great Britain by
CPI Group (UK) Ltd, Croydon CR0 4YY

A CIP catalogue record for this book is
available from the British Library.

ISBN 978 1 78816 537 2
eISBN 978 1 78283 710 7

My grandmother, professor and poet, who wrote –

have you seen, my friend?
on the peaks of inky, dark, rain cloud-topped mountains,
snowy white illuminating clouds appear sometimes?

and Prashant Kant, my uncle,
who could not see but showed me how to spot the
illuminating clouds.

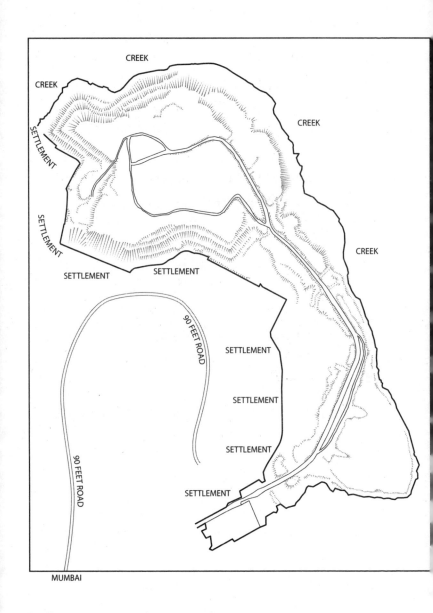

For illustrative purposes only

Cast of Principal Characters

At the Mountains

Hyder Ali Shaikh: Waste-picker at the Deonar garbage mountains; father of Farzana and her eight siblings

Shakimun Ali Shaikh: Hyder Ali's wife; mother of Farzana and her siblings

Jehana Shaikh: The oldest of the nine children

Jehangir Shaikh: Hyder Ali's oldest son and the second oldest of the children

Rakila Shaikh: Jehangir's wife, and mother of their three children

Alamgir Shaikh: Hyder Ali's second oldest son, who drives garbage trucks

Yasmeen Shaikh: Alamgir's wife and mother of their two children

Sahani Shaikh: The second oldest of the Shaikh daughters

Ismail Shaikh: Sahani's husband, who does odd jobs around the mountains

Afsana Shaikh: The third-oldest sister, and the only one to have left the mountains. A seamstress and mother of two

Farzana Shaikh: Hyder Ali and Shakimun's fourth daughter, and the sixth of the nine children

Farha Shaikh: The sister who comes after Farzana; the two often pick together

Jannat Shaikh: The youngest of the daughters

Ramzan Shaikh: The youngest of the siblings, a son

Badre Alam: Hyder Ali's cousin. He lives in the loft of the Ali's home

Moharram Ali Siddique: A waste-picker known for working night shifts and finding treasures in mountain trash

Yasmin Siddique: Moharram Ali's wife, and mother of their five children

Hera Siddique: Moharram Ali's oldest child; one of the few girls from the lanes to have made it to high school

Sharib Siddique: The older of Moharram Ali's two sons; he often misses school to pick on the mountains

Sameer Siddique: The younger of Moharram Ali's sons

Mehrun Siddique: Moharram Ali and Yasmin's middle daughter

Ashra Siddique: the youngest of the Siddique children

Salma Shaikh: A waste-picker; she arrived at the mountains with her two children more than three decades ago

Aslam Shaikh: Salma's older son, married to Shiva; the father of four sons and a daughter

Arif Shaikh: One of Aslam's four sons

Vitabai Kamble: Said to be one of the oldest waste-pickers on the mountains; she came to live at the mountains' rim in the mid-seventies with her husband and children

Nagesh Kamble: Vitabai's oldest son; he came to pick at the mountains as a ten-year-old

Babita Kamble: Vitabai's daughter

Rafique Khan: A garbage trader who also runs garbage trucks

Atique Khan: Rafique's younger brother, also a trader

In the Court

Dr Sandip Rane: A doctor who lives in a genteel neighbourhood near the mountains' rim. In 2008 he had filed a contempt case against the municipality for failing to close the mountains down

Justice Dhananjaya Chandrachud: The judge who adjudicated on Dr Rane's case in the Bombay High Court

Raj Kumar Sharma: A local resident who grew up in a leafy area not far from the mountains; he filed a court case in December 2015 asking for the mountains to be mended

Justice Abhay Oka: The judge presiding for several years over the court cases regarding Deonar

Introduction

I first met the waste-pickers of Deonar in the summer of 2013, when they began coming to the office of the micro-finance non-profit I ran in Mumbai,* looking for small, low-interest loans. They worked on the garbage mountains at the edge of the city, collecting trash to resell, they told me. I followed them back there, partly to find out what they did with their loans, but also to see this strange place, which I had heard of but, like most Mumbaikars, had never seen. I found a vast township of trash growing invisibly in plain sight – mountains that were more than 120 feet high, surrounded on one side by the Arabian Sea and on the other by a sequence of settlements strung along it.

Thus began my more than eight years' long entanglement with the Deonar mountains and their denizens. I watched the lives and businesses of four families unfold in their shadow. Most of all I watched a teenager, Farzana Ali Shaikh, grow into a life that seemed as unlikely as the mountains, rising precipitously with the desires that had flickered and died in the city. This book is Farzana's story,

---

* The city is referred to in the text as Bombay when that was the city's historical name, and as Mumbai after it changed its name in 1995.

her family's and her neighbours' story, and I am grateful for their permission to write about it.

I came to view the mountains as the pickers did: bringing the city's used luck, depositing its fading wealth in their hands. I attended hundreds of hours of court proceedings that aimed to control the city's waste, thinking every time that the mountains were about to move. I collected archival documents to unravel the rumours I heard. *Kachra train ni yaycha*, a picker had told me in one of my earlier walks on the mountains. *Garbage once came here by train.* It felt unreal, like many of the legends and lives around the slopes: a train service just for garbage? And yet it was true; years later I found myself at Oxford University's storied Bodleian Library, reading colonial records of how Bombay's garbage had indeed come to Deonar by train.

Deonar's mountainous township of trash created a world uniquely its own. And yet, wherever I went in the world, the pull of aspiration was just as unyielding, and as transient, throwing up waste mountains much like Deonar. A journalist friend had written of the 'waste Everest' outside Moscow. The mountains in Delhi were said to be nearly as tall as the Taj Mahal and had tumbled down in avalanches, as had others in Colombo, Addis Ababa and Shenzhen, killing people while I researched Deonar's more stable ones. One of the great urban legends of New York, I heard, was about the barge that floated off its coast, filled with the city's trash, with no state willing to accept it for burial. Then I met the former city official who had cut short a holiday to land the barge back in the city, the trash ending up at its own garbage mountains.

My years of walking the mountains showed me that, unlikely as the stories that emerged from Deonar's township of trash felt, most of them were real. Parts of them unfolded in one way or another in most cities. Waste masses even float in the sea, making islands. I came to see these mountains as an outpouring of our modern lives – of the endless chase for our desire to fill us with stuff. Our pursuit only lengthened these mountains, providing the raw material on which the waste-pickers built their lives, and left us unsated, searching for more, unseeing the world that our castaway possessions made.

The story that follows is of Deonar's mountainous township of trash and of the lives lived in its long shadow, but it is also a story of elsewhere.

1

Farzana Ali Shaikh rummaged on a mountain clearing on a hot April afternoon. The sun warmed her head and made lurid colours swim in her eyes. The smell of rotting prawns wafted up from the mountain. She jabbed her long garbage fork to push aside translucent fish scales, crackling prawn shells, entrails and animal dung, and scooped up the broken glass jars that had just poured out on the clearing.

Smoke and heat rose up, as forklifts shovelled glass away. It blurred Farzana's view of the trash strewn around her and brought up burning smells that mingled with the stench of decaying flesh. Scavenging birds swooped low beside her, searching for entrails. Farzana kept her eye on the glass and hacked her fork into the mess, keen to retrieve it. She didn't usually work on the *jhinga* or prawn loop, as this mountain was known. It was made up of remains from the city's municipal slaughterhouse and its vast port lands. That afternoon she and her younger sister, Farha, had chased a garbage truck winding up its unsteady slope.

Farzana worked quickly, shovelling glass jars, shards and saline bags that had fallen out of the truck into the large bag she dragged along. The truck had probably come from a hospital, and its contents would fetch good money. A straggly crowd built up around her, also eager for the glass. But, at seventeen, Farzana was tall, athletic and fearless.

Her eyes were trained to spot plastic bottles, wire, glass, German Silver – a metal alloy often used to make appliances and machinery – or cloth scraps. She snapped up her pickings before others could get to them.

She looked up to make sure that Farha was picking close by. It must nearly be time for their father to arrive with lunch, she thought. She clanked her fork into the glass heap again and, this time, brought out a heavy blue plastic bag. Farzana thought it must be filled with smaller glass bottles, which usually fetched a good price. She squatted on the warm fly-filled slope, untied the string and gently upturned the bag, expecting delicate glass vials to pour down, clinking and glinting in the sun. Instead a single large glass jar plopped onto the clearing. As she bent low to see what was inside, she could make out arms, legs, toes and tiny bald heads swimming into each other within it. She squinted, looked again and screamed. A few friends gathered to examine the jar crammed with floating limbs.

Farzana opened the lid and brought out a baby girl, a little bigger than her large, bony palm. The city sent a steady supply of dead babies, often girls, to the garbage mountains, along with its other expendables; mothers who couldn't bear to tell their families they had delivered a girl sometimes threw her in the trash instead. Farzana had occasionally unearthed them while rifling through rubbish. But as she tugged the baby girl out, two baby boys came up too, their stomachs fused to the girl's. The three had probably died together, unable to survive with or without each other, she thought. Farha said she had heard that lunar eclipses caused unborn babies to split or deform within wombs. This baby must have been born as three, she told the group.

5

Farzana stretched her arms out, cradling the life-less babies. She began to make her way carefully down the wobbly slope, holding them gently. Behind her, the mountain rose like a teetering hulk, made up of Mumbai's detritus, held in place with a topping of mud.

She waited for her friends to catch up. From high up on the next peak they could see the vertiginous trash mountains curve around them and stretch out into the distance. Together, the hills curled like a long sliver of crescent moon. Trash-made homes were dug into the inside of the moon's curve, and a shimmering creek arched around the outer edge. The creek ran into the Arabian Sea, which rimmed the island city of Mumbai. Rag-pickers such as Farzana called the garbage mountains *khaadi*, the Hindi word for creek. Nobody quite knew where the name came from but, standing high on a mountain clearing, you did feel as if you were floating in an undulating and smelly sea of garbage that faded into an unending expanse of glimmering blue sea in the distance. Farzana continued her walk through the rising and ebbing trash.

When they neared the creek, Farzana's friends dug their garbage forks into soft sand where the trash slopes petered into a rivulet. A few pickers came out of houses built on stilts, which lifted them above the trash at low tide and nearly immersed them in the waves at high tide. They walked over to see the babies and helped Farzana's friends shovel sand. The tide was rising and gentle waves inched closer to them. Torn clothes and plastic bags bobbed in the water and dripped from the branches of mangrove trees. Farzana felt a gentle breeze approach through the creek. It rustled through the old trees, through the leaves and plastic that filled their branches and shivered through her.

She lowered the babies into their shallow grave. Her friends covered them with sand and whispered prayers. They usually came this way later in the afternoons, to wade and swim in the rising tide. Farzana liked to stay until the setting sun faded behind the fetid hills, giving them a dusty pink glow, and the waves turned metallic. That was when she thought the mountains looked their best.

That afternoon they walked hurriedly back across the hills to find their father, who was waiting and hungry. Hyder Ali Shaikh was standing, tall, gangly and gaunt, on a quiet slope, his face lit up in a tobacco-stained grin. They sat down to eat. Both sisters wore salwar kameezes with cotton jackets to keep the mud and trash away from their clothes, and errant strands spilled out of the scarves they wrapped around their long, loosely bundled hair. While Farzana was prickly and quiet with teenage awkwardness, Farha, at fifteen, had stayed smiling and baby-faced. Over the lunch that Hyder Ali had brought from home, she told their father about their morning adventure. Uncharacteristically terse, he asked them not to venture near the graves again. *Ye sab cheez chhodta nahi hai*, he remarked. *These things have a way of not leaving you.*

Hyder Ali had moved to live in the shade of the mountains months before Farzana was born. He had come to Mumbai in his teens, from his village in Bihar. For years he had worked as an embroiderer's assistant. He enjoyed the long, quiet hours of filling fabric, tightly stretched out on the frame, with lacelike patterns. Half-made flowers, rising vines and wingless birds made shadows on his face and limbs, when he curled up to sleep under the frame.

Then a wife, Shakimun, and nine children followed, forcing Hyder Ali to seek a life outside the embroidery room that formed his world.

He had heard of the mountains that never ran out of work – vast dumping grounds at the edge of the city, where the remnants of everything that Mumbai consumed came to die. Nothing had ever officially been composted, incinerated or recycled. Instead it lingered on at Deonar, adding to the fetid and ever-growing mountains of garbage. Hyder Ali had heard that the mountains were older than the oldest pickers who worked on them, and larger than the biggest trash hills in the country. They stretched over 326 acres[1] and some rose more than 120 feet,[2] monuments to the increasingly ephemeral desires of the city's more official residents.

Hyder Ali's friends trawled the slopes all day, selling the trash they collected to traders who would sell it on, to be remade anew. They foraged for mangled plastic that could be pressed into sheets or pulled into filament. They traded glass bottles to be refilled with new drinks, metal to be melted into fresh parts for gadgets, and cloth scraps to be stuffed into toys and quilts or sewn into clothes. Hyder Ali had heard you could earn good money on these slopes, and their edges could yield space to make a home for his growing family. He heard the mountains sustained pickers, fed them, threw up treasures that had made fortunes and fuelled rivalries and ambitions.

So in 1998 he moved his family to a spot where a drain that ran down the mountains met a lane that curved around them. Their lane was called Banjara Galli, or Gypsy Lane, after the itinerant inhabitants who had left before city drifters replaced them. Farzana was born months later. Two more daughters and a son would follow, making it nine children who would come to fill the house they would build on these shape-shifting foothills.

At first Hyder Ali looked for embroidery commissions, while Shakimun strapped Farzana onto her back with a dupatta and waded into the township of trash hills. But finding work on his own was hard and soon he followed her into the rolling landscape of garbage. At first their rising stench made Hyder Ali throw up. His bony hands stank and, when he ate, he felt they transported the smell of garbage inside him. Hunger made him dizzy. Mountain trash swam before his eyes. He could not eat or sleep for days, whittling down his already-skeletal frame.

He developed a technique to protect his hands and appetite, clenching his toes tightly around cloth scraps while balancing himself precariously, on the wobbly slope, with his other foot. He bent his knee and lifted his leg, clinging onto the cloth, to deposit it in the bag that Shakimun held open for him. Hyder Ali often lost his balance in this acrobatic act and fell flat on his face into the muddy trash, amid a swarm of pickers. If he didn't get to something fast enough, someone else would. He had to discard his leg-curling and use his hands to work more quickly. As his hands and feet filled up with cuts and bruises from stumbling on glass and metal, he learned to dodge the stray dogs and birds that chased them for trash. Determinedly Hyder Ali, Shakimun and the children hung close to the khaki-and-orange trucks that relentlessly emptied the city's moth-eaten possessions onto the rising mountain clearings.

Hyder Ali liked to tell Farzana and her siblings that there was nothing he had not seen while trawling through

9

this sprawling necropolis. Everything that gave meaning to Mumbaikars' lives – from broken cellphones, to high-heeled shoes and gangrenous and dismembered human limbs – ended up here. He, like most pickers, believed that the spirits of people and possessions that had been sent here for unceremonious burial hung around the windswept slopes. On delivering the Urdu books that he found in the trash to clerics, he heard from them that God, who made people, also made spirits, and that the evil ones among them were called Shaitans.[3] Unseen and unheard but never the less tangibly present, they were said to be a manifestation of people's baser nature, their rising, unending desires. They gripped people, only to lead them astray.

Shaitans lived in filthy recesses and rose from smoke-less fires, the clerics had told Hyder Ali. Fires simmered, furtively and constantly, within the mountains' layers of decaying trash. He had seen smoke that rose from fires burning within the mountains, and flames that danced without smoke. At other times, flames erupted and moved like lightning across the hills, letting off swirling smoke, the two dancing together. Hyder Ali had nearly been encircled and trapped in these travelling fires. The Shaitans were bound to appear on the mountains – a dizzying accumulation of partly sated aspirations wreathed in fires and smoke, pickers believed. Shaitans arose from them and lay in wait for new homes and younger people to inhabit, they believed.

Hyder Ali had heard of friends who had been tripped on mountain slopes when they crossed the path of lurking Shaitans. Others warned him to stay away from certain hill slopes, or claimed they had encountered the tall, floating spirits known as Khabees in Islamic mythology, in their shrunken plastic-and-cloth-scrap homes on the edges of trash foothills, where they demanded rent. Hyder Ali's friend, Moharram Ali Siddique, had told him he heard a woman call out to him every time he neared the pile of white cloth scraps that he had collected on a slope, asking him to return her shroud from his neatly folded stack.

Hyder Ali knew that, of all his children, Farzana loved being on the mountains the most. She was the first of them to be born at their feet and had learned to walk on the gentle incline of trash foothills. As soon as she could make the short walk from their home, she had come wobbling over to them and it had been a losing battle to keep her away from them ever since. Shakimun sent him to get Farzana back, worrying she would get buried under the garbage showers that erupted from the emptying trucks. She had heard of children being mauled by dogs, of toddlers falling off garbage cliffs or tumbling down mountain slopes. Hyder Ali often found Farzana swinging from abandoned car fenders or digging for toys buried in the trash. He delivered her home, crying, and returned to work on the slopes. Farzana soon followed him back.

For months Farha and Farzana would remember the day they buried the babies as the day they got thrashed. When they arrived home, their eldest brother Jehangir was waiting for them, his face filled with rage. *Mardaani ho gayi hai? Bache gaad rahi hai?* he asked, his voice rising. *You think you've turned into men? Burying other people's babies?* Without waiting for their answer, Jehangir, who was eight years older than Farzana, slapped her and then Farha. He asked why they hadn't called him. He was at a clearing nearby that afternoon, he said. He would have taken care of it, or asked the municipal officials to. Don't get into these messes, he shouted. Nothing good ever comes out of these things.

Farzana couldn't answer. Tears choked her. Besides, fighting with Jehangir was never a good idea. Everyone at home knew that the anger of their wiry and intense brother was explosive.

In that long summer that stretched between her and adulthood, Farzana worked through the smoke that drifted over the slopes, the constantly burning fires, their sharp smell, the heat that turned humid as rain clouds approached, the new security guards who had arrived to patrol the hilly townships' hazy rim.

It would all end soon, she told Hyder Ali coolly. The baking sun would give way to Mumbai's long season of torrential rains, which would soak their burning township and quench the fires. That year the summer would also end in the holy month of Ramzan (known elsewhere as Ramadan), filled with day-long fasts and feasts that would occupy much of the night. And three days before the first fast, on 2 June 2016, Farzana would turn eighteen.

Hyder Ali later came to believe that it was in this long and boiling summer of waiting – the summer when Farzana found the glass jar filled with the lifeless babies – that the mountain spirits had entered his daughter, though at the time they did not know it.

The shadow of the Deonar mountains was longer than Hyder Ali knew, and breaking out of it was harder than he had thought. He had often asked Vitabai Kamble, who lived a few houses down the lane, for help in escaping it. He had first seen Vitabai as a rolling cloud of grey on the hills, draped in jewel-coloured sarees, chasing the arriving trash. Pickers said that she was among the oldest on the slopes, that she had seen the mountains before they were mountains. She herself spoke of the legends that floated in the mountains' halo, which said that they were older than the oldest pickers. Like most legends, some parts were true and others were not.

'On the morning of July 6 1896 there was a strong smell, as if sulphurated oxygen was generated over the north of the island and especially from the salt channels across Matunga and the vacant ground to the north. The smell seemed strongest furthest to the north,' Dr T. S. Weir, Bombay's health officer, wrote in the assiduously compiled administration report that the municipal commissioner sent to London every year.[1]

At this time, a migration of rats had been observed across Sewree, and I believe the smell was due to the decomposition of dead rats, for a number of bodies of rats were found in the suburbs. The Commissioner of Police and I happened to go over the north of the island on this morning in connection with arrangements being made for the inspection of traffic by the roadways into Bombay and we tried to ascertain the cause. The smell was most offensive, tainting the air, far and wide.

'A blue haze was often observed in the evenings of September and October and rainbows which I had not observed in Bombay for a long period,' Weir continued. 'At this season boils were very prevalent. On 9th of September a gale blew and the sky looked like a monsoon storm. In the evening, rain fell. A little time afterwards dead rats were found on the west foreshore.'

Days later Dr Acacio Viegas, a physician who practised in the Indian quarter of the city, was called to attend to patients stricken with fever. During his visits Viegas found nothing to explain their raging temperature and listlessness, other than a small red welt.[2] The next day, before he could diagnose their illness, their fevers spiked and they died. Using fluid extracted from their welts, he identified the disease as the bubonic plague. He began reading of more plague deaths in the newspapers.

By this time opium and the cotton trade had transformed Bombay from the rocky fishing islands that the British received from the Portuguese in the sixteenth century into one of the British Empire's most majestic and important trading ports. The British built a fort, reclaimed land from the sea to join the islands and, on the sliver that emerged, they built stately European buildings, complete with Indian flourishes. While the British lived in the breezy, tropical London-like area growing within the fort's walls, the lanes outside became packed with Indian migrants, drawn from around the country by the promise of work. Garbage and infectious diseases followed. Soon Weir began getting reports of hundreds of plague deaths a day. France imposed restrictions on Indian passengers and goods.[3]

Officials believed the disease had arrived in the city with pilgrims returning from a religious fair in North India.[4] Later colonial reports would conclude that it emanated from Yunnan, China, and arrived on trading ships from Hong Kong. It was carried through the lanes outside the fort by rats moving through the overflowing filth.[5] Over time, the garbage dumping grounds at Mahalakshmi, where Mumbaikars had sent their garbage for years, had nearly swollen into the homes around it, emitting smells, rats and diseases that sickened the residents nearby and threatened trade. But the campaign that Dr Weir planned to control the epidemic would grow, thorn-like, between the colonial administration and Bombay's residents. 'There is only one measure from which any effect can be expected and that is quarantine,' he wrote.[6]

Troops contained travellers arriving into the city in camps. They entered the slim Indian lanes around the fort, where they dismantled tiled roofs to let light into dark homes, emptied granaries piled with months of supplies and cleaned drains and sewers by flooding them with sea water that gushed back into homes. The returning waters brought dead rats, trash and all that the drains were supposed to purge. Soldiers searched homes for the sick and lined up residents outside, so that they could examine them for buboes. They burned patients' possessions, limewashed and quarantined their homes and kept their families in hospital for weeks.[7] Even the graves of plague victims were layered with quicklime or charcoal to contain the plague fleas within.

Fear and rumours gripped the city. Many Indians hid the ailing inside cupboards and protected them, with knives, from being taken away to hospital, afraid that they were being transported there only to die, alone.[8] One plague patient had jumped out of a moving ambulance and was later found dead, having walked a long way.[9] 'They had some idea that the ambulance would give them a shock that would kill them,' Weir wrote in the annual administration report. 'Men have said to me "You think we are like mad dogs, and you want to kill us as if we are."'[10]

Late one night Bombay's municipal commissioner, P. C. H. Snow, walked across this widening rift into the Indian lanes. He discovered a town growing unnoticed – one so tightly packed that the plague was bound to travel fast. In one room Snow found nineteen men, twenty-one women and seventeen children sleeping alongside each other. 'In fact, the room is a passage with a door in front between closed walls ... What can anything done outside this room do for the people in their misery inside?' he wrote.[11] As the city's budget surplus was wiped out by the fight against the plague, the disease was only spreading further, beginning to touch the edges of the constricted island city. Snow wrote of seeing patients walking the city streets in delirium and lying beside the road.[12] Some could be revived, but others were long dead. According to newspaper reports, more than 1,900 people died of the plague every week for the rest of the year. The recently built Victoria Terminus was packed with residents leaving Bombay.

On 14 October 1896, with plague-control measures

tightening, a group of Indians wrote to Snow. Enforcing the regulations would only increase the surge of leaving residents, they said.[13] Fleeing patients had already taken the plague to the historical neighbouring city of Pune and beyond. In both cities those who remained protested, often violently, as the Empire and its soldiers overran their homes, their persons and their rituals.

Late on the night of 30 October, Snow and Weir met the police commissioner, H. G. Vincent, at his imposing stone office, across from the city's busy electric-lit market. Shops had closed early and angry crowds swelled in the dark lanes nearby. Inside, Vincent pleaded for a retreat from the plague measures or, he feared, there would be riots. He and Weir worried that the Halalkhores, or waste cleaners, would join the crowds leaving Bombay. This could precipitate 'a vast panic and exodus from the city,' Snow wrote.[14] 'Bombay in a few days would have become uninhabitable, left to reek in a mass of sewage, sweepings and pollution, with no one at hand to conduct the daily routine of sanitation, much less adopt a single preventive measure against the plague.' The three officers withdrew their isolation measures for patients that night.

Instead they let the city's mosaic of communities pour into their own plague camps, hospitals and burial grounds and turned to pushing out the city's mounting refuse. With it, they hoped to edge out both the discontent and the diseases they had battled for years, including malaria, measles, mumps, chickenpox, smallpox, cholera and tuberculosis.

Early in 1897 the British officers identified an 823-acre marsh in the distant seaside village of Deonar, where they planned to send Bombay's waste from now on, replacing the overflowing, rat-filled grounds at Coorla and then Mahalakshmi. The government acquired the land from its owner, Ardeshir Cursetji Cama, that May.[15]

Cuchra or 'trash' trains, filled with the city's refuse, began arriving at the Deonar grounds on 7 June 1899, construction having been delayed by concerns that the smell would sicken travellers on passenger trains passing close by.[16] The municipality hired workers to empty wagons and fill the vast grounds, which were partly submerged in the sea and dotted with shrubs and an endless expanse of weeds. 'As the refuse contains large quantities of broken glass and old iron, frequent injuries occurred to the feet and legs of men emptying the wagons,' a municipal report recounted. 'The wounds were often very serious', delaying the clearing of wagons and the return journeys to the city. Workers had fevers and eye infections, and as the new loads of garbage had to be deposited further away from the end of the track, the work only got harder. Slowly the workers learned to live with the trash and injuries, and two trains of twenty-five wagons each began arriving every day.

A bund, or embankment, was built along the edges of the Deonar grounds to keep the sea from seeping into the site, and garbage from flowing into the creek, and Bombay's remains and their ghosts began filling them.[17] That year's municipal commissioner's report said that officials expected the grounds to emerge from the marsh, filled with trash, in twenty-three years. It would become 'a valuable Municipal estate', yielding more than 100,000 rupees as rent from farmers, who would cultivate the grounds, enriched with rotting garbage, and form the new edge of the extending city. 'It was thought that, by this method, a large area of waste, an unhealthy swamp, could be converted into fruitful agricultural ground,' the report concluded.[18]

And as Bombay kept growing, its remains did indeed slowly fill the distant bog at Deonar, draining trash from the city. Plague receded too. Officials dug streets to fix the drains, extend sewers, widen streets, open passages for the sea breezes and build homes for the growing migrant population. Beneath the streets they found older trash, deposited perhaps forty years before the city was built over it. *Cuchra* trains had ferried it away and continued to take the city's shed skins to the grounds for nearly nine decades, where they remained both in plain sight and out of sight. This arrangement had kept an uneasy calm between the city and its waste, until it erupted again, more than a century later.

In 1960 Bombay had become the capital of the newly formed state of Maharashtra. Its hastily extending edge began to touch the farms perching on their trash foundations and absorb them into the city. The grounds had fulfilled British administrators' plans, more than a decade after they left the country. Rains sometimes washed the garbage along the grounds' edges into the sea, drifting it back towards the city, but the shrunken grounds refilled fast.

It was a few years later that Vitabai Kamble had come to Bombay as a young mother. She and her husband had set up their home, made of plastic sheets and sarees, on a pavement in the mid-sixties. It was in central Bombay, across the street from the state-run television channel's newly built studio and its cloud-grazing antenna. When the breeze opened their billowy ceiling, the spindly antenna filled their eyes, bringing in the city's stardust. It helped Vitabai find her way back from wealthy homes, where she washed dishes while her husband did odd jobs. It was in the television tower-filled home that her daughter was born, and where Vitabai believed she lived the Bombay dream.

Migrant settlements like Vitabai's swelled and spilled out of the tenements that Snow had written about decades earlier, onto the city's railway tracks, along its stretching water pipelines, across its pavements and roads. But the city bulged with an aspiration that edged them out.

One day Vitabai got papers saying that the municipality had given her a plot of land, instantly elevating her to the status of landowner. The papers became her most prized possession. She bundled her children, her husband, her home and the land allotment papers into a municipal truck and they drove through the city until it petered out into saltpans and mangroves. When she saw the fetid dumping grounds and the chalk-marked section of rubble that was hers, Vitabai's dream of home ownership crumbled before her eyes.

Unlike her, others had fought the municipality's attempts to move them to Deonar. The rambling cloth-and-plastic communities around Vitabai's house in the city were often consumed by blazes in those years, and while their residents tried to reassemble their homes amidst the dying embers, the municipality took the opportunity to resettle them at Deonar. Many had filed court cases, alleging that the fires were set deliberately, intended to hand over their communities to developers so they could build apartments and office towers.[19] Expelled by Bombay's expanding concrete dreams, these extraneous people and their disappointments arrived at the grounds on trucks with almost the same regularity as the trains arrived with abandoned things, while the city stretched and rose over their homes.

The municipality could hardly remove them fast enough. Newspaper reports from those years say that Bombay's streets and pavements still overflowed with trash, people and their flimsy homes, which were so fragile they nearly walked away in the city's fierce monsoon winds. Garbage piled higher on the city streets through the day, bred flies and mosquitoes, stank and sickened the residents. *Cuchra* trains departed once in the morning and then again at night, when residents along its tracks knew to close their windows against the travelling smell; the municipality created a *Cuchra* Fleet, with trailers, donkeys and tractors to supplement the ageing trains. Together they filled Deonar's swamp with trash, all day and all night.

For those who held out, the city positioned the grounds' edges as planned communities for the poor. Newspaper reporters wrote about the wide roads and concrete houses. There were numbered blocks, tarred roads, a toilet for every ten people and large workshops to house their small businesses.[20]

But Vitabai, like most others, didn't get a home as described by the newspapers. She got a rubble patch edged with chalk, to ensure she did not spill into her neighbour's plot, causing a fight. It was filled only with the smell of the distant city's refuse, which she remembered as being much worse then than it was in later years. The truth could also have been that she got used to it: the smell had settled in her, along with the many wounds she sustained from being too tightly packed in with the ghosts of the possessions that Bombay had thrown away to make space for its dreams.

Their settlements turned the flower-filled swamps, at opposite ends of the dumping grounds' edge, into Lotus Colony and Padma Nagar, or 'the town of lotuses'. A string of small hamlets grew up between them, digging in to make the mountains' crescent curve. As you arrived from the city you came to Lotus Colony, which was followed by Baba Nagar – named for the mystics that once roamed its desolate marsh. No one was sure where along the curve Rafiq Nagar, also known as Rafi Nagar, ran into Nirankari Nagar and then Sanjay Nagar, situated in the deepest bend of the mountains' moon. It was named for the seventies politician who was known for demolishing Delhi's slums to make way for a modern city. Banjara Galli, where Farzana and her family lived, was part of it and had indeed been demolished several times. No one knew where the name of Shanti Nagar, or 'the town of peace', came from, for behind it was the wall behind which trucks endlessly rattled and returned after emptying onto the hills. It was followed by Padma Nagar, which concluded the township. Around there was Bainganwadi, 'the hamlet of aubergines'; Bandra Plot, named for the space given to residents coming in from the posh suburb of Bandra; and other plots – all named for the area's rustic past or the glamour of the incoming city.

As they filled and grew, the dumping grounds began to emanate a toxic halo. Nothing made it out; things only arrived. While Bombay came to be known as the 'city of dreams', Deonar became the sprawling necropolis of their remains: a noxious and wondrous world. Only its putrid air and water mingled, unseen, with the city's.

The fastest way for Vitabai to return to the city, for work, was to sit atop the stinking open-topped rakes of *cuchra* trains. Instead she, and others, began to empty the mangy wealth from their wagons, hoard it and sell it. Vitabai waded through the grounds' still-marshy tracts in search of treasures, stumbling on animal carcasses sticking out of the mud and encountering its ghosts. Often she turned back to find Nagesh, her eldest son, then her younger daughter following her. Forgotten, they made lives on all that the city spat out.

In 1992, as the cool winter winds lashed the mountains, riots had broken out in the city over the demolition of the Babri Masjid, a mosque in North India, and were hardly worse anywhere than in their lanes. Hindus believed the mosque was built over the birthplace of Lord Rama. Vitabai, a Hindu surrounded by neighbours that she had not noticed were Muslims, had stayed inside her house, sheltering neighbours for weeks. She heard of rioters dressed as police, neighbours going missing, the dead being flung onto trash slopes, and the living hiding with them. When she came out, some of her neighbours were returning home, battered, while others had begun the unending search for missing relatives.

Hindus had started to leave, aware of the ruptured air in their lanes. Some had moved across the creek, to the newly formed municipality of New Bombay or other distant but gentrifying fringes of the city. Bombay's lanes – where everything had lived on something else, languages ran into each other to make 'Bambaiya' and cooking styles melded together – became segregated. Muslims were moving to flinty, far-flung enclaves, and those who could not afford to settle even there arrived to fill the lanes around the trash mountains.

The clerics to whom Hyder Ali delivered the books he found in the trash had told him that when people settled, bringing light and cleanliness to the ruins, mountains and filthy recesses at the outer edge of society that Shaitans inhabited, the Shaitans left. *Naapaki mein rehna to Shaitan ko neota dena hai*, one of them had said. *Living in impurity and dirt is an invitation to the Shaitan.* But with nowhere else to go, pickers arrived to live in the shadow of the mountains and in the lanes, which had stayed unsettled even as they filled. Consumed in the hunt for overlooked wealth, Vitabai had stayed too.

Vitabai had first arrived at my office, on a warm April afternoon in 2013, to take a loan to buy what she could not pick. She was among the first mountain denizens to seek loans from the foundation I had set up with my father in the summer of 2010 to provide small, low-interest loans to the city's poorest residents, so that they could grow their businesses. After nearly a decade as a reporter, I wanted to do more than just write about India's rising economy and its lengthening shadow of slums and waste. While India's economy was fuelled by people buying – and taking loans for – new gadgets, holidays and weddings, I had written about how telecallers from banks hung up when they reached people in the slums and Mumbai's Muslim ghettos.[21]

We set up our office at the end of interminable, undrying clothes lines in a residential lane in the Sion area of the city. At first the only sounds were of trains passing by on the tracks behind it but, as word of our operation spread, the city's fish, fruit and street-food sellers, lunch-makers, cobblers and tailors began to drown them out as they filled our office. As I met vendors who exchanged garlic for household waste, which they then sold, and others who made most of the city's shoes, my brain slowly got rewired, showing me a different side of the city I had lived in for years. I asked how they made a profit on their meagre businesses (often several at a time), eliciting blank stares. They were not sure.

Hardly anyone I had met through the foundation fascinated me as Vitabai did that summer afternoon. She huddled close to the thin mattress I sat on, revealing hands and feet filled with fading scars, which mapped memories of the more than four decades she had spent on the rising trash. The mountains had lightened her hair, and I saw the thrill of chasing forgotten treasures dance in her silver-rimmed eyes. Vitabai's plucky energy and memories of her life on the growing mountains lit up my languorous afternoon.

I fretted about how would she would repay our loan, with her odd business. If you can only sell what you collect with your hands, how will our loans help you grow? I asked her in Marathi. *Kachra kadhi kami honar ka?* Vitabai quickly countered. *Will there ever be less trash?* She worked in one of Mumbai's fastest-growing industries, she pointed out. She offered to show me the unending hills she and other pickers mined. What she could not collect herself, she would use our loans to buy from others and then sell to traders. She quickly became my introduction to the world of the Deonar township – a place that before her arrival I knew nearly nothing about, but would soon, like so many others, become addicted to.

Soon after she took a loan, Vitabai brought in her daughter, Babita, for one. Weeks later, I saw Hyder Ali's lean shoulders and deep eyes rising behind her diminutive frame, as they walked through the long waiting area that I had fashioned out of a car garage. She had brought Hyder Ali, Moharram Ali Siddique and Aftab Alam, who lived nearby, to form a group that would take on a loan with her son, Nagesh. If one of them could not pay the weekly instalments, the others would.

Hyder Ali stretched languidly on the thinly matted floor across from me. With the sun streaming on his face, he began speaking, *Hamara gaon, Laluji ke bagal ka hai,* making a reference to the former chief minister of Bihar. Lalu Yadav was known for his humour and easy laughter – often at himself. I looked up from reading Hyder Ali's loan-application form. *Aap jante the?* I asked. *Did you know him?* He nodded sideways to say no. *Mile the?* I tried again. *Have you met him?* He nodded sideways again, breaking into a bony grin. But I understood that this was what he wanted to say about himself: the thing that the several-pages-long form, filled with personal details, did not ask. I came to associate humour and unfettered laughter with Hyder Ali too.

Unlike Vitabai and her family, Hyder Ali said he did not want to stay in the trash business. He leaned back, resting his hand on the lime-green floor mat, barely noticing the stripes it pressed into his reddened palm, and told me of his journey into the mountains' shade and of his dreams of stepping out. He wanted to use the money to set up an embroidery workshop, of the sort he had spent his youth in. He would bring embroiderers from his village to make bridal outfits to sell, in the city, for a commission. He hoped it would take him away from the hills, and would inch his family's fortunes upwards.

It was in the early 2000s, a few years after Hyder Ali settled at its rim, that Deonar probably became the world's largest trash township, of the kind where nothing had ever officially left or been treated. Fuelled by the city's swelling desires, the mountains had risen as high as twenty-floor apartment blocks. The city already stretched over the smaller dumping grounds in Gorai and Malad. The Malad grounds were handed back to a developer, who quickly topped them with glass-and-chrome buildings that housed call centres and entertainment-company offices, where executives got headaches and computers rusted too quickly. I heard later that this was known as 'sick building syndrome': scientists had discovered that gases from these hastily closed dumping grounds did not settle for years.[22] Instead they permeated the buildings that rose over them and sickened the people and devices within.

The city was at a growing impasse. The trash that used to be deposited at the closed Malad grounds came to the Deonar mountains instead, which were increasingly ringed by the expanding band of Mumbai's castaway people. They only waded deeper and brought out more of the trash they built their lives upon. The dumping grounds spewed out foul air and smoke, which the municipality countered by spraying herbal deodorant and disinfectant; it had to clear garbage from the city streets and pavements or it would lead to the same infectious diseases that British reports had recorded, on an unimaginable scale. But the mountains were beginning to intrude into the city that had ignored them for so long. If they got any taller, officials worried, sections could tumble down in dangerous landslides of garbage. Flights coming into Mumbai could crash into the peaks. Without any answers, the city allowed Mumbai's lengthening garbage caravans to keep emptying constantly on the rising hilltops.

3

Farzana's earliest memories were of watching her house collapsing into the muddy trash and rising from it again every few days. Hyder Ali had taught her older brothers and sisters to spot municipal officers on eviction drives while he was away at work. Farzana helped to empty the house, while they untied the bamboo sticks that they had brought back from the hills to make its bones. Then they stood aside and watched, giggling as the plastic and tin sheets they had collected to make its walls fell noisily in a heap.

In September 2000, three months after Farzana turned two, India's environment ministry had framed rules to manage waste.[1] Moved by the growing mountains of garbage around the country, the Supreme Court had asked the ministry to take control of trash, which was hardly mounting anywhere as dizzyingly as it did at Deonar. Among the many rules, encroachers such as Farzana's family were to be kept out of the township of trash. The municipality, tasked with meeting the rules, stepped up eviction drives, which had been happening, on and off, for years.

But as soon as officers turned their backs, the pickers' houses rose again. Chasing the city's constantly arriving remnants had become an illicit but unwavering addiction.

Squashed plastic bottles, bundled together in a load that almost matched the pickers in size, could get them through the day. A palm-sized emerald, which Hyder Ali heard someone had found, could lift their lives entirely. He watched *houdhi*, or pond-pickers, make bunds on slopes encircling the trash, fill these enclosures with water and then sift through the wet sand for gold dust mingled in the city dust. *Kisi ka kachra kisi ka bhangaar hota hai*, Hyder Ali told me, explaining his work and his township. *One person's trash is another person's scrap*. It all arrived endlessly, increasing the mountains. Pickers hoarded it, sold it, slept on it, ate it and inhaled it.

Five years earlier, in 1995, Bombay had become Mumbai. Its boxy socialist-era apartments, best known for squeezing a lot into very little space, were giving way to gated communities that brought First World amenities, complete with garbage chutes. In this world, stretching far into suburbia, buildings were named after trees, such as Cedar, Oakwood and Birch, which were never seen in the city's muggy weather. Malls, gyms and multiplexes arrived, turning Mumbai aglow with India's growing wealth. They were all filled with new things whose remnants came to the mountains, to be reborn only through the ministrations of the rag-pickers.

Growing aspiration brought plastic bottles that had contained purified water; takeaway boxes half filled with unseen foods; soiled nappies; and wires from new devices. Indians embraced sachets for shampoo, hair dye and ketchup. Their expendability provided a new thrill, even in families that had taken pride in passing things down through the generations. Glass and metal containers were replaced with plastic pouches and boxes made of tightly packed layers of foil, paper and plastic, which left homes when their contents emptied, but lingered for ever at the dumping grounds. Emptiness, sadness, longing and aspiration: it was all to be doused by new purchases and possessions.

At the township, in the growing gush that erupted from trucks, trash could be trash or it could be gold. While Hyder Ali, with his laid-back air, found only broken bits of cement flooring, his friend Moharram Ali, with whom he had taken our loan, found the long marble slabs that had recently come to fill Mumbai's homes. The city's growing wealth poured out onto the mountains, and Hyder Ali and Moharram Ali floated on its rising tide. But while Hyder Ali's languid approach yielded little, Moharram Ali's luck and drive brought Mumbai's moth-eaten treasures into his hands, and this pulled their lives and their children's lives in opposing directions.

As a toddler, Farzana wobbled and crawled around the jewel-coloured cloth-scrap hills that filled their home. Shakimun, Hyder Ali and the older children collected these scraps on the slopes, filling them into outsize bundles that they slung over their heads and that dangled in their eyes as they carried them downhill. Made of odd-shaped offcuts from city tailors' workshops, the cloth hills in their house would soon get sold to stuff pillows, quilts and toys. Then hills in new colours would rise afresh on their floor. Farzana took her first steps on this terrain at home, practising for the trash hills that rose behind them.

When he could not spot the older children on the slopes, Hyder Ali topped Farzana's head with useful finds. She brought mud to fill the drain that flowed down from the mountains along Banjara Galli. She carried chunks of cement slabs flecked with fading green, orange or silvery glass, or the dark stone blocks that were laid as flooring in Mumbai apartments in the seventies and eighties. Municipal guards sometimes chased her. As she ran down the unsteady slopes to stay ahead, Farzana often fell or dropped her floor slab. The mountain fragments that made it home were sold or thrown down to fill the watery bog beneath their home.

Hyder Ali enrolled Farzana at the municipality's Urdu primary school for girls nearby. Every morning she walked to school with her sisters, Afsana and Jannat. Every afternoon the breeze began blowing inwards from the creek, bringing a whiff of the mountains into their home, and drew her up the slopes. Standing on trash peaks, Farzana drank in the sea and its unconstricted gusts as she looked out for her other sisters, Sahani, Jehana and Farha, who worked on them. Soon the balance fell in favour of the mountains, drawing her increasingly towards them. She and her sisters spent the afternoons swimming in the creek and collecting cloth scraps to swell the pile their father made on a mountain edge.

Even amid the frenzied scrambles around the emptying trucks, Hyder Ali walked as if he moved to mellow music playing in his ears through invisible earphones. *Khaadi mein koi bhooka nahi jaata*, he had heard older pickers say. *No one ever goes hungry here*. It deepened his laid-back air. When he came to deliver his day's pickings on the pile he had accumulated on the slopes, it looked bigger than when he had left it. The children kept their household afloat. He could not keep them away from the slopes.

It was Jehangir, his eldest son, who had never been

to school, who fought with Hyder Ali to keep his sisters away from the mountains and at school. Jehangir hungrily chased the forgotten fortunes that had eluded his father. The deeper he sank into this giddy mountain addiction, the more he wanted to keep his sisters from it. He turned them back from the slopes, or towards the school whose four-floor building faced the mountains, a fading foil to their sickening allure. They were back the next afternoon, trailing the trucks.

Farzana was growing to be all arms and legs and what her sisters called *aadha dimaag*, or half a brain. The rising mountains had leaked into her mind, they thought. As the peaks rose higher, the rains gushed down harder every monsoon, bringing the slopes into their home. Farzana fell asleep to the clatter of rain and woke up to see her slippers floating close to her, amid unknown possessions that had flowed down the slopes. Blearily she folded her salwar over her knees and waded through the water to retrieve her books and shoes drifting through neighbouring homes.

Then she walked up the squelching slopes, away from school. She and her sisters dragged reeking wooden planks that Jehangir and their brother Alamgir, the third of the nine children, nailed to the walls at home and piled their soaking household on. At night they clambered onto the planks to sleep amid their belongings, while the mountain-filled waters sloshed below. When the rains paused, Farzana helped Shakimun throw out the water that filled their homes and bring out their damp provisions and the trash they had stored, which had turned to mush, to catch the sun peeking into their slim lane. She brought out her water-stained notebooks. Everything that she had learned had blurred.

Trying to catch up was futile. *Vaise bhi uske man mein gobar bhara tha*, her friend Yasmeen, who was a few years older and lived down the lane, would say. *Her mind was filled with cow dung!* The fragile-looking and outspoken Yasmeen, who would later marry Alamgir, was home only for the holidays. Her parents had enrolled her at a madrasa (Islamic religious school) in Gujarat, to keep her away from the mountains, and at school. Later Hyder Ali enlisted Yasmeen to teach Farzana to read the Koran, which had sunk without trace in Farzana's mind. The mountains filled her head, and her friends' heads too. Their school was emptying out onto the hilltops.

Moharram Ali's daughter, Hera, was elegant, imperious, sharp-tempered and one of the few girls from their lanes who had made it to middle school, further into the city. She was just two years older than Farzana and hardly ever picked trash. When Farzana walked to work, in the afternoons, she saw Hera leave for the Arabic, computer or tailoring classes her mother had enrolled her for. *Unke ghar mein safai kitni thi*, Farzana would recall. *Their house was so clean.*

Mountain air had elevated the tall and rakish Moharram Ali more than most others in their lanes. Farzana had heard how the mountains had delivered their fortunes into his hands. Her father called him Shaitan Singh, or Mr Troublemaker, for his gift for amassing trash. He was part of the small band of nocturnal pickers, and was among the mountains' most relentless treasure-hunters. Garbage trucks arrived through the night, but only the most fear-less picked through the dimly lit slopes, with only a few lights fixed on high masts. Jagged bits of glass and metal cut pickers as they walked up, garbage rained on them in dark clumps from emptying trucks. Moharram Ali fixed a torch onto the baseball cap that he wore back-to-front and took his pick of the trash under the moonlight, freed of the scrambles that erupted in the day.

On moonlit nights the creek, the rivulet and saltpans formed a glassy rim around the mountains. When he got to the trash peaks, Moharram Ali felt like he floated in the creek, along with the fishing boats he saw in the distance. The boats stayed out all night, trawling through the creek, in good weather. He thought they gave him company. He moved his head slowly from side to side, baring treasures in the torchlight. In the quiet and dark of the night he had found a silver idol of a Hindu goddess and a pillowcase stuffed with banknotes, buried in the trash.

While leaving, he often ran into the morning-shift pickers, coming into work. Hyder Ali and the others ribbed him, asking him to leave something for them. As the sun rose overhead, Moharram Ali often returned to chase the endlessly arriving trucks. He described his mountain fever like a love affair, telling me it was like how a person grows on you when you spend time with them. *Ek insaan ke jaisa lagaav tha. Khaadi hum logon to bulati thi. You know how you become attached to a person when you spend time with them? That is how I became attached to the mountains. They called out to me.*

He had told Hyder Ali that his father was the *mujawar*, or caretaker, of a saint's mausoleum in their village in North India. Their house was filled with musty books, bound in deep but fading colours. Moharram Ali and his father could not read anything in them except their faint prices – a few pennies. His father practised rituals passed down from his own father and, probably, from the books in their house. He chanted prayers that rose to fill up the rooms with heady smells and wafting smoke that took supplicants into a trance. When it all ebbed, the devotees, who came long distances to pray for miracles, often found their ailments cured. Moharram Ali had learned his father's courtly manners and enduring rituals. He told Hyder Ali that the prayers kept spirits away from him and brought mountain treasures into his hands. It fuelled the legend of Shaitan Singh in their lanes.

Jehangir had tried working night shifts too, in search of Moharram Ali's luck. Jehangir was ten then and, instead of mountain treasures, he had encountered only a *chudail*, or female spirit, who had died unfulfilled. She was draped in white, had her feet turned back and floated a little above the dark and mostly empty slopes. He had retreated to working in the day and begun to hang around instead with older boys, bullies. He learned to smoke and hurl the abuses that he heard them spout.

He began ferreting out the currency notes that Hyder Ali never seemed to have quite enough of to run the house. Their father found ways not to ask how Jehangir got them. Farzana heard, around the hills, that he had been drawn into the gangs' fierce fights for territory and the trash that came with it. At home, Jehangir thought his money gave him a voice in household decisions. Hyder Ali did not.

The two clashed over nearly everything, but most of all over Farzana. After her older sister Sahani dropped out to work on the mountains, Farzana, then nine, and Afsana, two years older, became the two oldest children at school. The boys had never been to one. While Afsana wanted to stay, Jehangir fought with Hyder Ali to keep Farzana at school, to give her a life away from the mountains. *Paak saaf rahein*, he told Hyder Ali, repeating what he had heard from clerics. *They should stay pure and clean.* And yet Farzana was on the slopes, after school, every afternoon.

Moharram Ali's wife, Yasmin, and their children hardly ever worked on the mountains. Yasmin spent the afternoons at home, watching cooking shows on the used television set they bought at a *kata* shop, where the pickers' collected trash was sorted into myriad categories and sold by weight. She got friends to pass on batter mixes that came in the trash, post-expiry, to try the recipes she saw. She tossed frozen peas into rice to make *pulaos*. Hera and Yasmin practised dropping spoonfuls of batter mixed with yoghurt into a pan and spreading it in slow, circular motions to make *dosas*, crisp like paper. They borrowed moulds to steam it into fluffy *idlis*.

For dessert, Hera got her friends to collect packets of batter mix for *gulab jamun*, when they saw it fall out of garbage trucks. Over long, slow afternoons they rolled the moistened batter into sugary dough balls, which they fried and then dipped in warm sugar syrup. They plopped the golden hot *gulab jamuns* into their mouths, spurting sugar syrup, amidst giggling and gossip. She saved any leftovers for the elaborate dinners that she helped Yasmin cook sometimes, and which Moharram Ali barely made it home for.

His luck was about to get better. One morning Farzana was leaving for school when a friend dropped in to say that Moharram Ali had found a gold necklace in the trash. Hyder Ali looked surprised. He hadn't seen Moharram Ali in days. Hyder Ali walked over to his house to ask if he really had dug gold out from the mountains. Moharram Ali said he had been at home, sick for a week. His fever had ebbed only last evening. The soft, sweet smell of steaming rice filled the house, but Yasmin would not serve dinner unless he brought some trash to sell. She had cooked with the last of her supplies.

Gaali de ke gaya to kuch to lana hi tha, Moharram Ali said with a grin. *I'd left the house with an insult – I had to bring something back!* He had walked up the slopes, hoping to find something easily, a bag stuffed with cloth scraps perhaps, and return home to eat. He switched on his torch, swung his garbage fork lazily into the slope and hit something soft and creamy. He dug around it and pulled out a tawny leather ladies' handbag.

He unzipped the pockets, rummaging inside to discover worlds so secret that women sometimes forgot to clear them out, even while throwing their bags away. Moharram Ali had found letters written in curly handwriting, delicate miniature bottles of perfume, monogrammed handkerchiefs that could be washed and sold as white scraps, and sometimes even crumpled currency notes, saved too safely from tight household budgets.

As Moharram Ali felt for zips and opened inner pockets that night, something flashed in the light. A gold necklace, with flowery patterns engraved on it. It was strung with black beads, the sign of a married Hindu woman. He stuffed it into his pocket and looked up to check if anyone had seen his glowing find. Pickers' lights moved around him. They were immersed in their own search for overlooked treasures. He left, his hand in his pocket.

When he got home, Yasmin and their five children were wilting with hunger. He pushed aside their cold dinner and brought his hand out of his pocket, asking Yasmin to see if his necklace really was gold or the cheap metal that women in their lanes wore. Since she had no way to tell, excitement and imagination carried them through the night.

Weeks later, Hyder Ali heard that Moharram Ali had opened his own *kata* shop, striking gold in the pickers' constant ambition: to become a small trader or, with some luck, even set themselves up in work away from the trash business. Moharram Ali and Hyder Ali, among others, would later tell me this was why they were taking successive loans from our foundation. They would pay the instalments unerringly, every week, and then borrow larger sums to feed their garbage addiction. Our office filled with more pickers from around the mountains' rim. Nowhere in the Mumbai slums where we worked did repayments come in as unfailingly as they did from the ones around the Deonar mountains. At first I ascribed this to our frail but intrepid loan collector, who had told them an alarm would go off in my distant office, next to me, if anyone touched her cash-filled bag or if she left without all the money that she needed to collect.

But when I walked the long, skinny lanes that ended in the mountains, I felt trash fever swirl among them. Pickers repaid our loans in order to hoard more and more of the rubbish that framed their lives and filled it. Their attempts to build lives away from its fetid but unyielding grip seemed fumbling and usually failed.

When I asked, some showed me the overfull *kata* shops they had opened with loan money, while others pointed to tin-sheet attics that they had built over their homes. We would climb vertical metal staircases into sun-filled lofts, which they hoped would be the starting point of their journey out of the garbage. These rooms hung over the hills and offered panoramic views of the city's refuse. I hunched to see sun-dried paper and plastic waft on the breezy slopes through the windows. The rooms were filled with half-manned rows of tailoring machines, which the pickers bought to stitch stacks of pre-cut shirts or jeans, while other rows were piled with shoe soles to be sewn onto glittery uppers. They were mostly sold in Mumbai's dizzyingly busy street markets. Piles of gauzy, brightly coloured fabric lined Hyder Ali's windowless and often-unmanned loft. The fabric would be covered with sequins soon, he would tell me, during my increasingly frequent trips.

Later we would retrace our steps down into his dark home. Unlike the unending garbage that rose behind him and filled his home, embroidery commissions were hard to get and even harder to deliver. Embroiderers would often leave Hyder Ali's workshop for better-paying ones. They'll be back right after the next festival, he would tell me for months, as the festivals passed by, one by one. He had struggled to teach Jehangir and his second son, Alamgir, the patient art of embroidery and make them his only assistants.

In those years Alamgir kept Hyder Ali's embroidery business stuttering along, while Jehangir rose with the mountains' gangs. The municipality, with its guards and police, hung lightly over mountain slopes, leaving pickers to their forgotten world and their unremitting chase. The year that she graduated from fourth grade, when she was about to turn ten, Farzana spent every day of the long summer holidays at the mountains. Forced by Jehangir to do so, Hyder Ali enrolled her in middle school. But when the new school year began, Farzana was still accompanying them to work.

Ghar mein reh ke kya karegi? Padhne mein man nahi hai. Hyder Ali mumbled to Shakimun, one afternoon when they were alone in their dark, crammed home. *What's she going to do at home? She doesn't want to study!*

Shakimun grunted to say she was listening to him, even as she carefully piled the slim edges of the gleaming steel dishes she had just finished washing on top of each other, in the cooking area.

Apni galli koi theek hai kya? Hyder Ali said, his voice rising. *You think our lanes are safe?*

Nahi, Shakimun said, so softly he could barely hear it over the din of falling dishes. *No.* The dishes flashed reflections in the room as she began stacking them up carefully again, until they rose high against the wall.

Kharche mein madad kar sakti hai, Hyder Ali went on. *There are expenses she could help with.* His workshop was failing, he said.

Jehangir walked in to collect something. Seeing him made Hyder Ali's mercurial temper boil over, shouting that if he didn't want Farzana to work, then Jehangir would have to make up the money himself. At eighteen, Jehangir retreated from the fight with his father. And so, at ten, Farzana joined the illicit army that hoarded the slopes all day.

4

In the summer of 2008, when Farzana dropped out of school and came to work on the mountains all day, a simmering battle to shrink the mountains and their halo reached boiling point. Dr Sandip Rane, a doctor who lived in a genteel neighbourhood near the townships' edge, had filed for contempt against the municipality, for failing to shrivel the Deonar township. It had only grown, in the face of court orders to fix it, he said, submitting photographs 'which show a film of gas over the waste', according to later court orders.[1]

A decade and a half earlier, when Rane set up his cardiology practice in the mountains' shadow, he had expected to see older patients with coronary disease. Instead his waiting room had overflowed with breathless children. He suspected their lungs were filled with the smoke he woke up to see rising from the trash hills nearby. Rane knew the residents of a neighbouring apartment building had filed a court case, in June 1996, asking the city to fix the hills and their smoke.

They watched the mountains light up with fires at nightfall, the residents said in their plea to the court. Dark smoke clouds drifted through the night into their homes, constricting their breath.[2] Fires rose and the smoke travelled until sunrise, they went on. They had heard that garbage traders got rag-pickers to light these fires so that lighter trash – plastic, paper and cloth – would melt away, leaving copper, silver, lead and other metals (the most expensive of mountain finds) for them to sell. Fine particles of toxic chemicals, or 'suspended particulate matter', left over from these fires hung thick in the mountain air, the level seven times higher than rules allowed.[3] They entered the lungs and bloodstreams of pickers and residents nearby, making it hard to breathe and rooting themselves deep in their internal organs. The fires left more than twice the permitted amount of lead in the mountain air, limiting the intellect of the children who breathed it in.[4]

The municipality's response was that the mountains lit up in 'spontaneous combustion'. The slowly decomposing garbage let off methane, which erupted in flames when it met the burning mountain sun. These self-ignited fires burned even on mountains where no new garbage had been dumped, officials wrote, suggesting that fires were bound to erupt from the dizzying accumulation of items packed together, and it was not their fault. The nightly smoke and smog in the petitioners' homes came also from fires that pickers lit for metal, officials said, and from the growing traffic on the highway that ran by their homes.

After the 1996 petition, successive judges had asked the municipality to settle a modern trash township elsewhere. Until it could do so, the judges had tried to make Deonar's ageing and sprawling trash township follow the waste rules. They had asked for its mess to be topped and pressed down with mud, to hold it all in place and make evenly spaced hills. They had set timelines to tarmac the dirt tracks that wound through the hills; to fix street lights around them; and to tighten security around their faint edges, so that pickers could not get in and light fires. They had asked for fire engines and water tankers to patrol, curbing the almost continually burning fires and their rising smoke.[5] They pushed for the trash township to change – to mirror the modern city whose wants fed it, and whose dark reflection it was.

Appointed to a court committee in 1996, the tall and unbending Rane sat in a portable cabin at the dumping grounds, watching over the project to bring the mountains into line with the rules, every Wednesday for years. He observed the illicit army that Hyder Ali and his family belonged to filling the slopes.

Hills got carefully formed, beginning near the municipal office where *cuchra* trains had once ended, delivering the city's shed possessions. The first hill, closest to the office, was reserved for offal waste. Others rose along the creeks' curve, filling up with everything else that the city discarded, layered with mud, ending in the eighth mountain, whose steep cliff dropped into the water.

Rane watched electric poles and wires arrive at the township to install street lights. But the lights had not come on. He heard that pickers stole them to buy drugs, or that cables snapped from the weight of the trash or from falling under its trucks. Later a few lights came, installed on high masts, casting a distant glow on the night-pickers.

The municipality fitfully began measuring the chemicals that hung in the mountain air, as the waste rules necessitated, often finding its air to be worsening. Doctors around the mountains told me that more than half their patients came in with respiratory ailments. They had asthma, bronchitis and persistent coughs. Pickers' weakened chests made them an easy home for tuberculo-sis and drug-resistant tuberculosis. An airborne infection, this ran rampant among the cramped homes in the lanes around the mountains. Pickers also arrived with Intersti-tial Lung Disease, which would thicken the tissue around their lungs, consuming them within five years of breath-lessness and coughing.[6] The patients who came with Chronic Obstructive Pulmonary Disease – the air sacs in their lungs weakened and their airways badly inflamed – would live longer, but doctors knew that in both cases there was no cure, only deterioration. They prescribed oxygen pumps, which they knew their patients could not afford.

'The problem is, you can't tell if a person is sick because of living near waste. You need an expert,' Marco Armiero, an environmental historian from Naples, told me when I began investigating the health problems that lay in the mountains' shadow. Mafia in his own region had brought toxic industrial waste from northern Italy and had strewn it at landfills, as well as on deserted country roads and on farms near Naples known for their produce, ripened by the balmy Mediterranean air. From long distances, drivers could see the flames from burning heaps of wires, lit to extract the copper within (just as Farzana had done with her slim pickings), making the region of Campania known as the 'Land of Fires'. Rates for some cancers had risen to twice the national rate around then, giving the area another name: the 'Triangle of Death'.[7]

For years, as the court hearings in Mumbai wore on, munic-ipal lawyers described how the municipality tried to keep the township out of the city limits, to prevent the trash leaking into the city's air and water. But the mountains crept in. There were nearly 13 million tonnes of garbage at the Deonar dumping grounds, officials estimated. How could it place a floor underneath it, as the rules required it to? The hills stretched over 326 acres. How could it make a ceiling to contain the air that blew into the city? A wall built on layers of trash would be unstable and bound to fall, they said. The lawyers pleaded for more time.

Rane sometimes heard of trials that the municipality ran to incinerate garbage and produce electricity, as cities elsewhere in the world did, as the court had requested. But Mumbai's garbage was too soggy from the rains, too gloopy from rotting food for the incinerator to work. The trash township spilled out of the municipality's attempts to shrink it.

Meanwhile the slim island city's open spaces had filled up. The relentless sprawl of suburbia had brought even distant places, which could have formed possible dumping grounds, into proximity with homes whose residents would be nauseated by the stink. They did not want open spaces around the apartments, which they had saved for years to buy, to fill up with the city's mess. Farmers did not want it to pollute their fields. Any open space the municipality found came with rival claimants.

In the years after the 1996 petition, deadlines to meet the waste rules and court orders came and went, but the mountains had not moved. The waste rules had outlawed them, mountain smoke sickened them and yet Hyder Ali and his ilk – the desperadoes of Deonar – still filled the grounds, carrying away all that was left. Clouds of flies obscured them and the guards' eyes glazed over when they looked at them, turning the pickers invisible as they continued to hunt for the dregs of Mumbai's fortunes. As the city, hemmed in by the sea, inched upwards, its garbage mountains and their halo followed, in step.

Under pressure from the court, in 2006 the municipality had appointed a private consultant, who delivered a report on resolving the problems at the Deonar township, the smaller mountains at Mulund and closing the trash hills at Gorai. Deonar's ageing waste could make for rich compost, the report said: a waste-to-compost plant could shrink the township. To get there, the municipality would spend more than Rs 10,500 crore (US $1.47 billion) on its three dumping grounds, nearly half of which would go into fixing the Deonar township.[8] It was the Mumbai municipality's most ambitious attempt to manage the city's waste since the Deonar grounds were settled more than a century before.

Early in 2006 consultants and officials invited bids for the projects. Officials worried whether a private company could really manage the Deonar township, where ragpickers fanned out on the slopes, their homes inched into the hills and gangs fought for trash.[9] None of the companies that bid for the chance to remake Deonar met the technical terms, and the contract was not given out. Trash arrival and its surreptitious removal went on relentlessly. More came than pickers could take away. It inched up on the mountains and spilled into the creek, stealthily swelling the township of trash.

Having waited for more than a decade for the mountains to move or shrink, Dr Rane had tired. In the summer of 2008 he filed his petition for contempt. In those twelve years the toxic cloud of Mumbai's festering possessions had only grown, he said. It hung heavily over the municipal ward around the mountains, where a quarter of all deaths came from respiratory diseases, Rane showed. In a ward further away, by comparison, it was less than 1 per cent. He presented medical studies that showed the haze was thick with the carcinogenic chemical, formaldehyde.[10] A different study showed that benzene, another carcinogenic, also festered in the mountain air, many times greater than at any of the landfills the authors looked at elsewhere in the world.[11] While it was below the permissible limits set in other countries, Dipanjali Majumdar, the study's author told me, those limits were for short exposure, not the nearly lifelong inhaling of benzene and other gases that the pickers experienced. She called the exposure 'chronic', and its health risks considerable: 'the gases emitted from the landfill and other pollutants in air cook a range of other hazardous dust and gases using sunlight in the atmospheric kitchen. These pollutants cooked in the atmosphere, called secondary pollutants, can cause severe air pollution and can even lead to climate change.' Those who lived in the mountains' halo had a life expectancy of just thirty-nine, living little more than half the lives that other Indians did.[12]

In search of answers, Rane began walking the sprawling colonial-era court's angular corridors as hearings to fix the mountains restarted. 'I am the kind of person who, if I train my guns on something, I don't give up,' he would tell me later. The municipality pleaded for more time. Justice Dhananjaya Chandrachud's patience wore thin, with a testiness seeping into his judgements: 'The rampant and unregulated dumping of garbage continues and, despite orders passed by this court, no serious attempt has been made to alleviate the problem.'[13]

Later, when I asked Hyder Ali what it was like being trapped in the mountains' deadly aura, he pushed out his bony chest. *Hamko kya hua hai?* he would ask. *Is there anything wrong with me?* He was healthier than anyone he knew, he liked to say, even after two decades of working on the rising tides of trash. He had seen friends silently replaced by their young children at the mountains, while they retreated to waste away in the lanes, consumed by tuberculosis. Others left to take the village air to help them recover, and never returned. While walking up the slopes to his work, he often passed pickers vomiting. Their ailing chests could not take the gentle uphill climb any more. Others had faded into the haze, their disappearance unnoticed in the unrelenting chase for the city's moth-eaten treasures. But Hyder Ali and his friends didn't think their treasure-yielding township and the livelihood it provided for them had anything to do with it.

5

Most mornings, when Farzana got to work on the trash peaks, she started by collecting the overripe tomatoes and aubergines that came in thrown-away food or sprouted from it with the rains. She waited for her friends' hazy figures to emerge on the rugged slopes and threw her pickings at them, making dark, wet splotches on their clothes. They swivelled in pain and confusion. When they spotted Farzana, her friends scrambled to look for their own tomatoes. They scoured through the trash that had arrived overnight for bits of watermelon or eggs and hurled them at her. Giggly tomato-fights ensued as they chased each other around the unsteady sun-filled slopes, rotting fruit in hand. Laughter and light were refracted in the halo of the forgotten mountains.

As the fights ebbed, drying pulp mingled with sweat and clung to them in the humid heat that hung heavily between the rain showers. Farzana bathed under the leaky taps of water tankers posted at their hilly township. The rest of her family, whom she joined at work, had asked to be spared her messy welcomes and perfect aim. Farzana and her daring spirit grew up together in the mountains' thickening fog and extending shadow. *Main pehle se hi aisi thi*, she would tell me breezily, when I asked later where she got her independence – her adventurousness – from. *I've always been like this.*

It was June 2008 and the school year had just begun, along with Mumbai's months-long rainy season. Farzana had come to work on the mountains all day. As she turned ten, dark monsoon clouds grazed and then cocooned the trash peaks. She watched trucks approach through the outer slopes. Filled with older trash and topped with rich mud, the hillsides had turned a glowing emerald with grass.

Drenched in wind and rain, Farzana walked among clouds, which also floated in the pools that filled the mountain troughs. At first the water looked clear, like the thick and empty plastic of the milk pouches that fetched the highest prices. Farzana collected the squashed plastic bottles that drifted, like bubbles amid lotuses.

As the rain continued to lash their township, the overgrown green slopes became muddy, the hilltops turned a molten brown. Farzana turned brown too, from wading thigh-deep into the mud. Dodging herds of cattle that their minders had brought to bathe in the water and graze on the grass, she slipped into the pools to bring out bottles, gloves or glass floating within. She came up for air, coated in muddy water, and saw her friends emerge, dripping slush too. She dipped back in for more.

Bags filled, Farzana walked downhill, collecting spinach, cucumbers and other vegetables for dinner. She looked for pumpkins growing under the rain-soaked trash and watched papayas clinging to the tall, spindly trees that sprouted from it. Farzana had heard that not everyone ate vegetables grown in trash. Some rubbed overgrown leaves, from plants she did not recognise, onto wounds to heal them, or chewed them to stay intoxicated and work longer on slopes.

When the rains receded, Farzana and her sisters began

their wait for Diwali. They were Muslims, like most others in the mountain communities. But on the slopes Diwali brought breezy winters and creamy candy-coloured sweets sprinkled with saffron strands, crushed cardamom, sliced pistachios or silver slivers that tumbled out of garbage trucks for days. City confectioners made hundreds of pounds of sweets, with disclaimers to consume them within a day or the fresh cream they were made with would sour. What didn't sell at the stores made it to Deonar for hilltop Diwali parties. *Hamara har shauk poora hua khaadi mein*, Hera – who came only to collect treats – would tell me later. *The mountains fulfilled our every desire.*

Balmy, fleeting winters gave way to unending summers. The township turned gold under the blazing sun, and Farzana watched trash shine or fade on the sun-baked slopes that rippled around her, edged by the glimmering creek. Plants withered quickly, leaving an expanse of dried mud and trash. Long, hot days were redeemed only by extended swims or by discovering puffy white boxes stuffed with ice-cream cups, long past their expiry date, in the trash.

Farzana knew the end of summer was near when thick bunches of blotchy red lychees began falling out of the emptying trucks. She bit through their scaly skin and pulled it away with her teeth. The juice within dribbled down her chin. She spun the fruit in her mouth, spat out the long black seed and swallowed the translucent white pulp, which cooled her as it went down, swirling the sweaty last dregs of summer with sweetness.

Farzana was suddenly growing to be tall, like both her parents, and athletic, like her mother. She poured her coltish energy into chasing the city's unending trash caravans. She watched garbage trucks lurch slowly up the rubble- and trash-filled slopes. As they got to hill clearings, she raced other pickers to reach them, clambering onto the trucks' side rails before they halted and began emptying. She leaned onto the trucks' edge so she didn't fall off, dipped both her hands in and skimmed the cream of the junk before anyone else could. She held onto the railing, turning and twisting aside when burning trash fell out of the trucks, ignited when thin plastic bags were jammed too tightly with garbage and still-simmering cigarette butts. She brought out hard-boiled eggs, or bags of crisps that she sat in a circle and snacked on with her sisters and friends. What they could not eat, Farzana enveloped in her outstretched arms and carried downhill for her younger sisters and brother.

Unlike his daughter, Hyder Ali worried about the remains of city people, their melted desires – the spirits that arose from them and were marooned on the mountains. To him they were an ever-present danger, hanging around the slopes, unobserved, only to ensnare his daughters. He told Farzana how he had seen unclaimed dead bodies tipped out of dumpers at the edge of the grounds, where trash hills ran into the creek. He had watched burnt ashes from Mumbai's cremation grounds being emptied on hilltops.

Passing on the rules he had accumulated during the years he had spent on the mountains, Hyder Ali reminded Farzana to stay away from the *jhinga* loop, the first mountain after the municipal office. His neighbours' son, Shabbir, called it *charbi ka tilla* or the 'mound of fat'. It was full of animal fat, dung and blood, and was treacherous and slippery underfoot. One of Shabbir's employees, flying a kite on the mound, had sunk into the squishy hill and had to be pulled out. Household trash was hardly ever emptied on it, and Hyder Ali believed spirits circled above it. Nearly eight years later, this is where Farzana would find the lifeless babies, with their stomachs melded together. But *usko bolenge nahi karna hai, to Farzana ko karna hi hai,* Sahani, her older sister, recalled, with a grin lighting up her almond-shaped, kohl-rimmed eyes. *If you asked her not to do something, Farzana had to do it.*

Some mornings her friends stopped by her home while everyone was still asleep. Farzana left with them and whichever sister she could wake up. They ran up to clearings where trucks had delivered trash from Mumbai's luxury hotels or the airport, and sat on the hilltops and ate hotel breakfasts. Hera would tell me later, pointing to Arif, their fourteen-year-old friend shrivelled by tuberculosis, that the bread they had eaten was as long as he was. They sliced breakfast rolls with cutlery that came in crisp airline packaging and slathered them with butter, jam or ketchup from single-serve sachets thrown away at breakfast buffets. Afterwards Hera left for school and Farzana and her sisters to chase the garbage trucks.

As Mumbaikars moved to wearing ready-made clothes, cloth scraps had faded from the slopes and Farzana had begun to collect plastic, copper wire and German Silver, rather than the bright offcuts that Hyder Ali had taught her to chase. She emptied her bag in her lane, accumulating long loops of electric wires and retrieving tight coils from within the gadgets that crammed Mumbai homes, but had to be discarded because they rotted in its salty coastal air and felt outdated as soon as they were bought. She burned the wire to recover copper, and stuffed broken television sets, rusted ceiling fans and video players into her burlap bag. She bashed stones on them, quickly covering her ears to muffle the sound of cracking. Sifting through the broken shards, she pulled out the metal frames of the television sets.

Collecting 2 lbs of trembling copper wire or German Silver, which could take a few days, earned up to Rs 300, compared to a few rupees for a couple of pounds of white cloth scraps. Farzana sold her haul and handed her money to Hyder Ali, who earned even less, his earnings shrinking with the waning supply of cloth scraps, his languid air and long breaks to chat with friends that he ran into at work. They told him how the cloth scraps now went straight from the textile factories to traders in their lanes.

The taller the mountains grew, the harder it became to move them. At court hearings in around April 2009 Justice Chandrachud had asked Mumbai's compact and erudite municipal commissioner, Jairaj Phatak, to go to the Deonar township to see the forgotten world with his own eyes.[1] Trailed by his entourage of civic officials, Phatak, who was an engineer and had recently completed a doctorate in economics, saw the halo of gas that ringed the mountains Rane had photographed, and on which Hyder Ali and Farzana worked. 'I was told that this smoke was not due to fire set by rag pickers but due to methane gas in the garbage, which starts burning, letting out smoke without anybody being near the spot,' Phatak wrote in his report for Chandrachud.

With contempt proceedings looming, Phatak returned to his office and rifled through the inspirational quotes that he assiduously accumulated. He settled on one from the American president Theodore Roosevelt, which he wrote out in his pocket diary: 'In any moment of decision, the best thing you can do is the right thing, the next best thing is the wrong thing and the worst thing you can do is nothing.'

Months after his visit, the municipality's lawyers announced that it had agreed on a plan. A few weeks later they gave a presentation in the courtroom, which was darkened for the occasion. The first air conditioners were just being installed in a few of the lofty, high-ceilinged courtrooms, and the long-handled ceiling fans, which had whirred noisily and drowned out court proceedings, finally fell silent. Creaky slatted wooden windows were closed, after years of standing open to catch a breeze.

On a screen installed in the courtroom a new Deonar township appeared. Officials showed tarred roads winding through the mountains, vents jutting out of trash peaks to release the fires trapped within, and a plant that would reduce their trash to compost. Half the hills would be shovelled to the side, freeing space for the compost plant that would feed Mumbai's fading gardens, officials said. Dried trash would also burn to fuel machines at factories nearby. The plant would create municipal card-carrying jobs for pickers on the trash hills, allowing them an official position, a pension and some security. If it all worked, Mumbai's waste would leave the mountains legally, as compost, for the first time in more than a century.

With contempt proceedings looming closer, Phatak and his colleagues re-looked at the bids that the two short-listed companies had made more than two years before. United Phosphorus Limited, one of the world's largest seed and fertilizer companies, came closest to meeting the terms. And so in October 2009 the municipality gave United Phosphorus the Deonar contract. It quickly convened a company with two partners; they called it Tatva.[2]

The municipality's plans had not worried Hyder Ali at first. The pickers didn't sell the food that rotted slowly on the hills. Besides, he had only ever seen the mountains growing higher, stretching further into the creek. The city sent enough trash for the pickers and the municipality's plans, he thought.

He and the children chose from more than a thousand trucks that streamed in every day. Long, lurching garbage caravans emptied on the hilltops, so that more trash could be accumulated in the apartment blocks and suburbs where it had begun its life. Farzana and her sisters bent low on hilltops to read alphabets stuck on the front windows of the khaki-and-orange trucks that passed below, indicating the city wards they came from. They raced to trucks that came from wealthy neighbourhoods loaded with saleable trash, gliding deep into the whirls of muddy pickers that surrounded them.

After she brought out everything she needed to sell, Farzana often emerged from the receding scrambles dragging felled branches or cracked bamboo poles that came from tree-lined neighbourhoods. She and her sisters dug them in, to stand upright on quiet hilltops. They threw burlap, plastic or long, dried-out palm leaves over them to make shelters from the beating sun, competing with the boys in making larger, better cabins.

Teetering on her teenage years, Farzana had acquired a sudden taste for gossiping in the interior of these cabins, in the lull between truck arrivals. They chatted over rice or instant noodles, ferreted out of trucks and cooked painstakingly over small fires they lit. City trash yielded slender, long grains of rice that were never seen in markets around the mountains. Sometimes they pooled money to buy spices and minced meat, then cooked it to go with the city rice and invited friends over. Younger security guards often joined them for parties, or to shade from the scorching mountain sun. They warned Farzana and her friends that they would shortly be replaced by new guards.

Soon Farzana did begin to see new officers, guards and machinery at the mountains, while municipal staff retreated to their office at the townships' entrance, from where they supervised the filling of mountains into trucks that faded away deep into the township. Mountains were shovelled onto others at the edge of the creek, clearing space for the plant. Rumours floated around the hills; it was hard to know which ones were true and which were not. Hyder Ali's deep-set eyes lit up in surprise when he saw that their lives, which had stretched out in the fog of delays and snags in contracting their township, would change. But even as he watched, the hills started to shrink.

A slim, empty strip opened up between pickers' homes and the trash. A wall began to rise on it. It would form the township's boundary, marking the hills within as Tatva's territory, and no longer the pickers'. Instead Tatva officials set up booths in the lanes around, offering jobs at the soon-to-be-built plant. Jehangir and most other boys signed up for them, hoping to have municipal employment that would make them legitimate on the mountains. New dreams settled in their eyes.

*

But Tatva staffers had discovered the fetid and secret world that Farzana lived in, and they knew it would be hard to manage. Soon after they arrived they wrote to municipal officials and asked for help. The mountains burned constantly, throwing up smoke, they wrote. The slopes were filled with the illicit army of pickers, overrun by cattle and their handlers, and their far edges were carved out between violent gangs. More than 200 garbage trucks arrived every hour in peak hours, delivering twice the amount of garbage that Tatva had been asked to handle every day. Pickers and traders believed it belonged to them. How could they even begin to deal with somewhere like this? they asked.

Beyond the mountains, a storm was gathering. Almost since its creation, Tatva had been embroiled in controversy surrounding the circumstances of its winning bid. The uproar had now made it to the State Assembly. The chief minister ordered an inquiry.

At Deonar, Tatva worked on, stretching the wall further, stranding the pickers outside. To begin with, Farzana walked along it and slipped through its cracks to work. Soon, however, the wall seemed unending and she could not make it through. Work stalled in their communities. Court orders and waste rules had finally arrived at the township.

Stuck now, Farzana hung outside the wall for weeks. She paced restlessly at its edge until she began seeing ropes fixed around the craggy stone edges of the wall. She pulled herself up and over, just as she had seen other pickers do, and got to work. Amid the shrinking mountains she found a pair of blue jeans lying stiffly against the unfiltered mountain sun, late one afternoon. She picked them up and held them against herself. She had seen actresses wear jeans in movie posters, as she sat in the buses or rickshaws that screeched as they inched slowly through the Lotus market, which had filled over time with stores, handcarts and stalls and was the tunnel that delivered their township to the city and new things from the city to them. Like her sisters, Farzana mostly wore salwar kameezes, with long dupattas to cover her hair. But she brought the jeans home, washed them repeatedly and saved them for the occasional family trips that Hyder Ali took them on. She kept scaling the wall to get in and work, watching the hills inside contract.

Dr Rane too had watched the wall stretch and the hills shrink. 'Everything I had asked for was happening,' he would tell me later. 'I saw sections of the ground getting closed for dumping.' In January 2011 he withdrew his court case.

The inquiry report on awarding the contract to Tatva came out that August. It said the bid process had some material flaws.[3] Report in hand, municipal officials wrote to the commissioner to ask if the Tatva contract was now to be rethought or scrapped. No response came. Instead a cloud settled over the mountain-shrinking project and the municipal card-carrying jobs.

6

Early in the monsoon of 2011 Jehangir was working on the mountains when someone came over to tell him that his plump boss, Javed Ansari – known as Shanoo Bhai – was walking to his house with a sword in his hand. Jehangir ran home, followed by Farzana, Sahani and the other siblings and watched as Shanoo slashed the plastic sheets that made up the walls of their house. When the roof collapsed, Shanoo walked into the heap of ruined plastic that was once their home, pulled out stones they had brought back from the mountains and laid down as flooring and threw them out into the lane.

Shanoo and other garbage traders had always fought to amass trash at the township. But as Tatva struggled to build the plant, the mountains began to grow again, the lanes around them swelled too and the life in them was pulled increasingly into the shadowlands of the trader gangs' control. Traders hacked cracks in the boundary wall, moved deeper, corralling hills and clearings, accumulated all that the trucks emptied and then resold it. Where pickers worked on their stretch of the mountain, the traders' lackeys also claimed the contents of their bags, paying them little or nothing, and reselling from their *katas* for a profit. Their presence was inescapable in the lanes, too, where the traders offered illegal connections to the electricity, cable

TV and water supply – and charged a fee for it. Traders' battles for control over the mountains, the township and the lanes around it grew increasingly vicious.

The legend in their lanes had it that some years ago Shanoo had taken on a murder charge for a rival gangster, in exchange for rights over garbage that was left on the hills adjoining them. Charges could not be proven in court, and Shanoo had returned home to induct the teenage Jehangir into the slim army that had helped to build his mountain fiefdom. Through a mixture of beatings and abuse, Shanoo had trained Jehangir to intimidate the other pickers and to fight other gangs with swords. *Shanoo ne hamare liye kya kiya? Hamne uske liye kiya*, Jehangir would tell me later. *What did Shanoo do for us? We made him.*

For months Shanoo had suspected that Jehangir was filling garbage trucks for his rival, Javed Qureshi, who was a rising man on the hills. Shanoo had seen Javed Qureshi's hills inching closer to his own territory and began to suspect that Farzana, Sahani and Farha sold their trash to Qureshi too. That evening in 2011 he had slashed their house as punishment. After that, the rain had fallen harder against the darkening light, turning their house into a muddy puddle. They ventured in, wading knee deep to find some fresh plastic sheets from the trash they had saved up, then strung them close around themselves and slept within its fragile protection.

Her sisters stayed away from Shanoo, picking surreptitiously, but Farzana left them behind, getting the boys who hung around the wall to push her over on days when it was freshly repaired. Inside, she chased trucks with them. If Jehangir found her playing marbles with boys, she would grin and show them her hand, tell them she'd be right back and follow him home, where she would get slashed with his belt. She hung out with boys too much: that was how she would explain Jehangir's beatings to me later. *Mujhe to vo bahut chahta hai,* she would beam. *He loves me a lot.* It was a kind of love that Jehangir had learned from Shanoo.

The two years Tatva had been given to build the plant expired in the winter of 2011, and the municipality had still not received permission from the state government to lease the grounds so that construction could start. Payment was now due for the plant, which had not been built. Payments were delayed. Negotiations continued. In May and July 2012 Tatva wrote to the municipality, reminding it to lease the vast township, so that it could begin making the plant.[1] The municipality in turn wrote again to the state government for permission to lease the Deonar township to Tatva. The state government did not reply, and the municipality did not reply to Tatva.

On 7 November 2012 Shanoo, who had recently been exiled and now lived in Navi Mumbai, after a trader he had beaten brought a court case, died in a road accident. His family and gang members brought him back to be buried in the Deonar cemetery. The graveyard, which was not far from the mountains, had filled up with poor Muslims who had moved into the area in the wake of the religious riots in 1992, looking for trash-made homes and endless work on the rising slopes. *Chori ka paani, chori ki bijli, aur ek gareeb ko chahiye kya,* a gang boss, who had arrived in an earlier wave of migrants, once told me. *Stolen water, stolen power, what more does a poor man want?* It was somewhere to live, and somewhere to die.

The new arrivals filled the thicket of lanes in the mountains' growing shadow and ended their days in the graveyard at its edge. Gravediggers looked for empty slivers of earth to inter the dead, who streamed in every day. They brought up half-consumed arms, legs and long hair still growing from bodies melded into the earth. The gravediggers quickly refilled the graves with mud sprinkled with salt or potassium and dug elsewhere, hoping that bodies that should have turned to dust in four months would have disappeared in two. Illness and violence – the twins that stalked the mountain slopes – meant the gravediggers filled not-yet-old graves with young, new bodies. *Yahaan boodha ho ke to koi marta hi nahi*, a cleric from these lanes told me, thinking of the funerals he conducted. *No one dies of old age here.*

For Shanoo's funeral, gang bosses from around the mountains' rim had set their rivalry aside for a day and streamed into the unkempt Deonar graveyard. They watched his teenage underlings make their way around the overgrown shrubs, tombstones and broken benches, organising proceedings. While leaving, several of the gang bosses asked Jehangir to stay in touch. *Collar upar*, his friend Miya Khan – known as Babu – remembered hearing, as he wilted in the sultry mid-afternoon heat and the uncertainty that lay ahead. *Keep your shirt collars – your spirits – up*. The hair that Babu had carefully piled into shiny *seeng*, or horns, to elongate his skinny frame, flopped limply on his face. Sweat soaked his shirt, sticking it to his back.

In the wake of Shanoo's death, Jehangir needed a new job: he became a father for the second time weeks later, on 9 December. His expenses were growing, and the legitimate job he had signed up for at the plant hovered forever on the horizon, delayed by Tatva's negotiations with the municipality. The gang, which was already sputtering out in Shanoo's exile, dissolved completely after his death.

Jehangir struck out on his own. He bought glass from pickers on the slopes, bribing or befriending guards to let him take heaps of glass out through the walls' widening gaps. Farzana and his other sisters washed and cleaned broken shards so that he could get a better price for them. Jehangir had watched Javed, and his bosses Atique and Rafique Khan, take over more territory on the mountains; he sold it at Javed Qureshi's *kata*, for more than Shanoo had ever paid him.

The brothers Rafique and Atique Khan had arrived at the mountains as children in 1975, when it was still a watery forest between the dumping ground and the creek. Atique, the younger of the brothers, remembered worrying about falling into the swamp when he first moved there as a ten-year-old. *Log daldal mein gir ke mar jaate the*, he recalled. *People fell into the swamp and died.* Regardless, his father and others had put down rubber tyres, plastic sheets and cardboard and settled in Rafiq Nagar on Deonar's marsh and the edges of the trash slopes. Police and municipal officials demolished their homes, but they kept resettling them, until the municipality finally acknowledged the settlement, making skinny roads and building a nursery school that tilted along the slopes' gradient.

The Khan brothers' father had started a restaurant where the brothers had begun waiting tables. They had filled mangroves with mountain mud and made plastic-sheet homes over them, which they rented or sold. But they knew that any fortune around here would have to come from trash. Around 2005 they cajoled their father into opening a *kata* shop in the mountain-facing stretch of road that was already filling up with them. Shop owners competed for pickers as they descended the slopes, carrying back bits of the mountains on their heads. The traders stopped at nothing to beat their rivals and redirect their trash, but Atique and Rafique brought a fierceness that had never been seen before.

In October 2009 Kadeer Shaikh, a rival of the Khan brothers, had died from stab wounds on the slim dirt strip between the mountains and their *kata* shop, even as a small crowd watched, immobilised. Kadeer's mother had refused to collect the body until Atique and Rafique were charged with her son's murder. But when police looked for witnesses to build their case, Kadeer's murder became unseen and unheard. Atique was kept in custody for a month while police investigations carried on and was then let off, burnishing the Khan brothers' image as the mountains' bosses. More accusations of threats and violence piled up, mostly unproven and unconvicted.

Soon after Kadeer's murder, the Khans' acolyte, Javed Qureshi, began appearing on their mountain clearings while the brothers worked from their offices at the mountains' edge. The Khans' name and their writ controlled life in the lanes of Rafiq Nagar and the mountains around them. Rooms in their skinny lanes opened out to damp, sunless alleys or rambling, sun-soaked trash slopes that petered into waves. Walking through the lanes could yield roosters, collected for prize-fights, couches spilling foam and ageing gangsters crouched against shrunken doorframes that blocked the sun. Cable television, water, trash, jobs: everything that made up life in the lanes was ultimately said to be controlled by the Khans and other gangs, as their cavernous sheds at the mountains' edge expanded.

With every delay in making the plant, the mountains were receding back into invisibility, while the gangs' grip on them, and the lanes around them, was extending. The brothers' men began patrolling their territory, which was strung with cameras that beamed footage of any intruders back to their headquarters. Jehangir's fortunes rose with Javed Qureshi, who lent him money for his sister Afsana's wedding. Jehangir sold his glass to traders, who would sell it on, to be melted into new shapes or refilled with new drinks. *Vo ek number ka aadmi hai*, Jehangir would tell me later. *He is a first-class person.*

Jehangir named his baby daughter Shifa, meaning 'healing'. He came to believe that she had mended his luck. His business with Javed Qureshi grew fast: the next year Jehangir replaced the family's plastic-sheet walls, the ones that Shanoo had slashed, with a few feet of bricks, topped with long layers of tin sheet. He made a loft, where he and his wife Rakila lived with their girls. *Iske aane se na unki kismet badal gayee*, Rakila would say about Shifa. *She brought luck in his life.* As his business grew, Jehangir hired employees – teenage pickers – who cleaned his glass heaps. Every few weeks he packed his younger brothers, sisters and the glass cleaners into the driver's cabin, while broken shards jangled in the back to sell to city traders. He dropped them at Chowpatty beach while he sold his mountain treasures.

Away from the mountains Farzana wore sunglasses, a

sun hat and long tunics with her jeans. She splashed in the sea, which was ringed by buildings nearly as tall as the mountains. While her sisters made castles out of the wind-blown sand, Farzana walked far ahead, along the gently curving shore, pressing her feet into the sand to leave footprints. She walked through a world she had known only through its detritus and turned back against the sun, every little while, to see how far she had come.

When they got there, mid-morning, Farzana watched college students arrive with their overfilled backpacks, there to escape class or shield gently forming relationships from prying eyes. As the afternoon wore on, groups of women in flowery burqa-like *ridaas* or sarees, with dangling handbags, came for a respite between the unbending mealtimes they laboured to meet in their claustrophobic kitchens. Farzana watched the shifting, lacy shadows, from the trees that lined the edges, fall on bejewelled honeymooners and couples throughout the day. They all sought the busy beach and its inadequate shadows, to escape Mumbai's cramped family homes.

Farzana felt, fleetingly, as if she belonged in this world of people whose lives were filled with things and who discarded trash, not hoarded it. When Jehangir came to take them home, she begged him to stay a little longer. They watched a deepening pink sky frame the rising skyline, the sea turn molten and the bronzed sun melt slowly into it, extinguishing its glow. Then they got back into his truck and drove through the snaking traffic, almost following the route that the city's trash took to reach them.

Behind the truck the remains of stumpy, torn-down buildings followed them, like lengthening shadows. The detritus created by Mumbai's never-ceasing construction industry was mostly supposed to be buried in far-flung quarries, else the cement, asbestos, rusted metal and chemicals they gave off could hang in the city air and settle in residents' lungs, sickening them.

Rafique, the older of the Khan brothers, was said to offer a way round these long and expensive quarry trips, which delayed new construction because rebuilding was usually permitted once the torn-down buildings were disposed of. Municipal officials working nights had seen trucks arrive from the city through the night, slipping through holes in the wall at the far end of the townships' official entrance.[2] They saw a secret suburb of grey concrete hills rise above the wall. When the hills got too high and wobbly, fires burned on them, water tankers doused them and bulldozers flattened the burnt remains. The debris hills rose again. It allowed the city's instant reinvention and was said to have lifted Rafique and Atique's fortunes too.[3]

Further along the mountains' broken boundary wall was a rambling estate where waste came from some of Mumbai's largest hospitals and was said to be Atique and Javed's domain. Pickers that the lackeys let in collected the thick plastic gloves, saline bags and bottles, which their landlord resold. Across both brothers' territories thin plastic sheets, shopping bags and garbage bags, which did not fetch much money, were collected and piled into trucks. Pickers had heard they went to factories in distant towns, where they were pressed into little plastic pellets and sold across the country and abroad.

Between the estates of debris and medical waste lay an empty space where the municipality planned to make a new graveyard. It had stayed vacant for years, officials worrying that rains and trash could come gushing down the mountain slopes, bringing up newly buried bodies. They began seeing it fill with debris from dead buildings instead, with the gangs inching their way across it at night. When I met him years later, Atique Khan told me that the brothers had retreated from the mountains after they were wrongly accused of Kadeer's murder. Their acolytes misused their name in running illegal businesses on the mountains.

In July 2013 Tatva had written to the municipality asking again for the lease to the township, so that it could mortgage it and begin making the plant that would lead to the mountains' closure.[4] In April the chief minister of Maharashtra, Prithviraj Chavan, had announced the formation of another committee to probe the terms of the municipality's contract with Tatva.[5] While it investigated whether permission could be given to lease out municipal trash townships to private companies, the township stayed in limbo.

It was at around this time that Hyder Ali first came to my office in search of the loans that he hoped would help him step out of the mountains' shadow. He began bringing friends, and Farzana often came along too. They sat in the long waiting area outside my room across from a pistachio-green wall painted, Warli style, with red stick-figures sowing, chaffing, harvesting and then storing their crop. Farzana asked Hyder Ali to explain the almost hypnotic movements. His mother had pounded grain for rich landowners in their village, since they did not own any land. They were paid only in small amounts of grain. This was the life he had fled as a teenager when he came to Mumbai, and now he fumbled and tripped, trying to tell her about it. Farzana wanted herself photographed against the map of everything that Hyder Ali had wished to leave behind.

When Hyder Ali and I chatted for too long, as we often did, Farzana poked her head into my room to hurry him along. She had to get back to work. I remember her as the awkward, tall teenager who wanted to accompany her father for a trip away from the mountains, but could not stay away from them for long. I did not know then that it was Farzana, her sisters and Jehangir who kept their household going and our repayments coming unerringly, while Hyder Ali's workshop sputtered out. While some of the other micro-lenders stayed away because of the gangs' stranglehold on the lanes around the mountains, I thought our unfaltering repayments came from being one of few low-interest lenders in them. I was unaware that Jehangir was by now a trusted lieutenant in the fiercest of the gangs.

In September 2013 Tatva wrote to the municipality saying that a dispute had arisen over the municipality's inability to lease the township to it and non-payment for its services.[6] It asked the municipality to form a dispute resolution committee to resolve the stand-off. Copies of the letter began arriving at a range of municipal offices.

In October the municipality wrote back, saying it would form a committee to resolve their differences. More letters from Tatva arrived at the municipal offices, attempting to set up the committee so it could begin work. No responses came. In December Tatva filed a court case to get the municipality to pay its dues for their work in clearing the site, as well as the failure to provide the lease to make the plant, which remained unbuilt.

Late one afternoon that winter Jehangir was buying trash on the hills when another picker called him to the creek. Jehangir ran down the burning slopes to find a small crowd collecting near the mangroves. As he got closer, he saw Farzana and Farha already standing around a boat that had run ashore in the sand. He craned through the crowd and saw the fading yellow sunlight glowing on gold. A middle-aged woman was sprawled across the boat, dressed as a bride. She was dead.

He asked Farzana to turn away but she stared, transfixed, at the gold bracelets that lined the woman's arms. They shone against her lifeless skin. They could hear police sirens in the distance and finally some policemen arrived, walking the last stretch over the garbage-strewn tracks. Jehangir saw them cover the luminous woman with a white sheet and take her away.

For weeks Farzana asked him if he had heard anything about the woman who had floated into the city's graveyard of possessions. How did she get there? she asked Jehangir, most evenings. Who sent her? All the woman's prized belongings had not been enough to fill the emptiness in her life, Farzana thought. Someone must have killed the woman and put her into the boat that had drifted into their town, Jehangir said. Like everything else on the mountains, he told her, the dead woman in her bridal jewellery had probably floated into their forgotten township to be forgotten, even in plain sight.

7

Legend among the pickers had it that expensive belong-ings could only have arrived at the mountains because they brought their owners ill luck. This misfortune would follow pickers if they kept any of these thrown-away trea-sures, they believed. Instead, pawnbrokers walked their lanes to rid them of their fortune-draining finds.

It was only in its infancy, but 2015 was turning out to be the year of dwindling fortunes. The sparring between the municipality and Tatva dragged on, in court and outside. In February a state-government inquiry concluded, pre-dictably, that the contract with Tatva should not have been signed before permission was obtained to lease the township from the state government, and that there had been irregularities with the tender process.[1] Soon after the report was submitted, the recently re-elected state govern-ment denied permission to lease out the sprawling trash township, drying up the plans to fund the compost plant and shrivel the mountains. The pickers would have to look elsewhere for better work and those elusive munici-pal cards. In these attempts, hardly anyone fell faster than Moharram Ali, once the luckiest of mountain denizens. Somewhere in the middle of Tatva's slow fade away from the mountains, he disappeared too.

Municipal officials had already been planning for a

new waste-to-energy plant at Deonar for several months; now they were staring at court orders that had said the township was to be closed that year. As the municipality began looking for funds, and a new company to build the plant, warm winds blew over the mountains, aggravating the season of fires. The monsoon, which usually calmed the fires for a few months, would not arrive until June.

That year water tankers posted at the township struggled to douse the fires for more than a week. Municipal officials looked on helplessly. Official correspondence also showed that in February the municipal commissioner had said there were several complications and risks involved in a waste-to-energy plant, especially one that the municipality would own jointly with a private company. It took back the fresh plans for a plant.[2]

The garbage caravans continued to arrive and Tatva shovelled their contents onto the hills, as it had for more than five years. In court, it pushed for the appointment of an arbitrator to award its unpaid bills and damages for being unable to make the plant. Municipal lawyers countered by saying that Tatva had worked for years, while awaiting permission; it was content, they suggested, with piling trash on the hilltops rather than making the plant. It had paid Tatva for the work it did. Mediation was not written into their contract. At the township, broken fragments of the wall stood stranded – a reminder of the future that had so nearly arrived, before it sank into the trash that the pickers had waded through their whole lives. On 19 March 2015 Justice Shahrukh Kathawalla granted Tatva's plea for mediation with the municipality. That winter, arbitration proceedings would begin.

*

I had thought that Moharram Ali, with his endless plans, courtly manners and shining luck, would be one of our first borrowers to enter the middle class. With prospects of the job he had signed up for at the plant fading, he told me of new businesses that he had set up to supplement trash-picking, every time he came to take loans. As well as the *kata* shop that he had started after finding the necklace on the slopes, he rented out rooms for a commission and took masonry jobs. It was the best time to be a masonry artisan or *karigar*, he would tell me.

Just as the mountains were said to add a few feet of trash every day, so the straggling communities at their rim were always growing too. Mosque towers were rising above tin-sheet dwellings, and I had watched corner shops in the Lotus market turn into internet cafés, cake shops and clinics. Farzana had told me of a new sweet shop, which made a dessert that melted in the mouth like cotton, soaked in sweet milk.

But years of treasures falling into Moharram Ali's hands had made him unused to the slow grind of masonry. Struggling to deliver commissions on time, he returned to his village often, bought a small plot of land, took loans and spent months building a house on it. Stretched too thinly, he now found his glow beginning to fade. When he returned, the pickers who sold him trash for his *kata* sold to others instead. There was no trace of it in our meetings, but his fragile fortune was slipping out of his hands, replaced by growing debt. He took larger loans from us, repaying unfailingly and always telling me of a new plan that he needed them for.

Yasmin, his wife, struggled to run the house while he was away, and ran up her own debts. The necklace that

Moharram Ali had found often floated in her eyes. She thought about the night she held it in her hands and felt her life was about to get better. She came to believe the necklace had brought ill luck to its owners, which had followed her family too.

Hera, who had inherited her father's long nose and good looks, dropped out of high school. Months after she turned eighteen she took a loan from us to buy a used tailoring machine and began to stitch curtains. Sharib, their eldest son, whom Moharram Ali had wanted to learn driving so that he could work at the plant, picked trash all day. At fifteen, he was still baby-faced but seemed suddenly taller, his eyes blurred under his floppy hair. For years Yasmin had berated him for picking at the slopes after she dispatched him to school. But with Moharram Ali away, she began keeping his money, settling Sharib in the grip of the mountains that she had wanted to keep her children away from.

She tried enrolling him at night school instead. Sharib returned home soaked in mountain mud after class had begun, fell on the food that Yasmin could rustle up and then stretched on the floor, hardly ever making it to class. Later Yasmin would say that, with Moharram Ali away and creditors at her door, she had become addicted to Sharib's earnings. She watched his smile turn scarce and brown. She turned away when she saw him chew the tobacco that stained it. She knew that it kept him working through the long, hungry days.

When she came to drop off garbage bags or refill water bottles, Farzana began seeing Yasmin in her house collecting the slim, long strips of fabric to be stitched as borders for sarees or kurtas, which Jehangir's wife, Rakila, gave women to stick beads on, in pencil-marked flower patterns. Neighbours streamed in after the mountain pickers left for work, collected these pieces and exchanged gossip, with children in tow. Farzana wondered why Yasmin took work that fetched only a few rupees, for borders that were longer than herself; her family had always floated a little above the others in their lanes. And yet Yasmin was there most afternoons, telling them that she needed to stay busy while Moharram Ali was away.

By the time he got back, Yasmin was desperate. Moharram Ali returned to stalk the mountains' overlooked riches and waited restlessly for his luck to turn again, bringing treasures back into his hands. Then his father called to say that he had fixed his youngest daughter's wedding – that of Moharram Ali's favourite sister. Moharram Ali left to sell the village house in order to fund the wedding, returning to struggle with his dwindling fortune and his growing debt. Without my knowledge, he borrowed from others to repay us and take more of our low-interest loans. In his lane he moved secretly, avoiding creditors. Yasmin struggled to send him to work just as she had once struggled to send her sons to school.

She decided to step in, taking a loan from us to start a *vada pav* stall at the market on 90 Feet Road, which ran along the mountains' curve and was named for its width. Yasmin, Hera and Mehrun, her middle daughter, fried potato patties and green chillies that sputtered in the pan and brought tears to their eyes throughout the afternoons. She handed them to Moharram Ali, in oil-stained newspaper, to slice into fluffy buns and sell as the market came to life at dusk. Reluctantly he set up the kind of stall that he had kept in business for years. Then friends dropped by. Yasmin heard he gave them free food. The stall folded, adding to their string of failed businesses and swirling loans. She faltered on our repayments, making new loans unavailable to her.

She handed her nose-pin to Rakila and asked for a loan to start a new business. Yasmin bought groceries to start a meal service for the artisans who made shoes or clothes, or who filled them with embroidery at the many workshops sprouting in the lanes. Her first customer, an embroiderer, began taking a lunch box, eating his dinner at home with Moharram Ali and retreating into the dark lane with him to giggle over their glowing phones. The embroiderers' payments got sucked into buying the family's food supplies; Yasmin could not add new clients, their business shut, and Rakila wore the nose-pin for months, while Yasmin looked for loans to retrieve it.

At home Moharram Ali raged at Yasmin for his stained clothes, for not pressing his feet until he fell asleep and for her steadily growing quagmire of debt. Pouring over loan-repayment records in my office, I was surprised to see his name among the delayed repayments. Amidst it all, Hera had turned nineteen – one year over the sanctioned age for girls in their lane to marry. At Rakila's house, the women told Yasmin to find the striking and fiery Hera a match before she got too old.

One of them told her about a relative in the upscale Mumbai suburb of Bandra who had a son with decent job prospects. Yasmin borrowed jewellery for herself and Hera and took Moharram Ali, whom she said was a successful trader, to meet the family. He smiled and looked the part, helping to settle the wedding. Hera would finally slip out of the mountains' grasp, as Yasmin had always wanted. And yet pulling it off required more money than they had.

Yasmin went to Rakila's house and enrolled her and Hyder Ali to start a *bishi*, an underground Mumbai system for raising larger sums for desperate times. The *bishi*'s members contribute fixed instalments into a shared pot every month. One of the subscribers is able to withdraw the pooled sum each month, minus a commission for the organiser – the payout rotating until everyone has been able to withdraw from the pot. Yasmin's offer was even better. She would collect the instalments and return double the amount, including interest, every month, she told them. Hyder Ali joined so that he could grow his embroidery workshop when he got the increased amount, and Rakila planned to take on more beadwork. Moharram Ali often asked for these instalments, to make his own repayments. Yasmin resisted. They argued.

In September 2015, weeks before arbitration proceedings between Tatva and the municipality were to begin, the municipality served a pre-termination notice to Tatva, which it would later enforce on 22 January, 2016. Tatva was to leave the Deonar township on 31 January 2016, only six years into its twenty-five-year tenancy.[3] Until the municipality could begin fixing things afresh, the township would continue to take in more of the city's reeking secrets, employing only the illicit army of pickers.

One night when Yasmin brought the instalments home, Moharram Ali asked for them again. He would replace them soon, he said. Yasmin refused. With their parents' voices raging within their home, glowing in the dark lane, the children stayed out. Later they slipped in and slept on the floor, before the voices quietened. In the morning Yasmin was sleeping next to them. Moharram Ali was not. When Yasmin sent Sharib and her younger son Sameer to look for him on the mountains, he was not there. She asked Hyder Ali to go to the 90 Feet Road market, but it was deserted, the shops had not opened.

Around noon the *bishi* organiser made his way through the small crowd at their home. He asked Yasmin for the instalments. But when she opened her wooden cupboard and looked under the clothes where she had hidden the money, it wasn't there. She upturned clothes and the broken dolls that Moharram Ali had got from the mountains for Mehrun and Ashra, their younger daughters. Moharram Ali had left with the money.

Days later, when Hyder Ali walked to Yasmin's house to ask for his money, which had vanished instead of doubling, he saw her beaten-up television set, washing machine and Hera's sewing machine being carried out through their lane. Creditors would sell them to retrieve what they could. Yasmin's room was filled with others pressing for their money. Farzana began seeing Yasmin lock her house from the outside, before they arrived. Our loan officer returned to tell me that Moharram Ali had disappeared, Yasmin was untraceable and both of their repayments had stopped.

A tired disappointment replaced the dreams of gold in their lanes in the winter of 2015. The failed compost plant had become one of the mountains' ghosts, even before it materialised. Tatva's staff were leaving to work elsewhere. The latest court deadline to stop dumping garbage at the Deonar township – to fix it or settle a modern trash township – had passed months ago. Garbage caravans arrived unabated, letting Sharib and Sameer work and keep the house going.

Yasmin had pulled twelve-year-old Mehrun out of the free municipal-run school to manage their home, and enrolled eight-year-old Ashra, her youngest daughter, who had been at a private English school, in it. Ashra returned with dishevelled hair, which Yasmin tried to tame, and empty notebooks that she did not notice. As their household suddenly curled at its edges, words began to get stuck within Ashra. They came out fitfully, and sometimes only in her intense green-eyed stare.

Ashra was hardly ever in class and doodled even when she was,[4] Shireen Mohammed Siraj, Ashra's third-grade teacher at her new school, called to tell Yasmin. Days later Yasmin walked slowly through the school corridor, looking down at the floor, which was wet and slippery from the children's water fights, and seeing the mountains seeping in through the classroom windows. In the principal's room, a couple of burqa-clad teachers were speaking to a burly consultant who had been assigned to supervise the area's schools. *Pen se nahi likhte par whitener jeb mein rakhte hain*, one teacher said. *They have not started writing with pens yet, but they carry ink whitener.* The consultant nodded knowingly; he had seen students inhaling the ink whitener in stairwells around the mountain schools. Yasmin and her teacher Siraj decided that Ashra needed remedial classes.

Lallu, Ashra's cousin and classmate, came over to walk to school with her every morning. He tucked his blue-and-white striped school shirt into navy-blue shorts that bunched up under his school belt and hung down below his knees. His socks were rolled underneath them and over his kneecaps. He wore a clip-on tie, pressed his hair down with oil and slung the school bag that seemed to out-weigh him over his shoulders. He waited at the door while Ashra searched for a bit of her uniform, or nursed an upset stomach inside. She often emerged only after Lallu left, singing made-up ditties of lines that she heard Yasmin say to creditors, and dancing with the flies on the loose stones that covered the drains.

Lallu picked trash on the mountains or went through their lane's overflowing dustbins, after school, to supple-ment his father's earnings from selling medicinal herbs. He pushed his mother, who was Moharram Ali's sister, to apply for a bank account or an identity card, when teachers asked him to. In their walks to school he reminded Ashra that the municipality would deposit a rupee in her bank account for every day that she attended. She stared ahead.

Yasmin began to notice that, some afternoons, Lallu returned home without Ashra. Siraj said she was not at class. When questioned, Lallu said that Ashra had left with a tall, slim man. Worried that a creditor was trying to kidnap Ashra, Yasmin asked who it was. Moharram Ali, Lallu reported back: he had hung outside her school until Ashra spotted him, ran up and hugged him. They walked nearby, getting a snack, with Moharram Ali asking Ashra to keep their meetings secret. After this discovery, and on Hera's instructions, Ashra made Moharram Ali walk her through Rafiq Nagar's skinny lanes.

They entered a lane just wide enough to fit a person, with a slim open drain, flattening themselves against the wall to let others pass. At the passage end, not far from them, Ashra saw a leafy old tree rising from the watery swamp. Moharram Ali turned and unlocked a room, and a small childlike woman followed him in. This was Shabana, his new wife, he said. He had left home with her, to escape the unending wait for jobs at the waste plant, money to repay the mounting loans and treasures to tell friends about. The next morning Hera, her friends and Yasmin followed Ashra through Rafiq Nagar's lanes and rained blows on Shabana, whom Hera had heard was even younger than her. They returned home, with no one to wait for.

For weeks Ashra came home to find Yasmin curled up on their thin single mattress or speaking to Hera through tears. *Mere karze ki vajah se gaya*, Yasmin said. *He left because of my loans.* She should not have collected *bishi* instalments and tempted Moharram Ali, she said. She wished he hadn't found the gold necklace that had upturned his luck, her marriage and their lives. The two of them had piled on debt and new business plans, thinking mountain luck would turn their way again. Instead the loans had grown, teetered, tumbled and consumed them while, Yasmin believed, the necklace had turned away the mountain luck. Only the debt had stayed, piling up.

When Yasmin returned home from one of her money-seeking trips one afternoon in January 2016, Hera pulled out a marriage certificate with her photo stuck next to Wasim, from the lane next to theirs. Mountains rose from his doorstep, and their rubble formed its floor. Wasim had liked Hera since they were at school, but she had seemed out of his reach. He had dropped out of middle school while she went to high school. He picked trash; she wanted to be a teacher. He seemed destined for a life on the mountains, and she for one away from them. Then the mountains had tugged her back. Wasim heard that Hera lived inside a padlocked house, flashing her anger to keep creditors away, while her friends had married. During Yasmin's long absences the pair of them had gone to the municipal ward office close by and got the marriage certificate.

Both mothers feared the scandal that the clandestine marriage would evoke and planned a small wedding party. When Moharram Ali heard, he called Yasmin and said he wanted to attend, although he had no money to give. Hera refused. She could not bear to have him watch her finally bind herself to the mountains that she had nearly left.

She wore the simple red dress that made up her whole trousseau. Wasim's family walked over to Yasmin's house as the early winter dusk fell over the mountains and their lanes. A priest came for the ceremony, followed by a small party. The women chatted inside the house, and Sharib served snacks to the small group of men spilling into the dimly lit lane outside. As he turned back, Sharib thought he saw Moharram Ali's hazy figure at the edge of the group. Sharib went inside and asked Yasmin what he was doing there. Hera heard them and kept up her smile. When Sharib came out to serve soft drinks, his father had vanished.

As night fell, Hera walked over to Wasim's house, taking the disappointment that would set up home within her. Her plans joined the many dashed dreams that filled the mountains' shadow that winter; shaking off the curse of the city's trash and their fortunes had proved too hard.

8

Three nights after Hera's wedding, in the early hours of 28 January 2016, Hyder Ali awoke in his bed, before dawn. His chest burned. He rubbed his eyes, opening them sleepily, seeing a haze. He shut them and tried again. A pale mist floated in the dark.

He slung a shirt over his favourite blue-check lungi and woke up the children. He walked carefully into the outside room, letting out his goats and chickens, hoping it would quieten their racket. Alamgir and he stepped out into their slim lane, which was filling with smoke, swelling and floating ahead, taking their long-forgotten township into the city.

Hyder Ali cursed the new migrants who filled Banjara Galli these days. One of their workshops must have exploded, he mumbled. They stumbled through their lane, bumping into the hazy figures of neighbours, to reach the mountains' edge, filled with light. Flares lit up the night sky. Fires raged on the mountains as far as they could see, with black smoke spiralling above. There was not an inch that was not burning, Alamgir remembered thinking.

Jehangir, who was already there, told them he had seen the fires simmering since the afternoon. Watching them grow into the night, he, Alamgir and the others were not sure who to call. Tatva was in the middle of its long-drawn-out departure from the mountains. Its contract was to end in three days. They couldn't find the guards.

From the crowds gathered at the edges of the mountains, Alamgir heard that the fires had started at the far edge of the township, on the eighth mountain, which was mostly in the Khans' control. The creek curved around it, winds were howling in from the sea that night and the fires travelled with them. By 3 a.m., when Hyder Ali and Alamgir arrived, the fires had blazed through much of the township.

Alerted, municipal officials spoke to Tatva officials, who told them they were working to douse the fires with the bulldozers and earth-movers they had on hand. But as the night stretched on, they could only watch as the fires grew and travelled deeper into the hills. Hoping to take decisive action, the municipal officials on night duty wrote a memo to their counterparts at Tatva, asking for fire engines.[1] But with smoke filling the cloudless sky, cellphones became unreachable, officials were not sure where Tatva's staffers were on the grounds and the memo was never delivered, they would later tell their superiors.

Ahead of the watching pickers, an impenetrable wall of smoke built and rose. As the sky turned flame and then blush, officers began calling their bosses in the municipal corporations' solid-waste management department and asked for water tankers and fire engines. They finally entered the townships' fog around 7.10 a.m., winding slowly through the flaming hills.[2] Garbage trucks, blinded by smoke, blocked their way. Firemen saw pickers working amid the wafting mist. They heard dogs whining within it.

The firemen stepped out, uncoiled their hoses and pointed them at the flames, but even before they turned on the water sprays, the fires extinguished themselves. Other fires calmed under the hoses' rain, only to travel through secret passageways within the hills and erupt magically on distant hilltops. The water they sprayed ran off the slopes without cooling the blazing innards of the mountains, which were more than 120 feet high. The firemen sprayed on, amid the rising flames and smoke, not knowing what else to do. The wind and growing smoke made the firemen sick, with four of them being taken to hospital.

Through the windows of her fourth-floor classroom, Ashra watched the mountains blur to smoke that morning. Coughing fits had woken Yasmin before light and she had tried to wake up Ashra. Half awake, Ashra had said she was coming down with something. Her throat and eyes felt scratchy. She could not go. But Yasmin was irritable too, so Ashra caved in and went to school, tripping over garbage and goats on the foggy walk.

She walked up the stairs to her classroom, where the sea breeze was blowing the smoke in, clouding the shrunken communities below and filling their classroom with a sharp burning smell. School shut early that day, and Ashra was home again soon. Coughing and teary-eyed, the children were edgy from the screeching of the fire engines below. Teachers wrapped up classes early, thinking they would make up the next day when the fires quietened.

But the smoke clouds were only growing and travelling further. Firemen had not found underground water storage tanks or hydrants at the township.[3] Instead the copious toxic smoke and seemingly magical dance of flames – which Mumbai's fire chief, Prabhat Rahangdale, would later tell me landfill fires were known for the world over – were rising and swelling. Residents in the high-rise buildings that had edged closer to the mountains and nearly ringed them felt it burn in their chests, coughed through the night and woke to see a gauzy veil floating around them. In their vertiginously high homes and offices they felt dizzy, for reasons that had nothing to do with height.

As the mountains drifted further into the city, they arrived in places worlds away from Banjara Galli. From high up in their glass offices, Mumbaikars took pictures that captured the faint outlines of monolithic office towers suspended in woolly smoke. They posted the images on social media, adding captions that asked if they had woken up to a dystopian nightmare.

Television news headlines about the strange fog settling in the city were accompanied by NASA satellite pictures that showed a trail of dense white smoke rising from the mountains, gusts from the creek carrying it deep into the slim finger-shaped city, hiding it. After eleven decades of being hidden in plain sight, the Deonar mountains had returned to Mumbai, carrying burning fragments of every resident's life and memories.

The municipality had invested in new khaki-and-orange garbage pickup trucks to take away the trash that piled up outside the apartments that Mumbaikars spent their lives working to buy, the cavernous offices they spent their working weeks looking out of, and the malls and multiplexes they retreated to on weekends. Every day the city was renewed, shedding its debris into the overfull black plastic bags that lined street corners and filled the garbage trucks that ferried it quickly away to the Deonar mountains, where it accumulated silently. As dusk fell, city residents watched flames glow at the city's far edge; the stench and smoke itched in their chests, running down their eyes as tears. More than 50 fire engines, fire tankers and water tankers were at the mountains.[4] But the fires were only growing.

The next day police filed a case against three young boys for lighting the fires. A woman had seen them running away from the blazes in the dark. The case was also filed against Tatva for negligence; it would later be closed as mistakenly filed.

The fires burned, unrelenting, turning into an embarrassment for the state government. On the streets and in the media, residents and opposition politicians protested at its failure to douse them. The water that it was spraying on the undiminished fires took away from the city's drinking supply, they said, but the fires were only growing.

As the mountains' toxic cloud inflated over Mumbai, the city's air pollution measured 341 on India's newly launched Air Quality Index (AQI); the acceptable limit was 200.[5] Around the mountains it was higher. Particles of burnt garbage hung in the air, keeping the suspended particulate matter – the most harmful form of air pollution – at 192 micrograms, nearly twice the permissible level. Nitrogen oxide was at 97 micrograms; it should have stayed below 80 micrograms.[6] It mingled with the sun's heat to create the growing smog, making breathing around the mountains hard and sapping already-weak lungs. Mumbaikars should stay inside to avoid inhaling its air, residents were advised, although that would hardly protect those in the lanes around the mountains. Doctors all over the city reported seeing patients with smoke-induced breathlessness, scratchy chests, coughing, giddiness, nausea, fever and watery eyes.

The cloud hung over the global investor conference, designed to be Mumbai's glittering showcase, that was taking place from 13 February 2016. City and state administrators had spent months cleaning and prettying the usually gritty city. Driving through Mumbai's gridlocked traffic, I had begun seeing slim road dividers fill up with newly planted petunias, purple, pink and white. They overflowed from baskets that were strung from street lights and hung over my car, swaying wildly in the same sea breeze that fanned the flames on the mountains. Oversized electric versions of traditional Indian oil lamps appeared on traffic islands. I heard they would light up, to greet investors into the city.

Other slivers of open space filled up with larger-than-life lion cutouts. One was filled with colourful Lego blocks, another with rusty nuts and bolts, a third with twirly machine parts. Looking for lions became my pastime while waiting for Mumbai's perpetually stationary traffic to move. A red lion on a billboard perched high over one of the city's busiest intersections. They were all mid-stride: a lion on the move was the symbol of the Indian government's newly launched 'Make in India' campaign. The national government, elected a little over a year earlier, hoped it would attract foreign investment in its struggling manufacturing sector.

Prime ministers and presidents of several countries, and a galaxy of global corporate bosses, were due to arrive within weeks. In the city's new business district, metallic screens in the style of Mughal-era *jaali*, or stone lattice-work, were welded together to make conference pavilions, which would fill up with stalls showcasing how cutting-edge products could be made in the state. Traditionally these lacy patterns were hand-carved in stone to let light and air pass through long, winding passages in medieval fortresses, allowing sunlight to stream in and casting filigreed shadows.

Prime Minister Narendra Modi was to inaugurate the event on 13 February. At the opening, a lion would appear on the giant television screen onstage and then leap into life, like the country it represented. The hologram would stride through the auditorium filled with international investors, a symbol of the global economic powerhouse that had awoken.

Instead, the mountains and their smoke seeped in through the metallic screens, casting their fetid shadow on the half-made pavilions, just weeks before the conference. It was as if a primitive and discarded city drifted through the new one, dogging the steps of the striding lion. The organisers worried about how they would sell the promise of new things amid the burning detritus of the old; about whether guests would pull out because of the toxic air quality.

Worried by what I could see around me in the city, and by everything I heard from wealthy but breathless friends, I had gone to the mountains' edge to see how our borrowers were doing. I found that the smoke cloud was all over the city except in the mountains' shadow. I ran into Hyder Ali sitting at his doorstep, chatting with friends. This was not new, he said. He had seen fires since he started working on the mountains nearly two decades ago. He had even sprinkled silver powder to quell them.

I asked how Farzana was. She must be at a friend's place, he told me airily. It's what she did these days, he added, before going on about the fires he had seen. I looked ahead and saw Farzana walking towards us, filled-up garbage bag in hand. Farha trailed behind. Farzana must have made it to the mountains, Hyder Ali said, looking unsurprised and lurching up to see what she had. Farzana opened her bag to show him the still-warm mangled metal she had collected.

We continued our discussion of the pictures I had seen of the fires in the newspapers. *Ye to kahin bhi liya rahega*, Hyder Ali said. *These photographs could have been taken anywhere.* Another picker who had dropped in to chat pointed out that fires burned on the mountains all the time; these ones had only made it to the news because sea breezes carried the smoke into wealthy homes. Some of that was true. Some of it Hyder Ali and his friends told themselves so that they could keep working, or taking their children's earnings, collected from the burning mountains.

Farzana, Sahani and the other children walked the mountains all day. *Hawa jahaan daudti thi, vahaan dhuaan daudta tha, aur uske peeche peeche ham*, Sahani said. *Where the wind blew, smoke followed and we followed behind it.* As Farzana walked up the slopes, they sent heat shocks through her slippers, which crumbled under her feet. The smoke that rose from them burned in her eyes, throat and chest. She took to wearing black lace-up shoes she had found. She waved burlap to clear the air, so that she could see the unrelenting garbage caravans that still arrived. She followed their approaching headlights, searching for a way through the growing fog. She trailed them as they got to the far end of the township, to empty on hills that the fires had not yet reached.

Tatva's guards had left and policemen had come to support the firemen. They tried keeping pickers away from the burning slopes and unloading trucks, but the pickers, long practised, evaded them. When the trucks emptied tightly packed plastic bags on the warm slopes, nearly-dead fires erupted again on the hilltops.

Phugawalas, or 'plastic people', such as Farzana sifted through the slopes with forks, trawling slowly for bits of the remaining plastic that had escaped the fire's heat. Speaking of how she became one, Farzana had told me, *Itne tarah ka tha ki kuch na kuch to mil hi jata tha. Safed, kala neela, paani. There were so many kinds that you always found something. White, black, blue and the colour of water,* or transparent. But now it was all melting away, and instead the fires brought up metal, the most elusive and expensive of mountain finds.

She watched the *chumbakwalas* trace the slopes with magnets tied to sticks – this was the 'magnet people's' time and Farzana decided to join them. She bought magnets from the 90 Feet Road market, then tied them onto long sticks that she waved over the burning trash slopes. Bits of nails, coins, wire and dismembered gadgets flew up through the smoke and ash and stuck to her home-made metal detector. She prized the hot metal away with a thick old scarf and stuffed it into her bag. Farzana bought water and *vada pav*, Mumbai's ever-popular potato burgers, from vendors who walked the slopes, so that she could stay out longer, tracing the mountains with her magnets all day. Did the flames and smoke scare her? I asked later. No, she said. Did they make her sick? I asked. Why would they?

she replied, not remembering how she coughed, although I did. She earned more than she had before the fires, she said.

The *chindiwalas*, or 'cloth-scrap people', to whom Hyder Ali belonged, were mostly out of work on the slopes. Instead they collected scrap bundles from tailors in the city and sifted through them at home. Like them, Hyder Ali stayed home. Unlike them, he hardly worked.

From the mountain tops, Farzana watched the municipal and police convoys stream in. Tatva's contract had ended while the fires raged and it had left the township, sending the municipality Rs 36.19 crore in unpaid bills, days later.[7] Municipal staff were returning to manage the mountains. Farzana watched bulldozers demolish the homes and shops that crowded the mountain's entrance, so that the fire engines could enter easily. She turned back down to wave her home-made metal detector over the mountains and fill more bags with metal to sell.

I read, in the newspapers, that the municipality had called experts and scientists, who suggested that a range of chemicals be thrown over the burning township. But trash burned in layers buried far below their reach. The fire department fielded frantic calls from residents of distant and varying neighbourhoods every day, as the breezes blew the smoke in their direction, making them sick. Fire engines splashed water from new angles to change the direction of the smoke clouds that Farzana felt rose in shapes like people, floating in the air.

Was it the fire beyond Rafiq Nagar that I was asking about? Yasmin enquired, surprised. She had not seen it. She didn't think Ashra's racking cough had anything to do with it.

Over several trips I watched Sharib sprawled face-down on the floor, turning just when I thought he was asleep. I watched the soles of his feet turn red, purple and then a puffy black from the burns accumulated on the slopes. Fluid oozed out of these blisters. Yasmin told me he could barely stand or walk. But when she nagged, I saw him lift himself up and limp out of the door to work, with blister fluid sticking to his slippers. In the last few months Yasmin had become caught in a tangled mess of debt and despair. Sharib provided their only steady income, even if it was meagre. She could not let a fire disrupt it. So at night Yasmin warmed castor oil and rubbed it on his soles, or applied potions whose recipes were passed around their lanes. It was all he needed, she said.

Uparwale ne mere bachon ko bahut taakat di hai, she would tell me when I asked again if the fires had caused the coughs that rang in their home. *God made my children very strong.* At first she had got Ashra cough syrup that the doctors prescribed. But when Ashra began running through bottles without getting better, Yasmin stopped buying them. It only drained her household budget. She didn't see the fires. She didn't feel them. Others in their lane also worked so hard through the fog that they didn't see it at all. They did not feel it burn in them.

Desperate now, municipal and fire officials hitched water hoses onto the forklifts that usually shovelled mud and garbage, to extend their reach deeper through the fog to the burning hills. Alamgir and other pickers sat atop the swinging forklifts as they drove into the blinding smoke, directing the drivers deeper into the glowing mountain recesses. He jumped off just as the forklifts dived in, shovelling aside trash to unearth the blazes burning deep within. Water tankers moved in to spray water and coolant on these fires. Then the forklifts blanketed the uncovered fires with gravel and debris from unburnt hills. I asked Alamgir what it was like inside the toxic smoke clouds. He was a little above them, he told me, sitting on top.

After days in which the aviation authorities had worried that the smoke could prevent planes coming into land at Mumbai airport, the smoke retreated from the city just days before the 'Make in India' conference. The chief minister made a pitch for Maharashtra being the country's most developed, industrialised and investor-friendly state.

Thousands of foreign investors and Indian business heads drove through the lacy pavilions in golf carts, exploring investment opportunities. India was one of the world's great consumer markets, officials told them. Months before the conference, $5 billion had been committed to making iPhones in the state,[8] because India was soon to have the world's second-largest number of cellphone users. Cool February evenings were filled with Bollywood galas on Mumbai's beaches, walks through its colonial-era naval dockyard lit with fairy lights, and fashion shows that showcased the state's hand-woven textiles.

Hyder Ali spent his days sitting outside his house, chatting with the friends still left in the lane. Some had moved out, to the homes of friends or relatives outside the city, to exorcise the smoke that itched within them, fogged their minds and trickled down from their eyes as tears. Others ran through expensive medicines that did not soothe their burning chests.

Although Hyder Ali would not admit it, the fires were unlike any he had seen before. The city's discarded desires had burned like the fires in hell that clerics had told him about. Jinns and Shaitans arose from them, they had told him. He waited for Farzana and the other children to return in the evenings, with warm trash and new stories that swirled about the mountains.

He heard that the mountains would shut for ever now; that cameras like blinking black eyes would hover over their peaks; and that they would move outside the city. Some of the stories he heard were true, while others were as hazy as the smoke that floated above him in those days. I watched him turn bonier, his eyes sink deeper into his face and his hair turn grey and then startlingly orange. Later I heard that he had applied cheap, chemical-infused henna to hide his sudden crop of grey.

9

The fires had relented just enough for the conference to get under way; within days the distant simmering hills erupted again. Flames spread across 5 acres near the creek, which the fire engines would struggle to reach. Engineers at Deonar's municipal office looked up with dread as the night sky glowed amber. Then, surprisingly for a February night, it rained, spoiling outdoor events at the conference that evening and soaking into submission the fires that could have raged for days.[1]

Weeks before the fires first broke out and officials, politicians, television and camera crews came to swarm over the mountains, the diminutive and greying Raj Kumar Sharma had walked around the townships' broken wall in his puffy high-waisted trousers, with a camera slung around his neck. He had slipped through its gaps to photograph the mountains, filled with waste-pickers and nearly emptied of security guards. He took pictures of the municipality's security cameras that did not work, and was captured on the gangs' cameras that did.[2] He photographed the empty guard posts taken over by drug addicts, assiduously cataloguing the township's brokenness. His photographs would bring the township into the city again, in a different way, injecting a new urgency into the attempts to resolve it.

Sharma had lived in an airy terraced apartment,

minutes from Deonar's trash township, since the fifties. It was in a leafy lane in Chembur, a neighbourhood with a gentle, fraying charm. Down the street was RK Studios,[3] where some of the Hindi film industry's greatest dreams had been made. Sharma's home had once belonged to Lalita Pawar, one of RK's favourite vamps. She was best known for having a glass eye and a tough demeanour that occasionally yielded to reveal a golden heart.

Sharma's family had rented the apartment and, when Pawar's movie career waned, with the trips to RK Studios fading away, they bought the house from her. The Chembur, in Sharma's childhood memories, was full of fruit orchards and picnics sprinkled with stars. He had heard and smelled the open-topped *cuchra* trains pass by, at night, to reach the Deonar township. He had watched the mountains grow precipitously; and now, greying, he was full of ingenious ideas to mend them. He walked the mountains and travelled the country in search of solutions, and returned to push them with the municipality and in court.

His photographs and his petition that arrived on the judges' desk, the fires and the news headlines that followed, had forced Justices Abhay Oka and C. V. Bhadang to reopen the case. The still-simmering mountains provided a dark and urgent backdrop as the arguments began. In Justice Oka's outsize wood-beamed courtroom, along the court's angular and winding ground-floor corridor, Sharma asked the court to set a new date to close the mountains. The municipality's lawyer argued to keep the Deonar township going for a little longer. Restricting garbage flows, as Sharma had asked for, would mean trash hills being built in the city, sickening the residents, he said.

Oka (pronounced Oak) was the fourth most senior of the court's seventy judges. He had shiny black hair, neatly pressed down in a side parting, a toothbrush moustache and was a commanding presence in his stately and always-packed courtroom. He often heard more than sixty cases a day, with a break for lunch – a rate of work which meant he could cut through the obfuscation that lawyers indulged in, to buy time and avoid commitment. An impish smile often played under Oka's moustache, as he perched his face on his palm and asked lawyers to turn to page numbers and paragraph numbers, in their written petitions, that contradicted their own arguments. That afternoon, Oka bore down on the municipality's lawyer.

He pointed out that the municipality could not start redirecting its garbage caravans, across the creek, to the site in Karvale village in Navi Mumbai, which had been selected a decade ago for a modern landfill to replace the Deonar township, in the near future. It turned out that the land was dotted with tribal settlements.[4] Their owners had resisted selling and moving out. They had attacked municipal officers when they went to measure the land to settle a purchase price. Even when officers returned with police protection, they had not been able to survey the sprawling plot. The municipality had to keep the Deonar township going a little longer, its lawyer said.

In the busy courtroom Oka's impatience was palpable. He confronted the municipality's lawyer with the more than a decade-and-a-half-long failure to meet regulations and previous court orders. Oka reminded him that the municipality had a legal obligation to manage its waste responsibly. In the orders that he later passed, Oka noted caustically that the rules 'are being observed only in breach'. Dumping of garbage at Deonar was illegal, he said.

From Sharma's petition, Oka drew out the lawless bubble that had grown on the mountains, for display in the courtroom. When the fires erupted, there were too few cameras installed and none of them worked. The boundary wall was broken, the township's edges carved up by gangs. Security guards were nowhere to be found on the site. The mountains burned even as the lawyers argued, Oka pointed out. He seemed incredulous when the municipal lawyer said that the city's waste could fill Deonar's rising hills for longer. How could the city's shadow have space, when Mumbai was sprawling outwards and growing upwards? Oka's look suggested.

On 26 February 2016 Oka passed orders stating that the municipality had allowed reckless construction and development in Mumbai, without thinking of its mounting flow of trash and the reeking township that it emptied into. In fuelling the growth of the city and its township of trash, the municipality had violated its residents' right to life, as protected by the constitution, which included the right to live in a pollution-free environment, Oka wrote. He stopped fresh construction until the municipality came up with a plan to manage its waste and shut down the Deonar mountains, although the tearing down and rebuilding of old buildings, which made for most construction in the space-starved city, could continue.[5]

Oka set a deadline of 30 June 2017, a year and half later, to stop dumping garbage at Deonar. He established a committee, made up of a former administrator, a police officer, scientists and Sharma, to ensure his orders reached the mountains – a committee to oversee the municipality of castaway belongings.

On the mountains, pickers had told me there was a court case to close the township. Since it had only swollen since I began going there, a few years before, I too assumed that the court orders were among the many official plans that had not penetrated the mountains' halo. But when I read about the orders banning new construction, I knew that – in a city where wealth and aspiration were reflected in dizzying real-estate growth, and some of its greatest fortunes were made through its skyscrapers – stopping fresh construction would send tremors through Mumbai's heart. The court order had finally brought the mountains into the city, connecting residents and their detritus with the distant mountains that had exploded in flames and smoke.

On 19 March 2016 the mountains were bathed in the glow of fires that belched dense smoke into the city once again. Flames travelled across the hills, and the city woke up to the now-familiar smoke and sharp smell of burning from Deonar. A television channel's headline described it as a 'smog shroud' that had fallen over the city again. In the mountains' shadow, doctors struggled to cope with snaking lines of breathless patients, to find ventilators for their sickest patients. They tried to revive a breathless baby who, newspapers later reported, died.[6]

While fire engines tried to subdue the fires, schools around the mountains, which had remained closed for more than a week in January, shut again. At other schools further away, students were not allowed to play in the school yard or were asked to wear face masks – flimsy shields between them and Mumbai's deadly air.

This time, tired authorities were full of conspiracy theories. Such raging and uncontrolled fires could not possibly be accidental, they said. Even though the authorities had asked Tatva to leave, they claimed the company had left a burning township and large bills, aggravating the already-angry municipality. Much of what Justice Oka's judgement identified as the municipality's failings, its officials thought should have been laid at Tatva's doorstep. After all, it had been managing the mountains when the fires broke out.

With the fires still burning, Vitabai heard Prakash Javadekar, India's environment minister, was coming to the township. She took Nagesh, her eldest son, and walked to the municipal office to meet him, following Nagesh's large grey curls to the front of the waiting crowd.

With the midday sun warming her head, her life on the forgotten mountains played in Vitabai's mind. She wanted to tell Javadekar about it. She thought of her fading scars, of how, at first, the mountain smells had made her stomach churn, even after eating four *vada pavs*. She thought of how Nagesh, the skinny ten-year-old who began trailing behind her on the slopes, had turned shapeless and grey on them. Her friend Salma Shaikh had brought her son, Aslam, to the mountains as a toddler, and her younger son, Rafique, as a 100-day-old baby, strapped to her back with a saree, after her husband died. Salma had kept them in a shelter that she made with dried leaves that fell from the trucks. While she worked, Aslam had wobbled out of the shed, picked trash and grown to middle age on the slopes too.

Vitabai wanted to tell Javadekar that pickers such as

herself had made a life on the mountains. They could not have burned them, as the news swirling around them suggested. She knew traders' lackeys lit nightly fires for metal. *Ani amcha maran. And we are to die.* She wanted to tell him that, as one of the mountains' oldest inhabitants, she had picked up after the city for decades. She dreamed of having an official job doing so, a municipal identity card that would turn their secret army into legitimate workers. The card would make officials leave them alone, instead of threatening them, asking for bribes or detaining them for being trespassers.

The long convoy arrived. The crowd jostled restlessly outside. The strong burning smell and fear of new eruptions hung thick in the air. Vitabai and Nagesh waited in the hot sun until the official cars drove away. No one stepped out of the vehicles. They returned home dispirited. In Delhi, Javadekar told reporters that the fires revealed the contractors' carelessness; a team of environment-ministry officials had visited Deonar and would investigate what had happened.

Weeks later, Farzana was bent over her metal detector when the police lined the mountains again. She heard that Rahul Gandhi, an opposition politician, was coming. She and Sahani followed pickers to the municipal office. Gandhi walked on the trash hills while photographers clicked; he was dressed in white and looked pink and flushed amid the pickers' tanned bodies and muddy clothes. Farzana did not know that the photos would be printed on posters that were stuck all over the city to showcase the state government's and municipality's failings.

At the same time, pickers from their lanes were getting hauled in for questioning, and some were arrested. There were no cameras on the mountains, said a junior super-visor at Deonar.[7] To penetrate the mountains' fog, police relied on rounding up pickers, to interrogate them about the fires and the dark world of the mountains. They asked about suspicious happenings in the days leading up to the fires. The mountains and their inhabitants, which had grown for so long in a bubble of secrecy, were suddenly visible, their bubble stretching thin, threatening to pop.

10

Together, Oka's order and the endless fires had diverted
most garbage caravans to the grounds at Mulund and the
new hills at Kanjurmarg, where trash hills were to be
dehydrated until they turned to compost. Farzana and her
sisters did what they had always done when the trucks
dwindled: they walked to what they had heard was Atique
Khan's estate. They reminded the lackeys who guarded it
that they were Jehangir's sisters and slipped in to fill up on
what they called *ganda maal. Dirty stuff.*

They tied handkerchiefs around their faces to keep
away the rising smell of boiled flesh, and sifted aside dis-
embodied limbs and gangrenous fingers. They collected
freshly steamed syringes with their backs cut off, so they
could not be refilled; saline bags; water bottles; and long
bloodied swabs of gauze and cotton. For every three filled
bags they handed over to the lackeys, they could keep the
fourth for themselves. Farzana filled frantically, hardly
feeling the unknown blood stain her, the syringes poke her
and the broken glass bottles cut her. Syringes jabbed them
a lot, Sahani told me later on, but they just tied something
around their wounds and kept working, not feeling the
pain. It was the only thing better than picking from the
municipality's garbage caravans.

Bags filled, the sisters walked back home, the smell

of people's steamed remains clinging to them. The smell stayed stubbornly on them, even after they washed. *Koi hadsa dekha to man mein reh jaata hai*, Sahani would say. *What we see lingers in us.* They would never return, the sisters decided, as they had done for years. But in a few weeks they would be back, as they always had. The garbage trucks were dwindling.

I'll act like I beat you, and you act like you cried. One municipal official who managed the mountains had reminded me of an old Marathi idiom to explain the official shadowplay that had let the city's detritus acquire its dark afterlife at Deonar. Its contract apparently said Tatva was to make the boundary wall, including the break where nightly convoys entered with the remains of buildings to make debris hills. I read the municipality's letters to Tatva saying it would fix the wall itself, while the police settled a booth across it.[1] For years the booth had stayed unmanned, the wall broken, the convoys streaming in while the Khan brothers and their rivals were said to have amassed dead buildings, dead people, leftover hotel food. As the city's water lines, power lines and sewers stopped before their stretching lanes, pickers had little choice but to cling to the gangs' largesse, their love. It nearly strangled them. But now, as the fires lit up the forgotten trash township and the shadowy private estates within it, the municipality and police had to reel them in. The mountains began moving from under the feet of its illicit and invisible residents.

Manoj Lohiya, a police officer who had been tasked by the police commissioner with bringing this secret world out into the open, gave an interim and then a final report saying the failure of the plant meant that methane stayed trapped within the mountains and seeped through them, hanging in the mountain air. That night in January 2016 fires had begun at the far edge (in what was said to be the Khans' territory). Sea winds had howled, swelling the flames, taking them within the trash hills and into the sky until they were out of control, Lohiya said. The delay in the arrival of the fire engines had taken the fires further into the city.

As they started building a case against the Khans, police began walking the slopes, discovering the world Farzana had always lived in. They saw cameras and lights surrounding hills staked out by gangs – as Sharma, the petitioner in court, had. Getting caught in their gaze brought out lackeys to defend the gangs' turf, unlike the municipal cameras that, once installed, did not work.

The sprawling private estate of medical waste within the township was settled not long after the municipality had cut out a far corner of the township to make its medical-waste incinerator in 2007. While municipal trucks made rounds of the city hospitals, bringing their waste to the incinerator, Atique Khan bought a small pickup truck. It was said to make trips to the city's largest private hospitals, unofficially redirecting it to this estate, where pickers sorted it and lackeys resold it. Farzana had learned the names of some of the city's best hospitals from the drivers of trucks that veered away from her on hill clearings to this estate.[2] It was not trash meant to be strewn on the hills for pickers. And yet, for Farzana, it was too good to leave: thick plastic from saline bags, medicine bags and glass containers that sold well. She had followed these trucks to the edge of this territory, pleading for entry. But that summer, as police began walking the slopes, fewer trucks came to this estate. What made it to the incinerator blew toxic clouds into the air that the pickers barely noticed.[3]

Police discovered that the clashes for dead possessions had led to gangs lighting fires in rivals' territories at night, burning away their rivals' fortunes. In letters written to the state's chief minister, the police commissioner and others, one of their rivals referred to the Khans as *Matti Mafia* or 'Mud Mafia'. The Khans' attempts to control life in the lanes were throwing up power struggles of a different sort too: Farzana's Banjara Galli formed the overlap between two of the area's fiercest gangs. Life on the mountains was controlled by the Khan brothers, and life at home by their namesakes, Atique and Rafique Shaikh (no relation to Salma Shaikh or Hyder Ali Shaikh), also brothers.

The Khans provided satellite television in Baba Nagar, and I had seen minions who claimed to work for the Shaikhs, especially their brother Shafique, collecting power bills in Banjara Galli. Atique Shaikh's face featured on police posters around their lanes, with a headline saying 'Wanted'. Farzana's family, like most others, only used legal power to accumulate bills that made them exist in the official records, which they hoped would eventually help them show that they were legal residents. They bought illegal power to keep costs low, and the army that patrolled their lanes placated: any payment delays could lead to disconnection, threats and abuse. Throughout Farzana's childhood their lanes had been lit through the pickers' ingenuity. But since I began walking them in 2013 I had invariably run into these foot soldiers collecting payments, even though police busted their illegal network several times.

The Shaikhs, who had started out picking trash and grabbing pickers' garbage-made homes, had later retreated to build flourishing careers in business and politics. They were also charged with a number of crimes. Rafique's third wife, Noorjehan, was the area's corporator – an elected representative in the municipal corporation – allowing them to raise the area's concerns with officials. It was Noorjehan's responsibility to ask why trash in the lanes around the mountains was not cleared, speaking on behalf of the lanes near where the city dumped its own garbage endlessly.[4] At one of her campaign events, Rafique had brought a bottle of muddy tap water and emptied it, to show area representatives and municipal officers that they were failing to provide drinkable water. It was through these shows of largesse from mountain bosses, the trickles of sustenance from the municipality and leftovers from gang wars that life came to Farzana's lanes. And it was within their tangles that it stayed stuck.

On the edge of the Shaikhs' territory, along the 90 Feet Road that Farzana's lanes nearly opened on to, the police said Khans' lackeys collected fees for parking the pickup trucks, auto rickshaws and taxis that pickers had saved up to buy, so they could build lives away from the trash. The owners of these vehicles told officers they had been threatened, intimidated, beaten or their vehicles impounded if they did not pay up.[5]

The police and municipality set out to reclaim this forgotten world, which had grown so tangled while they looked away. Mumbai's municipal commissioner had announced that it would become a prohibited zone: anyone, other than municipal staff, seen on the trash slopes could be a fire hazard and would be detained or fined. It threatened the fragile grey economy that had grown up around the mountains and their bounty. New guards had replaced the ones Farzana knew, and there were more patrols on the mountains than she had ever seen before. Construction workers dotted the edges of the foothills. Once again they began fixing the mostly broken boundary wall and brought barbed-wire rolls to top it.

Farzana heard of pickers being turned away from the mountains. She heard of friends getting into work before dawn to evade the guards and cameras that were to begin watching the hills. With the city's glare glinting through the mountains' halo, their world was beginning to spoil at the edges, crinkling their lives and shaking their futures. Farha waited for unguarded moments to get in and work. Hyder Ali perched himself on the ledge that jutted out from their wall, where he often spent his afternoons. He walked over to the mountains' edge sometimes, not picking trash, but hoarding the stories that pickers carried with them when they returned, inhaling their worry and growing gaunt before my eyes.

One evening when Farzana returned home she saw the wispy Salma Shaikh sitting outside the house, filling in Hyder Ali on the events of the day. Salma had draped her flowery orange saree around her shoulders, drooping, as if weighed down by the mountains. As she got closer, Farzana saw Salma run her fingers around a plastic necklace, which she later heard was retrieved from a trash bag. It gave her an elegant, worn air. Farzana heard Salma softly hurl the insults she had accumulated over four decades on the mountains at the new guards. Hyder Ali listened, looking bemused.

Arif, her fourteen-year-old grandson, had taken to

working pre-dawn to avoid the guards, Salma told them. He kept picking trash one morning, as the sky turned from ink to rose to gold. Guards had come into work and spotted him, half-filled bag of plastic bottles in hand. They chased him, waving their sticks frantically, Salma told them. Arif ran down as fast as he could, stumbling over the wobbly slopes, drained by the persistent cough and fever he had caught from his father Aslam, who had tuberculosis. He struggled to stay ahead of the guards and their flailing sticks.

Then Arif felt a sharp and piercing pain in his foot. His knees buckled and he fell into the sun-dried trash. He turned his foot, to see that a rusting nail had pierced through his thin slippers and made a deep cut in his foot. Blood gushed onto the warm, torn plastic bags and glinting tablet strips. Guards closed in on Arif as he slumped on the slope, in pain.

They let him go, with a warning never to set foot on the mountains again. Salma had taken Arif to get an anti-tetanus injection and his foot wrapped in a gauze bandage to keep him from limping. *Beta kabr mein ek pair hila ke aaya*, she told Hyder Ali, talking about Aslam. *My son already dangled one foot in the grave.* She had only Arif for help, and now she was alone.

When her softly delivered invective abated, Hyder Ali suggested that she get the non-profit organisation that gave them identity cards to complain about the guards who had chased Arif. What could they do, if pickers kept sending their children to the slopes? Salma replied. The volunteers would ask if they had given birth to children only to send them here, she said. She knew she had to help Arif build a life away from the mountains, but they were all she knew – the only thing she had passed on to her son and grandson.

I had come to believe the best mountain views poured out of the elegant, bristling Salma. When the mountains' weight had pressed her down and put the grit in her soft voice, they had forgotten to take away the whispery softness, the lingering mischievousness that clung to her like the paper scraps she sometimes picked.

She had tried to get Arif employed as a waiter or dishwasher, she told them. But his sickly face, chipped tooth and bony frame made him look younger than his fourteen years. He got work only on days when there was a big wedding and the caterer was so desperate for staff that he could persuade himself that Arif, in his rumpled white shirt and frayed bow tie, looked eighteen. Most days, Salma admitted, Arif tried creeping back to work, before light, on the mountains, often getting beaten, getting warned, getting detained.

Another evening Farzana found Hyder Ali at their doorstep, talking to a newly married picker with a thin moustache. He had gone to the mountains to relieve himself, early one morning, and looked up to find a black eye buzzing high over him, he told Hyder Ali. He had heard the television news crews that hung around the mountain edges these days used small flying cameras to bypass security and to film the seething mountains. Pictures of him relieving himself would reach his newly acquired in-laws back in his village, he told Hyder Ali. He had told them he worked in an office. They would see where and how he lived in Mumbai, on the television news. He would crumble in their eyes, he fretted.

When he left, Hyder Ali went inside the house and put

on the television set that he had bought at a *kata* shop, had repaired and that now perched high up on the wall. Farzana emptied her bag outside and heard Hyder Ali flick through the channels, looking for news reports on the mountains, as she sorted through the day's pickings. Most talked about leaked police reports that said the pickers had lit the fires at night, at the behest of their bosses, the garbage traders. More *kata*-shop owners and pickers were getting arrested. Farzana emptied the bag she had brought back, sorting through syringes, saline bags, swabs and meal trays. She had had to go back to the medical-waste estate again.

11

Through April 2016 the township stayed warm, heat building from the seething fires and rising summer. Fire engines, forklifts and the assistants who hung off them dotted the slopes. Municipal officials and assorted consultants worked on the mountains, and police filled the lanes around them. Everyone was here to fix the mountains' seething mess, which had suddenly and unexpectedly frozen the endlessly inching-upwards city. The pickers' subterranean world had been discovered and they were being evicted.

I searched for Salma for weeks before I ran into her, walking slowly down Banjara Galli one afternoon. She had been in and out of hospital because of the fires, she told me. *Ghabrahat*, or 'mortal fear', was the only way she could describe the range of symptoms that paralysed her, none of which were directly related to air quality. Her blood pressure had shot up. She had visited doctors and swallowed medicines secretly, so that she didn't alarm the already-sick Aslam and Arif. The week she felt better, fires had erupted again. Salma's blood pressure increased so much that a blood vessel had burst in her eye. Everything had blurred; the world looked different. She needed surgery to fix it – a procedure she later chose to remember as cataract surgery.

As the summer warmed, the mountains were shrinking. Mumbai's sultry, humid heat sucked out any moisture left within, deflating them. Madan Yavalkar, a municipal engineer who had managed the mountains for years and knew them better than most, had described the mountains' seasonal inhalation and exhalation in the municipality's fire-inquiry report, written in Marathi:[1] 'At the height of the monsoons' fury, when rainwaters seep into the mountains, they expand and when the summer sun draws out the moisture, they contract.' As I walked the lanes that summer, I felt the mountain luck deflating too.

Guards often turned Farzana back from the slopes. When she sneaked in, she saw the township emptied of garbage trucks, as she never had before. She spent boiling, windless afternoons waiting for the trucks at mountain clearings. The relentless flow of trash gushing onto hilltops, tumbling down slopes, tangling into mangroves and flowing into the creek, the endless torrent of castaway possessions that Farzana had always seen, had now slowed to a trickle. In just a few months the amount of garbage dumped on the mountains had dropped by one-third. Until Deonar's hills cooled and consultants drew up a plan to fix them, the caravans would move mostly to the municipality's smaller garbage mountains at Mulund, and to the modern, new ones rising at Kanjurmarg.

Farzana usually worked with Farha, who chatted and played around to fill the unending afternoons, the sun warming their heads, and the steaming mountains their feet. The days stretched thinner when she waited with Jehana, her reedy eldest sister, who lived in a tin-sheet room sprouting from the boundary wall with her husband and six children. The two watched the slopes stir in the smoke tendrils that still rose from the trash. In the midst of long silences, they waited for the breeze, or a glimpse of trucks winding through the bumpy roads below.

Seeing a truck emerge from the hills propelled them to their feet, sprinting to the clearing that it would empty at. Other pickers swooped in from the silent hills, falling on the trash with the day's pent-up energy. These short bursts of scrambles for garbage were fierce and desperate. Sometimes Farzana found herself on newly empty and uncontested clearings, once the territory of gangs. The growing police glare had shaken the brothers' grip on the mountains. Trash that had only emptied in their estates began appearing elsewhere in the township.

Shovelling around with her long fork threw up used hospital gloves, or 'bloodied hands', as Farzana called them. It was the only one of the mountains' handouts that she could not bear to see or touch. Looking at the stiff, white blood-stained fingers made her stomach churn. She turned her face away, glancing back from the corner of her eye to hook them onto her long garbage fork and scooping them into her bag. She picked empty saline bags, tubes, medicine bottles and packaging. Finding thick hospital plastic made up for the days when the guards turned her away.

It was during these burning months that Farzana and Farha chased a truck carrying hospital waste to the prawn loop on a slow afternoon. It was then that Farzana reached into a bag that she thought was full of little glass vials, but brought out the glass jar filled with the three lifeless babies joined at the stomach, joined in their flickering lives, joined in death. After she had buried them in the soft sand at the edge of the township in the evening, Jehangir slapped Farzana when he heard what she had done. *Padne ka hi nahi yeh sab mach mach mein. Kuch achha nahi hota is sab se. You should not get drawn into messes. Nothing good comes out of them.* Why do they give birth to them, Sahani had asked, if they want to send them here?

Things were going to get better, Farzana wanted to tell Jehangir. The fires that had raged all that year were receding. Her birthday, on 2 June, would bring the rains and keep the mountains soaking and cool. She would turn eighteen – an adult whom Jehangir could not slap, Farzana thought, wiping away tears. Adulthood was close, and Farzana kept slinking through the closing wall to work. She needed to save up, buy herself jeans and have a party to mark her transition. But as the summer wore on, sometimes the guards threw Farzana's carefully filled trash bags under the buzzing bulldozers and sent her home. She watched pickers get beaten if they lingered on.

Wilting under the tightened security, the older pickers tried a new strategy: making themselves visible. In her lane Farzana saw posters and banners strung up for protest marches in the city. Pickers wanted to work on; they wanted identity cards to make them exist officially. Weeks after the environment ministry team visited but did not meet Vitabai, it seemed to have heard her. The government brought out new waste rules that said pickers were to be involved in segregating and sorting the city's trash. But while Vitabai and Salma were about to become legal waste-pickers and sorters, they did not yet know it. The rules did not reach the township, and the guards still shut them out. Increasingly pushed out of the mountains and their livelihoods, they still struggled to emerge from their hilly netherworld, now spoiling under the sudden heat.

Vitabai took several long bus rides into the city for the protests. She heard of pickers who went to meet Maharashtra's youthful chief minister, Devendra Fadnavis. But, at the township, more guards swarmed. Vitabai felt the tenuous life that she had built on trash slopes crumbling.

One afternoon she emptied her bag in the lane, while Salma and I watched and chatted with her. She separated takeaway food boxes, plastic-coated wires to be scraped away with a knife, and picked out a metal ring topped with a tortoise. Vitabai knew that wearing mountain finds could bring her ill luck. But she had heard that people in the city wore tortoise jewellery as a prescription for good fortune, and occasionally it found its way into the trash. She fiddled with the ring, unsure of what would work, weighing the luck of the tortoise against the danger of finding it on the slopes. She slipped it on. *Marna to hai hi ek din*, Salma shrugged. *Pehen ke marein. We are going to die some day. Better to die wearing what we like.*

Stuck outside the wall, with mountain luck teetering and ebbing, Vitabai made the rounds of friends' homes, asking for the phone numbers of wealthy people who needed help cleaning their homes. She hoarded them, just as she had once collected the phone numbers of truck drivers who sold first dibs on their garbage. She took more long bus rides into the city, filling in for friends needing a day off from cleaning jobs and hoping it would lead to more lasting work.

I ran into Salma, whose blood pressure was still raging, more often than I met Vitabai. She worked when she could, and at other times I found her crumpled against the wall in her other sons' house, where she had moved so that Aslam and Arif didn't have to support her. Most of all, I found her stuck, waiting, outside the mountain wall.

Grounded by the fires, the guards and with everything seeming hazy, Salma agonised over how she could make a fresh start, away from her century-old benefactor. She thought of taking the four-hour train ride to Surat, buying sarees from its famed wholesale textile market and selling them door-to-door, in their lanes. But she had seen Vitabai's son Nagesh, and others, bring back bags of sarees they couldn't sell, because no one in the lanes had enough money to buy them. Nagesh defaulted on our loan repayments, as did others. He was not seen around Banjara Galli or the slopes. His phone was switched off. When our loan officer asked Vitabai, she told her that Nagesh had moved to the village. But neighbours felt they saw him at night.

Sabko paisa dena hai to aur kya karega? Salma snorted, when our loan officer asked about disappeared borrowers. *When you owe everyone money, what else would you do?* Years of picking trash meant that the delicate skills of embroidery or tailoring, which some of her newer neighbours practised, had bypassed Salma's bruised hands. Their lives having braided into the mountains over four decades, she and Vitabai had nowhere to go, and knew nothing other than collecting trash. Edgily Salma waited for her blood pressure, and the security, to ease so that she could return to them.

Salma had worked mostly alone for more than a year since Aslam's cough began racking their home through the night. After he ran through bottles of cough syrup, Salma had taken him to a free charitable hospital deep in the city, where she had heard pickers took their persistent coughs. She had returned to work, freeing Aslam to make the hour-long bus ride into the city's crumbling and congested old quarter. He waited irritably for doctors to see him, while horns blared from the street outside and from the flyover that ran above it.

Bargain-hunters filled the streets behind the hospital. Together the maze of lanes was known as *Chor Bazaar*, or Thieves' Market. When Mumbai's grand old homes were dismantled, the good stuff came here, and the rest went to Deonar. Frayed family photographs, oversized chandeliers, hand-painted Bollywood posters, rusty aeroplane models and broken irons lay under jumbled piles and layers of dust. Wealthier shoppers came in search of hidden gems amidst the household junk, as Salma did at Deonar. New things were added. They were scraped to look old, and old things polished to look new. They were laid out together to earn shop owners the small fortunes that Salma and Aslam could only imagine earning from mountain trash. Pickers sometimes washed and patched trousers that they found in the trash and sold them here.

Salma had returned home after long days on the slopes to find Aslam slumped against the wall, the bright-blue T-shirt he often wore hanging more loosely over his shrunken frame each day. A shadow had come over him. He walked little and shaved infrequently. His cough was echoed in the skinny Arif. With Arif, Salma tried dragging back trash-filled bags that nearly outsized them. A bag filled with plastic bottles, which matched Salma in size, would fetch Rs 50 (a little over 50 cents), she showed me. She needed several of them to buy Aslam's medicines and keep their family of eight, with Aslam's wife, three more boys and a three-year-old girl, going. She kept Arif working, hoping it wasn't too late to treat his cough but worrying that it was. She didn't know that Aslam had stopped taking his medicines or making the trips to the far-away, free hospital.

A flower trader had asked Salma to help with the impending gush in demand during Ramzan, asking her to string the fresh flowers he bought from Mumbai's wholesale flower market, so that he could sell them in the city. One afternoon, when I went to see her, Salma rested her back against trunks piled up with the family's belongings and sat between heaps of sweet-smelling tuberoses, roses and jasmines in their long, dimly-lit room. She bent forward to catch the sun and thread her needle. Amid jabbed fingers and perfumed hands, she learned to braid the flowers in intricate patterns. She made flower blankets that were laid out in the city's filigreed mausoleums, to make wishes come true. She made garlands that brides and grooms hung shyly around each other when they got married; and wreaths that were laid at the feet of the dead. Most of all, she made flower braids that adorned women's hair, masking the smells of cooking or the fish they sold, enveloping them in the heady, aphrodisiacal fragrance of jasmine instead.

Aslam sat next to her, with tiny crystals making shining reflections on his gaunt face: he was sticking them onto a peach-coloured skirt in long paisley patterns. It would later be stitched into a bridal outfit and would hang in Mumbai's markets. Salma and he would each earn Rs 30 for their work, just about enough to afford a thinly stretched meal for everyone. They had begun getting Aslam treated for his tuberculosis at the government-run GT Hospital in the city. Outside the house, he played with a Frisbee that he had fashioned from an empty medicine carton.

Salma's little granddaughter flitted over her flowers, asking for two rupees, while Salma tried to work. *Toffee lena hai*, the girl said, blocking the sun as she bent over to catch Salma's attention. *I need to buy toffees.* Salma waved her away, trying to get the slight jasmine stems through her trembling needle.

The girl bent lower so that Salma would look up at her. *Ek jhaad lagaya hai*, Salma said, pulling the thread out of her half-made flower braid. *I've planted a tree.* It will grow money along with flowers, she continued. I'll give you the money as soon as it flowers. Befuddled, the girl went out to play. The sun fell further into the house, and Salma slumped against the piled-up trunks and went back to braiding flowers.

Fridays were unfailingly busy for her. It was the day that devotees visited the city's milky, marble mausoleums. Entreaties to the saints buried there rose through the crescendo of music and heaving crowds. Worshippers draped flower blankets over the tombs of the saints to propitiate them. They bent low over the tombs, swathed with brocade and flowers and wreathed in incense, and whispered their petitions, hoping the saints would hear and make them come true.

Salma could not afford bus rides into the city herself. She still believed that her flower blankets could keep diseases away from her family, and security guards, drones and cameras away from the mountains. Ramzan was not far off and she hoped that, through her blankets, her prayers would reach the miracle-inducing saints of Mumbai.

No one was sure how Farzana avoided the guards and made it to the mountains as often as she did. After the long waits for trucks, she brought bags filled with plastic, wire and television sets that fetched the highest prices, squashed bottles that earned a little and the wispy carrier bags that earned the least. But it was getting harder. Some days Farha and Farzana returned home with nothing, ate and clambered onto the long wooden planks tacked to the edges of their house and slept early, tired from the endless waiting.

One night Farha woke up to the sound of Farzana muttering insults, her voice rising to threaten someone. In the dark, she called out to Farzana and asked who she spoke to, but Farzana carried on. Farha called louder, waking Farzana, who muttered, confused, that she was not speaking to anyone. Both sisters drifted back to sleep. Farha reasoned that Farzana was seeing guards even in her dreams.

Around the end of April 2016 Farzana and Sahani were walking up towards the seventh mountain after lunch, to collect plastic bottles. After a while Farzana looked up for air. Tea vendors walked around them with kettles. The late-summer sunset was at least an hour away. She looked downhill, to where a crowd had gathered around the Khan brothers' warehouse. Policemen were bolting it shut. Others photographed the scene, or fixed barbed wire around the private suburb of hills within the municipality's township of trash.

For a few days afterwards, the army from these estates waved down trucks and directed them to different parts of the township. Farzana and Sahani decided they were changing tack, to dodge the police. It was nearly a week before they heard that policemen had arrested the Khan brothers that same afternoon, charging them under the stringent Maharashtra Control of Organised Crime Act

(MCOCA), which allowed for long periods of imprisonment without bail.[2] Police would later also arrest Javed Qureshi.

Jehangir was called for interrogation; others melted into the skinny lanes or returned to their villages to escape attention.[3] Officers had shut all the private hill clearings in the township, including Jehangir's own. He was in and out of the house, his restless energy turning nearly frenzied as he met traders, offering his trash to anyone who might take it.

Mumbai's summer stretched ahead, moving slowly. Farzana worked with Farha on a mountain peak on an afternoon suspended in sun. They waited for the breeze and the garbage trucks to begin drifting their way. Their feet were clammy in the socks and lace-up shoes they wore to keep from the heat shocks that the mountains still gave off.

Farzana was looking for glass to give to Jehangir. It only made him rage at her. There was never enough to fill a truck and make the trips into the city to sell it, he told her. But not knowing what else to do, Farzana and Farha tried collecting more. As the two walked up a steep hill, Farha tripped on a discarded shoe jutting out of mud and fell backwards on her bag.

Glass, boiling hot under the sun, cut through the material and made a long, serpentine cut on her back. Blood stained the shards within the bag. She screamed until Farzana called Alamgir to take their injured sister home. Neighbours followed her howling progress to Hyder Ali's house. She would need stitches to repair her back, but Hyder Ali didn't even have enough money for the rickshaw trip to hospital. He spilled the tobacco powder that he and Shakimun chewed into Farha's cut. It burned her back, intensifying her screams. *Ye to door se chilla rahi thi*, he said. *She's been yelling from miles away.*

As the cut on her back filled slowly, to make a dark, curling tobacco-filled scar, Farzana and the others had taken to calling Farha 'snake woman'. They believed that mountain luck had carved itself into her back. It drew glass and other mountain treasures into Farha's hands, even amid the mountains' diminishing fortunes, even amid tightening security and the city getting nearer. It would stay in her through the mountains' endless cycle of turning fortunes.

12

Throughout the summer of 2016 Farzana and Farha watched the assorted consultants bore holes and lower tubes into the mountains to measure the fires still seething within. They heard that some of the vents would stay within the mountains, to release these secret fires and their smoke. They also heard that the consultants were mapping the township in order to pick a sliver of it for the waste-to-power plant. More than a year later, when I applied to the municipality's solid-waste department for information on the height of the mountains, I was sent this map, carefully created with images from drones that had flown low over Farzana that summer.[*]

On a long, warm afternoon Shakimun squatted next to Sahani, the second-eldest of the sisters, at the mountains' rim. They watched as Farzana arrived with a cloth pile, leaving them to sort through some fashionably ripped jeans (and others irretrievably ripped) while she turned to walk back up the slopes for more. Shakimun, sitting with her arms hanging off her bent knees, waited until Farzana had walked far enough out of earshot, then spoke softly to Sahani in the lilting dialect she had brought from her

---

[*] This map, obtained through the Right to Information Act, was used to create the map at the beginning of this book.

village, decades ago. *Raat mein ajeeb harkatein karat hai. She says strange things at night.* Shakimun was worried: the mountains, with their chaos and poison, were bubbling out of her daughter in nocturnal mutterings and odd behaviour. Farzana was born to the mountains, and their contours had shaped her, body and mind. But now she seemed trapped within them, and they were wedged inside her.

A neighbour had taken Farzana into the city for a trip, along with her own children. She returned in the evening, swearing to Shakimun that she would never take Farzana again. Farzana had felt faint and needed chips, but not the sweet ones they got. The salty ones were too salty. Without them, she was so drained of energy that she could not walk to get the bus back, leaving them all stranded for a while. She was always weak in those days, Sahani would remember. She always had a headache, a stomach ache. Always.

At night, more of the family heard her say things that Farzana, when woken from sleep, would insist she did not say. Mohammed Salahudin, who had lived a few houses further down their lane, had recently moved out, but often returned to wash away unwanted traces from the pickers, with his prayers and rituals. But just as Salahudin began chanting, Farzana got up and turned to leave. Sahani tried to hold onto her, but Farzana was already out of the house. They looked out, but she had vanished. Hyder Ali pronounced that this was a *Shaitani harkat* – the doing of the Shaitans that rose from the discarded desires that had burned on the mountains for months.

Hyder Ali tried taking Farzana back for the prayers, but she never sat through them. Later he asked Salahudin to pray over an amulet, and then got Shakimun to tie it around Farzana's arm. He hoped these portable prayers, and the few fasts she would keep during the holy month of Ramzan, would dislodge the Shaitan settled within her, which was perhaps a remnant of all that lay abandoned on the slopes. He asked Yasmeen, Alamgir's wife, to supplement these protections with her Koran-reading lessons. In any case, he thought, as Farzana entered the marriage market, being able to recite a few verses would also improve her prospects of finding a husband.

Yasmeen got Farzana, Farha and Jannat, the youngest of the sisters, to cover their heads demurely and sit facing the buttery-yellow Mecca mosque that she had painted against a pink wall, while she spoke a verse:

Do you not see how God drives the clouds, then joins them together, then piles them into layers and then you see the rain pour from their midst? He sends down from the skies mountainous masses of clouds charged with hail, and He makes it fall on whom He will and turns it away from whom He pleases. The flash of His lightning may well nigh take away the sight. God alternates the night and the day – truly, in this there is a lesson for men of insight.[1]

Yasmeen's baby son, Faizan, crawled out of Shakimun's arms and tried to get into hers. By the time she had settled him, Farzana had slipped away. She just would not hold the Koran in her hands, Yasmeen recalled, frustrated. Teach those who want to be taught, Farzana countered; the class was meant for Farha, not her. For Farha enjoyed the class, believing the verses washed over the burning mountains, rinsing away their smoke and the smell that itched in her.

Out in their lane, Farzana followed a trail of coloured cloth scraps blowing down the slim passage with the dry summer breeze, taking slow, long steps, stamping them down and walking towards the mountains.

Sometimes she took a winding route so that she could poke her head into Mohammad Khalil's cool, dark house. He was one of Sanjay Nagar's oldest residents and collected only coconuts from the mountains. Hindu rituals hardly ever began without breaking a coconut to bring luck. Sometimes I felt that the rapid growth of new things – of rising wants in the city – could be measured by the cracked shells that arrived at the mountains. With our loans, Khalil had begun to buy them from wedding halls, car showrooms, new apartment complexes and temples. Every time he came for a loan he showed me his plastic-encased bank passbook, swollen with more savings than I thought used coconuts could yield. He would have a big wedding for his daughters in his village, with his savings, he told me. Relatives and friends there would not know that his money had the smell of spent luck.

Khalil had made a makeshift bamboo-stick conveyer belt, curving around the edges of his room, filled with drying shells. He would also sell their velvety husks, to be made into matting. They filled his house with an intense, heady smell. Farzana stood outside, took in the scent of drying coconuts, then wound her way to work.

One afternoon as she sat on a mountain peak with Farha, the beating sun keeping her anger boiling, something happened to Farzana. That morning Hyder Ali had told her that he had no money for her to bribe the guards to 'unsee' them. Farzana had left without breakfast, then waited for the guards to pass by in order to get on the slopes, not eating lunch, either.

They saw two trucks emerge, following the winding, potholed mountain roads. As they turned to chase them, the trucks diverged to move towards different loops, turning the sisters in opposite directions. They argued over which one to follow, each worried they would miss the contents of the dwindling trucks that were gone in an instant these days. Farzana's anger, seething throughout the day, flashed, their voices rising as they saw other pickers emerge from the hills and move towards the trucks.

But even as Farzana saw Farha wave her fork closer to her, goading her towards the trucks, Farzana slumped on the slope. Farha tried calling out to her, shaking her, but her sister would not stir. The sun warmed her inert face. Not knowing what else to do, Farha looked around for Jehangir or Alamgir. She shook Farzana again, but she was unmoving. Farha saw the emptied trucks make their way back into the city. Farzana stayed motionless among the castaway possessions.

When Farha returned with Ismail, Sahani's husband, and his brother Saddam, they found Farzana lying unconscious on the trash peak, glowing against the sun. A small crowd had gathered around. Ismail filled Farzana into his arms and brought her slowly down the slopes. Shakimun mumbled frantic high-pitched prayers as Ismail brought Farzana in and laid her on the floor. He called Salahudin, who prayed over a bowl filled with water, which he then splashed on Farzana's face. She woke up to see a small crowd around her and slapped Ismail. Why had he brought her home? She needed to get back and fill her garbage bag, which was still on the slope. Shakimun asked Farzana to stay home and help her with her embroidery, filling a red tulle sleeve that wafted in the air, its tiny crystals giving flashes of a rosy hue.

When Jehangir came home that evening, he ignored Shakimun's story of how a Shaitan had tripped his sister on a mountain slope. He took Farzana to a doctor nearby, who examined the pale inner rim of her eyes and told them that she was very weak. Working in the sun must have made her feel dizzy and faint. Jehangir got her the multivitamins the doctor prescribed and asked Farzana to make sure she didn't skip meals. He asked her to stay home, not work on the mountains any more, as he often had. Farzana returned to the slopes the next day.

Shakimun sought treatment for her own diagnosis of Farzana's sickness. She had heard of a healer across 90 Feet Road who was so holy that he didn't even let the shadow of a woman fall on him, as she told Hyder Ali. With such discipline, he could make anything happen, she thought. She got Yasmeen to write down Farzana's name, explaining that she had been gripped by a *Khaadi ka Shaitan*, a spirit from the mountains. She dispatched Hyder Ali and his cousin Badre Alam, who lived in the loft above, to the room filled with incense and supplicants, with the slip. They returned with more *taveezes* – talismans – for Farzana.

On some days Sahani ran into Farzana on the slopes and they picked together, as they always had. On others, she found Farzana home in the afternoons, as she never had been before. Often she was muttering, Sahani told me, or crying. *Andar andar tha. Baad mein bahar nikalne laga*, she said. *At first the Shaitan flickered within my sister. But then he started pouring out of her.*

It was bound to happen if she worked during the afternoon, Ismail told Sahani when she tried telling him of

Farzana's affliction. The thing about Shaitans was, as he would explain to me later, that they came out in the day from around 7 a.m. to 2 p.m. and then from midnight to around 2.30 a.m. *Iske liye main uske baad hi kaam pe jata tha. Unka saya pade hi na,* he said. *I worked only after that, so their shadow didn't fall on me.*

But as word began to spread in the lanes of the mountains' spirit that had got stuck in Farzana, neighbours dropped in at Hyder Ali's home, often with thoughts on her ailment. One of them pointed out to the anxious Shakimun that Farzana had spent all winter on the burning mountains, within the toxic halo of smoke. A lot of mishaps happen at the mountains, she told Shakimun. They were all burnt. Farzana must have inhaled something. But to Sahani, the answer was clear: they needed a bigger healer. They decided to take Farzana to the mausoleum of the Sufi saint, Hazrat Shah Jalaluddin Shah, who was known for exorcising seen and unseen ailments from people on Thursdays.

A short bus ride dropped them at the far end of the close-by suburb of Chembur. On their way to the Dargah, the shrine that they had heard was nearly as old as the city itself, they walked past oil refineries that spewed air as noxious as the Deonar mountains' halo. Baba Jalaluddin, buried within, was said to have ensured that the sprawling British-made refineries that came to ring his mausoleum could never cover it.

When the mountains' rim had grown crowded, and new arrivals continued to build slim, double-storeyed bedsheet-made homes that hung over the city's roads and inched onto its train tracks, the municipality had sent them here to settle a tenement town. It grew within the halo of the refineries, close to the halo of the mountains. Baba Jalaluddin had come to be known as *Shahenshah-e-Chembur*, or the 'Emperor of Chembur', presiding over a kingdom of poisonous chemicals and disease.[2]

That evening Shakimun, Sahani and Farzana stood in the courtyard of his shrine. It was lined with old trees, simmering cooking pots and outsize drums. Shakimun and Sahani walked ahead, drawn by the shimmering green trellises that stretched across the mausoleum's silvery, glass-topped inner walls. They turned back to see that Farzana had stumbled and fallen at the doorstep. Akbar Bhai, the healer they had come to see, came out to help. When Sahani told him that Farzana worked at the trash township, had begun to babble through her sleep and had fainted, he said, *Gande saye ne pakda hai. An unclean spirit has gripped her.*

As the sun slowly began to cool and retreat from the courtyard, Sahani and Shakimun watched it fill with people and their aches and troubles. At six, Dargah staff began beating drums. Some people came out with their feet chained, others alone and sat in the courtyard, to be in the presence of Baba Jalaluddin. Shakimun, Sahani and Farzana stood in the crowd and watched. As the Dargah's healers coaxed out the stirred spirits through the sound of their drums, Sahani watched loose hair and bodies swing and then blur to the quickening beat. Their bodies slammed on the ground and rose, to the sound of the drums again. As the sky darkened, lights came on, the drumming ceased and the whirling bodies fell on the floor, drained. Akbar Bhai told Shakimun to bring Farzana for eleven Thursdays in a row, so that Baba could extricate the Shaitan.

At home, Shakimun flopped onto the plank they had fixed to the outside wall so that Hyder Ali could sit and watch Banjara Galli go by. Sahani said she could not go to the Dargah again; that the swaying, falling bodies had frightened her. Budhi, the plump old woman who had squeezed onto the bench between Shakimun and Sahani, said she could go instead. Budhi's silvery candy-floss hair and soft, plump frame had begun appearing with the dark, and she would settle to sleep on the bench soon after it was made. *Usko dekhne vala koi nahi hai na*, Shakimun would tell me of how they had come to take Budhi into their home, already swollen with people. *She has no one to look after her.*

That year we had moved to a new office, in the outsize and derelict basement of a building in a surprisingly quiet and leafy Mumbai lane. Even that immense office had filled up as Ramzan approached and the demand for loans went up, as it did every year. The month of fasting and prayers was meant to set followers on a path to God. Our borrowers took loans to buy fruit or juicers and set up stalls for people to buy food to break their fasts with. Others set up trinket stalls, and clothes and shoe shops, on bedsheets laid out on pavements. I often asked our loan-takers how splurging on luxuries sat with the need for abstinence from desire and purification. They told me it was the small indulgences that made the long abstinence possible.

I ran into Hyder Ali in the crush one day and asked what he needed a new loan for. He would revive his *zari*, or gold-thread embroidery, workshop, he told me. Didn't I know that Eid – the culmination of the month of Ramzan, with its early-dawn to post-sunset fasting – was when women wore their best clothes? he asked. Unsure of his workshop's prospects, I changed the subject, asking after Farzana. *Vo kaisi hogi? Theek hai*, he replied lightly. *How would she be? She's fine.*

Later another borrower from Banjara Galli told me how Farzana went to Baba Jalaluddin's Dargah on Thursdays, and that a Shaitan had gripped her. Only the healers there could get it out, she said. I moved on to her loan application. After she left, I called one of our volunteers, Roshan Shaikh, who lived in a tenement building near the shrine in the refinery's halo, to ask her about Farzana's predicament. Farzana must have been standing with her hair loose, she interrupted, before I could finish asking why a girl would be taken to the Dargah. She didn't believe in all this, Roshan told me, but still ... the girl was in the right place.

A young woman from her own building had recently been cured by Baba Jalaluddin of one of these invisible but toxic lovers, Roshan went on. The family had quickly got her married to someone outside the city, so that the jilted Shaitan didn't repossess her.

Girls these days! They dab scent on, pin flowers into their hair and go where the spirits lie in wait, Roshan fretted. It was how the girl must have got trapped, she said, although I had not named Farzana or mentioned that she worked on Deonar's slopes. *Shaitan aashiq ho jaate hain*, Roshan concluded. *Shaitans fall in love with them.*

13

The morning of 2 June 2016, her eighteenth birthday, Farzana emptied the money box she had been filling for months. She walked to the Lotus market and bought herself a pair of jeans. After all, this was it: she was finally an adult. She watched lights getting strung through the long, chaotic street, ready for Ramzan. Pickers carefully piled up hills of prayer caps, shoes and fruit on the pavement, on the road and on folding tables that straddled the two. The fasts would begin within days. Farzana went to the packed sweet shop where she usually bought cream clouds floating in sweetened milk with her carefully saved money. That day, it was cake, wafers and chocolate.

Turning back for home, she saw pale-grey clouds hanging over the mountains that rose ahead and hung like hulks over their communities. Sisters, nieces and nephews dropped in to wish her a happy birthday through the afternoon, but Farzana had left her bags at home and gone to work. All of the sisters had been the same since childhood, Sahani often told me. They got fevers if they missed walking the mountains for even a day, and their bodies ached. Farzana couldn't stay away.

In the evening Farzana wore her jeans with a new long black top filled with multicoloured patterns. She wore gold hoops in her ears and made up her face. The house filled slowly with all the Shaikh siblings, their spouses and children. Only Jehana, the eldest, stayed away; her husband thought he had seen her with another man at work and hacked his garbage fork into her head, making a deep, bloody gash. That evening he sat at their doorstep, while Jehana stayed inside. At Hyder Ali's house the others huddled around Farzana as she cut the square cake with her name written in white sugar icing.

Even as she sliced the cake and began serving it, Ismail began teasing her, saying that this was the year Farzana would get married ... but to whom? *Tere se acha dikhna chahiye!* Farzana replied. *It better be someone nicer-looking than you!* Ismail threw something at her and they chased each other around the packed room, bumping into the others and trying not to trip on Faizan, Alamgir's nine-month-old son, who crawled around them.

Hyder Ali sat next to Jehangir, who had been in the middle of moving out of the house for months and looked ahead as he spoke. Jehangir had his own trash business, his own motorbike. Why would he live with his family or share his money with them? Hyder Ali asked caustically. Jehangir didn't respond. He, Rakila and their three children ate at home, but walked over to sleep in a house he had recently rented nearby. Soon they would be gone, and Alamgir too was hoping to follow his brother, with a new job driving a garbage truck. If that happened, Farzana would become the oldest of the children who handed money over to their father, to keep the household limping on.

Look for a husband for Farzana, Jehangir said, turning to Afsana, the only one of the sisters whose marriage had taken her out of the mountain's shadow. He didn't want someone from the dumping grounds. What if it closes down?

Farzana turned sharply away from Ismail. *Mujhe karna hi nahi hai bhai. I don't want to be married!* She wanted to stay, she protested, to stay home with him – tears running down her powdered face.

Three days later the sun stayed behind the clouds, which were gathering slowly through the day. Farzana was picking on a trash peak in a gentle breeze. She did not notice them darken until, a little before sunset, she was drenched in the monsoon season's first showers. That night she slept fitfully, to the sound of thunder. The holy month of Ramzan had begun before dawn. When she stepped out into their lane, it glowed before first light under a canopy of freshly strung silver bunting, hung above it. Farzana, fasting, already felt hungry.

As the rains doused the fires, the official plans to make the plant intensified. The municipality had asked consultants to plan for a plant that would consume 3,000 tonnes of waste – more than half of what arrived at the township every day. In court committee meetings, experts were sceptical that such a big plant would work at once; it could perhaps be made in phases. Justice Oka's deadline to stop dumping at Deonar's hills was only a year away, and the fires that had burned all winter were on everyone's minds. A project that had glimmered and faded for decades felt full of a sudden urgency.

Farzana worked on, watching the outer slopes turn emerald with grass, just as they had when she first came to work. Lotuses bloomed and melted in the rain that rose in the troughs. She forked over old trash, gloopy from the rains and charred from fires. A few weeks earlier Shakimun had accompanied her to Baba Jalaluddin's Dargah, unbraiding her long hair so that the spirit did not get tangled in it when Akbar Bhai teased it out of her body with his incantation. Alone amid the crowd of entranced people, Farzana did not move or sway to the rising drumbeat. The spirit had retreated from her, the healer told them. The job that should have taken eleven weeks was done in five. Shakimun returned home, relieved.

But friends who awoke before dawn and went to relieve themselves at the foothills began seeing Farzana in the dark. Farzana, who had always been with one of her sisters, was now walking alone on the dimly lit slopes. They took to calling her *Khaadi ka Bhoot, 'ghost of the mountains'*. She had begun returning to the slopes before light, before anyone woke up, often with money to buy food there. She got to work early to beat the guards, she said. She came home around dusk, with the day-shift pickers. When Shakimun sent her a message to come home for lunch, she heard that Farzana would buy food from one of the vendors who roamed the slopes and would stay on. Salahudin had told Shakimun that mountain spirits didn't leave easily.

One afternoon, after waiting hours on a mountain top, Farzana and Farha saw a truck winding its way along the dirt track towards them. Mud splashed as they ran alongside it on the hills, chasing it to a clearing. Farzana watched breathlessly as its trash emptied out. Farha threw herself at it, jostling with the others who had gathered around. She looked up and found Farzana still staring at the mushy trash fallen around them. Others pushed her aside to get at their pickings.

Farha went on collecting squashed bottles. She kept an eye out for Farzana, who stood still, gaping. She called out to her sister, who did not seem to hear. She came closer and prodded Farzana tentatively with her garbage fork. Aren't you going to lift up your fork? Farha asked, thinking of how long they had waited for the emptying truck. Pickers jabbed around them. Are you starting a fight with your older sister? Farzana retorted angrily. *Akdi nahi uthaegi to ladna padega*, Farha replied. *If you don't pick up your fork, I will have to.*

Farzana swung her garbage fork, aiming it at Farha, who cowered and stumbled away, surprised. Farzana followed her, fork in hand. *Badi behen ko maregi? Are you going to hit your older sister?* Farha heard Farzana repeat as she ran off downhill. Farha laughed as she ran, thinking they would stop soon, clutch their sides, catch their breath and collapse on the slopes, laughing. But when she turned back, she saw Farzana's eyes filled with rage, her fork dangling in front of her. Farha stayed ahead. Farzana tripped clumsily on the loosely packed slopes, but kept after her. Farha's chest burned. The air was heavy with unshed rain, making it hard even to draw breath. But Farzana's fork was close behind her, and Farha kept stumbling forward.

She saw pickers around them stop their work to watch. She heard some of them call out, asking Farzana to stop, but Farha felt her sister getting closer. She heard Alamgir call out to Farzana. But Farzana's footsteps stayed close behind her.

Farha heard a scuffle and turned back to see Alamgir grab Farzana tightly from the back until she fell on the slope. Farzana held onto her fork even as her long, curled-up limbs rose and fell with deep breaths. Alamgir wrested it away and lifted his sister in his arms. He was the tallest of the siblings, sinewy where Jehangir was wiry. Farha heard someone say the humidity was shortening fuses on the slopes these days as she trailed behind Alamgir, breathless and befuddled. Farzana slept in Alamgir's arms, heavy with exhaustion. He laid her down on the floor at home and began telling Shakimun about the rage that had gripped her, speaking softly so he didn't wake Farzana up. The mountain spirits had not receded.

Just as the city's assault on the mountains had assumed a new urgency, the family decided they needed to step up their efforts to exorcise the mountains from their daughter. Shakimun asked relatives and friends. Many had stories of mountain spirits gripping their families: Hindus had seen the Khabees, spirits from Islamic mythology, while Sahani believed she had been possessed as a teenager by a Hindu goddess. Some asked Shakimun to take Farzana to the shrine of Mira Datar, the patron saint for exorcising spirits in Mumbai.[1] A fifteenth-century boy saint, buried in the neighbouring state of Gujarat, Mira Datar had powers to unclench the grasp of spirits stuck inside people that were so legendary they had led to the creation of a green outpost of his distant mausoleum on a busy street in Mumbai, close to the city's vast port lands. It featured the same spirit-cleansing rituals. Farzana tied green glass bangles to the shrine's walls with a thread, hoping it would elicit the green bangles worn by Marathi brides and others who came into the city, and a calmer life.

Three days later, Shakimun told Sahani, Farzana cried through the night, tormented by the mountain spirit. Over the weeks, more healers came to visit, more talismans were tied on and Farzana kept returning to work before dawn, with no memory of it all. She only once remembered going to the shrine in Chalisgaon, hours away.

In the city the builders' association had appealed against Oka's order to stop construction. They should not be penalised for the municipality's inability to manage its waste, for its failed plans, they pleaded. But Justice Oka was immovable. Until the mountains were dealt with, there could be no new construction in the city. Soon the builders appealed in India's Supreme Court.

In their attempts to fix the township, Tata Consulting Engineers looked at waste-to-compost plants and power plants around the world.[2] They were concerned, as other consultants before them had been, that Mumbai's waste did not contain enough plastic, paper, cloth or wood scraps to burn well as fuel in an incinerator. Nearly half of what arrived at the township was mushy food waste, saturated by the monsoons, and would not burn easily. The plant might work only seasonally, in fits and starts, the consultants worried.

But that May a new report that the municipality had commissioned arrived from the National Environmental Engineering Research Institute, showing that the calorific value of Mumbai's waste, which allowed it to burn well and produce power, was high, higher than in the other cities the report studied.[3] The city's habits had changed: Mumbaikars sent rice straw, coconut husk, good-quality plastics and paper, giving the waste a high calorific value. The waste had indeed become more combustible. The plant that at first seemed as it would not possibly work might now work.

*

At Farzana's home the spirits seemed to recede with each incantation, only to return. More suggestions poured in. Farzana was not to treat the slopes as an open-air bathroom, as pickers usually did. The spirits rising from desire could catch you when you least expected it. It was how desire was: it could grip you, trip you, then not leave you.

Yasmeen's mother told Shakimun to take Farzana to the shrine of Makhdoom Shah Baba along the Mahim Bay. Known as the *Qutub-e-Kokan*, or 'shining star of the Konkan coast', along which Mumbai lay, the saint had drawn aches and pains from across the city and beyond. The lanes around the shrine were filled with the possessed, the dispossessed, disabled and others that the city had stretched to breaking point.

A scholar and saint, Makhdoom Shah Baba was said to have lived seven centuries ago and held court at the spot that later became Mahim's police station, nearby. His annual feast began with a procession led by the station's senior inspector, increasing Makhdoom Shah Baba's glow. Musicians were said to have come on barges to play at the feast. The fair that went with it spilled onto the beach that stretched behind the Dargah, illuminating the Mahim Bay and holding up traffic movement in the curving finger-shaped city every year. Shakimun felt sure it was the Mahim Dargah that would bring out the Shaitan lodged in Farzana.

One afternoon a borrower from Banjara Galli told me of Shakimun and Farzana's trips to the Mahim Dargah. As I processed loan applications for the stalls that mushroomed in Deonar's markets around Eid, I hesitated to ask more about Farzana. That year, I heard, the festive haze that I had seen in the markets around the mountains, made up of the sweet smoke of luridly red rotisserie meats and light from halogen lamps, filled an empty market. The pickers had little money with which to buy anything there, leaving them pale and washed-out.

When the borrowers left, I called Roshan, our volunteer. Why wasn't anything working on Farzana? I asked. None of the medicines, the talismans or the rituals I had heard about seemed to make any difference. *Kabhi kabhi usko pata chal jata hai, Hazri ke liye ja rahein hain, to vo thodi der ke liye bagal mein baith jata hai,* she said. *Sometimes when the Shaitan knows you are going to have it extricated, it comes out and sits next to you, to escape for a while. But it comes back.*

14

As Eid approached in Banjara Galli, fragrant smells wafted into Moharram Ali's house and filled his wife Yasmin's head. She had nothing to offer in return for the food she smelled. She owed its makers money. She told them fasting gave her a headache and she needed to sleep through the evenings to get over it. But she didn't fast.

Moharram Ali had tried to work further along the mountains, through the fires. Many months later, when I met him, he dismissed the smoke and changed air in Banjara Galli that were unsettling life in the lanes, in his airy, elegant manner. Mountain air doesn't 'suit' everybody, he told me. But he had worked there most of his life – a bit of smoke didn't bother him, he said. He would not admit that things had changed, that the mountain air no longer suited his family. As security tightened, Moharram Ali dropped into the family's house at night to pick up money that he said he had left behind in his hasty flight. When Yasmin tried calling him, to ask for Eid expenses, his phone was switched off or went unanswered. Friends stalked their home to retrieve loans they had given him. But they never saw him. The legend of Shaitan Singh – of Moharram Ali's invincible luck – had flamed out untraceably, gutting his family.

The market stayed open all night on Chaand Raat, the first night of the crescent moon that would bring Eid. The settlements glowed against the dark mountains, and pickers spilled into the market to bask in the moonlight, shop with whatever money they had and eat. Others set up stalls to sell bangles, henna cones, spice bundles to layer into *pulaos* and edible silver to set, quivering, on sweets, hoping to earn money away from the trash. Hyder Ali had told me that Shaitans, creatures of the dark, stayed away in the glow of that night.

Moharram Ali returned Yasmin's call that evening; she had not wanted her boys to be draped in the mountain filth while their friends wore new white kurtas for Eid prayers. In the months since their debts had mounted and Moharram Ali had left, Mehrun and Ashra's clothes had inched up and tightened till they no longer fitted them. He would take the girls out to buy new clothes, he said, and would send her a set. Yasmin did not know how to tell Sharib, who was filled with rage against his father, that there was nothing left for him or his brother. She went, instead, to ask friends for a loan.

Mehrun and Ashra met Moharram Ali in the market, which was luminescent with fairy lights and bejewelled shoppers. Mehrun wore a sullen pout, thinking about everything Hera and Sharib said about their father. Ashra held Moharram Ali's hand and kept up a chatter that he could barely hear as they wove through the crowd. They passed butcher's shops without customers, with long, bony carcasses that hung, partly carved, for days and attracted mostly flies. They avoided piles of fruit on the pavement, which had rotted on carts until the sellers threw them away. Enchanted, Ashra pointed at dresses whose sequins glittered under the halogen lamps, their stiff taffeta layers making it seem as if someone was inside them, as they hung on bamboo poles. Moharram Ali's face fell when he heard their prices.

He tried directing her towards cheaper clothes that lay in dark piles. Ashra shook her head: no. Mehrun saw Moharram Ali's face crumple even as Ashra's lit up, like the lights filtering softly through the fairy-like dresses. In the end Mehrun said she could do without new clothes, and Ashra quickly picked a long, creamy lace dress filled with gold sequins, which came with a long skirt and trousers. Mehrun and Ashra, holding her outsize bag, walked back to Sanjay Nagar, while Moharram Ali took his empty wallet back to Rafiq Nagar.

Yasmin came home a little later, with Rs 2,000 (little more than $27) that she would not have to return: *Fitra* was charity given on the last night of Ramzan. The next morning Sharib and Sameer bathed, wore their new white salwar kurtas and went out for prayers. Yasmin thought her tall, strapping sons, scrubbed of their coating of mountain grit, looked better than any of the friends whose homes they visited to collect *Eidi*, or money as blessings, and sample the treats their homes were redolent with. Ashra wore her gold dress with the skirt, got Mehrun to make braids in her hair and left for a friend's house. Yasmin thought her children looked so nice that no one would notice she had not lit her stove on Eid.

For years the mountains and their lanes had emptied out in the wake of the festival, as pickers took trips into the city, stretching the festival to Baasi, or 'stale Eid'. They visited far-flung mausoleums, colonial monuments and rocky beaches. But that year the mountains darkened as soon as Eid was over, the lanes stayed full and creditors returned to Yasmin's door, hungrier than before.

Yasmin was often out and, when she was away, it was twelve-year-old Mehrun who faced them, with no money and little to say. Yasmin thought the creditors would retreat in the face of a child. Then one afternoon she ran into a creditor whose money Moharram Ali had disappeared with, as she entered their lane. She told him, as she usually did, that she would return the money when Moharram Ali returned. The creditor interrupted: if she didn't have his money, she should send Mehrun to his house at night, as payment for the debt.

Unlike the other Ali children, who were tall and strong, Mehrun was fragile, almost breakable. She seemed translucent, with her milky complexion, permanent blush and hazel eyes. Her presence in conversations at home was gauzy too, conducted mostly through glances. Both Moharram Ali and Yasmin had told me that she looked just like them. *Mera bachpan hai ye,* Yasmin had said. *She is my childhood.* In the moves that the family had made since Moharram Ali's disappearance, the dolls he had collected from the mountains for Mehrun and Ashra had disappeared, the sewing machine Mehrun had used to stitch clothes for them taken away by creditors. *Kabhi socha hi nahi ki vo gudiya hai aur main insaan,* Mehrun told me during the long afternoons I spent at their house. *I never thought they were dolls and me a person.*

Yasmin had begun keeping her door locked. I heard of Moharram Ali's disappearance, his reappearance in a different part of the lanes and Yasmin's own evasions soon afterwards. When I asked other women in the lane, I was told that Yasmin did not live there any more, her house was locked. I asked them to say, if they did meet her, that I had not come seeking money, but to ask about her and her precarious situation. Then one day I heard a voice say, *Dhoondh rahe ho? Are you looking for me?* And when I looked up, I saw Yasmin. She unlocked her house and I walked in, surprised to see Mehrun inside. *Aaj kal aise hi rakhti hoon*, Yasmin told me, with an embarrassed smile. *This is how I keep the house these days.*

She needed money to send Mehrun and Ashra to an orphanage or a hostel, away from her creditors and her troubles, Yasmin told me. The creditor's words played in her mind. A friend had told her about an agency that hired women to carry babies in their wombs for wealthy but infertile couples; she told Yasmin that women from their lanes had been applying to be surrogates, a job that could pay them lakhs of rupees. With the mountains closing on them, it was the only way to make good money in their lanes, and Yasmin, then thirty-seven, queued up at their office in Dreams Mall, a shopping centre in a suburb nearby. She signed consent forms and went through medical tests but was not selected.

With the rent for their room due days ago, Yasmin travelled to a hospital across the creek, where she had heard a doctor was looking for a surrogate. The hospital was unlike any she had seen before: there were no sick people or medical smells in its softly lit beige lobby. She got chatting with the burqa-clad woman sitting next to her. They were unlikely to be chosen unless the younger women failed the tests, she said; she had already moved from surrogacy to medical trials. She got paid several thousand rupees for a few days of popping pills and medical tests, she commented. Yasmin begged the woman to take her along.

A few days later, when she got the call to join a trial in the city of Baroda, nearly 250 miles north of Mumbai, Yasmin left Mehrun and Ashra with Moharram Ali and asked Sharib and Sameer to sleep at a *kata* shop. Then she took the five-hour train ride north and returned, days later, with a few thousand rupees, which she used to rent a new room and make some repayments. A week later she got another call. It was a woman she had met at the test centre, asking if she wanted to go for another 'study'. Yasmin told her she would meet her at the train station. With the putrid grip of the mountains fading away, she slid into the dark underworld of medical trials.

At test facilities, managers ushered her into quiet air-conditioned rooms. Women who tested anaemic or had low blood pressure were sent home, usually in tears. Others were taken into a room where someone explained long legal contracts stating that they willingly participated in the test and would not hold the company responsible if trial drugs made them sick. Yasmin could not read a word of the Hindi script they were written in and relied on the verbal explanation to sign the contract. Mostly she tried not to listen too hard.

Over the months Yasmin showed me contracts for contraceptives, epilepsy drugs and pills for heart conditions, among other trials. I saw Mehrun's name listed as the beneficiary, if something were to happen to Yasmin and money was due to her family. The drugs were usually being tested by an Indian organisation on behalf of a large Western pharmaceutical company that had developed it for use in international markets, where it was illegal to test unapproved drugs on people. But without human testing, companies would not know whether the medicine worked and what side-effects it had. So it was Yasmin, and the other such women, on whom the future of global drug discovery rested.

For a few days Yasmin and the other women stayed at the test facility while scientists and doctors kept them under observation to see if any drug-induced illnesses developed. Some women threw up, got headaches, dizzy spells or fevers. Others sat up on their beds, in dormitory-style rooms, recounting stories of the disappointments and struggles that had filled their lives and had brought them here. They wiped away tears in the dark.

As she waited for sleep in the eerily quiet, air-conditioned test facility, the meeting with the creditor floated in Yasmin's mind. She had asked a friend's husband to speak to him before she left. Nearly everyone in their lanes owed him money, the creditor had said. When he asked for it, they said they could hardly work on the mountains, and that they would pay when Yasmin did. She told him that Moharram Ali had disappeared. The creditor said he was nearly broke himself. He regretted it, but he had to force Yasmin.

Cold and awake in bed, Yasmin thought of her visits to orphanages. She would have to show that she was divorced or widowed in order to enrol Mehrun and Ashra. But Moharram Ali still dropped in sometimes, and she wanted that more than divorce. The next morning she awoke to days filled with elaborate meals, laid out to give the women strength. Yasmin and her new friends dissected recipes and planned to replicate them for their children, when they got home with the money.

A few days later the tests were repeated to ensure the drug hadn't caused any side-effects, and Yasmin and the others were paid and sent home, with the instruction that they were to be back in a month or so for a final check on how they had reacted to it.

She returned with money, and sometimes even gifts. She bought a tin of ghee for Hera, who was pregnant. The next time she got a box of peanut brittle, which she knew the children liked and had not eaten for a while. Creditors dropped in as Yasmin entered Banjara Galli. She handed over her money, curled up on her mattress and napped, to the hum of the children around her. Sharib and Sameer saved up to get her a boiled egg or beetroots; she had told them they were fed beetroot salad at the trial facility to ward away the anaemia that the drugs could induce.

Sharib brooded for days after Yasmin returned from the medical trials. He was apprenticed with a mason, when he could not get to the mountains; soon he would find a construction job and earn enough to repay their loans, so she would not need to go any more, he told his mother. Until then, though, she repaid the undiminishing debts, serviced with a rate of interest about which she had no idea. When her creditors found Yasmin, she just handed over whatever she had.

Every time Moharram Ali called in, Yasmin thought he might be back for good. But it was always the same: he took some money, hung out some hope and left again. The mountains, which had yielded gold into his hands, now bore down on him. Winds howled on the slopes and rains lashed them. When he walked through their passes and clearings he slipped and slid. Guards patrolled even at night, and the torches they waved in curly sideways patterns to catch pickers in the dark moved in his mind in the day.

When he was on the mountains, Moharram Ali felt they smelled gingery. The smell mingled with the stench of rotting trash, made him nauseous and clung to him. In fact the municipality had given a Rs 1.5 crore contract to spray herbal deodorant on the mountains for a year, to quell their stink.[1] Opposition politicians had asked if it was not somewhat indulgent to spend so much on perfuming trash mountains. But the contract was given and forklifts moved through the hills, spraying the disinfectant and deodorant.

Although she was on the trash slopes more often, Farzana had not noticed the smell. Mumbai's garbage convoys were returning and she was consumed in chasing them. But they often emptied mud and concrete, rather than trash that she could sell. Every year the municipality fixed roads and bridges before rains lashed the city: Mumbai's pounding rains could wash away homes that were too old or too new, and their debris piled up in heaps around the city and arrived at the mountains for weeks. Farzana saw mud, gravel, bits of old roads and chunks of concrete emptying at the mountains all day, burying the old trash and pressing it down. Moharram Ali heard that all the gold had melted with the fires and would not be found again.

15

Days after Eid, which was on 7 July that year, Farzana had awoken late one night. *Mujhe chod do. Main kuch nahi karoongi,* she cried aloud, to a roomful of people who had submitted to sleep. *Leave me. I won't cause any trouble.* Her painful sobs rose slowly, filling the house until everyone was up.

Neighbours came, expecting to see a fight, only to find Hyder Ali and the others standing around Farzana. They watched bewildered as she sat on the mattress, crying. *Chod do. Main vapas nahi aoongi. I won't return. Leave me alone.* It was probably the guards she saw in her sleep, Jehangir thought. He should never have let Farzana go back on the slopes after the doctor told her not to. It was the Shaitan, Shakimun knew, pressing Budhi into service for immediate relief. Budhi chanted and splashed holy water on Farzana. The family waited sleepily for the prayers to work. But Budhi had exhausted them and retreated outside, before sleep overpowered Farzana.

This would have to be the year that the stubborn spirits left, Shakimun decided. Soon after Eid she restarted the incantations, manifestations and collection of talismans. Healers waved lemons in slow circles around Farzana and then eggs, then spattered them on the floor to release the spirits. They burned a lock of her hair in a weak, rain-dampened fire while reciting Koranic verses to draw out the spirit entangled in her.

Shakimun returned to the Dargah at Mahim with Farzana. Outsize cooking pots boiled and steamed around them: Makhdoom Shah Baba was known for feeding the city's hungry. On wheeled wooden boards, limbless people circled around the mother and daughter. Old, bent people stretched their arms out, asking for money to buy food, in Baba's name. Plates of food arrived, paid for by a wealthy patron, and the gaggle around them drifted away. They saw the *mujawar*, or caretaker, they had met before, sitting at his shop front. He did not seem surprised to see them and resumed his prayers for Farzana. Then a few days later, when Sahani walked in at home, Farzana was sitting alone, resting her chin on her muddied and drawn-up knees. *Vo dikhta hai*, Farzana said. *I can see him*. Sahani followed Farzana's eyes, which stared straight ahead at the kitchen counter. *Vo baitha hai*, she continued. *He's sitting there*. But Sahani couldn't see anything, she recounted to me later, and worried that her sister was going crazy.

The next Thursday the *mujawar* at Mahim sat Farzana in the courtyard, which was filling with others seeking separation from spirits. Shadow flowers streaming in through the grill with the fading sunlight. Woody smoke from the burning bark of the loban tree rose and mingled with the misty sky. It thickened to clear the fog within, as the drumming began. People sitting in the courtyard stirred. They swayed slowly at first, and then faster as the drums picked up. They ached and swirled in pain to the beat. By the time it abated, the sun had set and the court-yard was bathed in the cool purple light of the Mumbai monsoon. But Farzana had stayed cool too.

She was at the mountain slopes before dawn broke the next day, telling her friends that she had only been away for a trip. The city's attempts to shrink the mountains were picking up too. Did she know, pickers asked her, that Tata was coming to take over the mountains, to turn the mountain waste to power? They were nearly here. They had begun asking me the same question. While I doubted that Tata Consulting Engineers' consultants would mend the mountains themselves, I thought that some part of one of India's largest industrial groups surely could. Jehangir had heard that Tata officials had already taken plastic and paper from the slopes and used it to generate some power at their campus across the creek. If it worked, mountain plastic would begin going to their facility, he had heard. Prices for plastic would go up. He asked Farzana to start picking the thin plastic carry-bags that did not fetch much money at the *kata* shops, but which would get fed to Tata's plant. Optimism began to rise again in Jehangir.

At Mahim, though, Farzana's spirit remained stubbornly in place. Shaitans stayed elusive in the glare of a crowd, but clung hard, like desire itself, the ageing *mujawar* told them. The following week he would trick the Shaitan into believing there was no one around, so it could reveal itself, and then would drive it away, in a *parda hazri* – a manifestation within curtains. No one but the *mujawar* and Farzana would be there.

That afternoon Sahani and Shakimun stayed at a distance while the *mujawar* took Farzana into a room at the back of the shrine. After a while the *mujawar* came out, triumphant: it was a Shaitan from filth, he said. It's gone now. Sahani interrupted him, to say yes, Farzana was a trash-picker – the *mujawar* had got it right this time. *Ab vo theek ho jayegi. Bas vahaan vapas jaane mat dena. Unka saya rahta hai,* he said. *She will be fine now. Just don't let her go where he caught her. They linger on there.*

Jehangir agreed that Farzana needed to stay at home, although he didn't believe in the spirits, but in the doctor's diagnosis that the mountains had poisoned his sister. She was not to work at the slopes, and he asked her to sleep on the mezzanine floor, with his family. He would watch over her. Shakimun had asked friends to look for a match for Farzana. Until then, she would keep Farzana home and teach her to cook.

And yet often when they called her down for tea, in the mornings, Farzana was not there. They were not sure when she had climbed down the steps, opened the door and left. Even the goats tethered at the door had not bleated, Shakimun noticed. Friends told her they saw the *Khaadi ka Bhoot* on the slopes, before daybreak. She bought *vada pav*, samosas and tea at the mountains or ate at the restaurants near the municipal office and stayed out all day.

Shakimun sent Jehangir, Alamgir, Sahani or whoever else she could find to bring her back. But Farzana was never at the mountain they heard she was at. She had left with the emptied garbage caravans, getting to clearings before trash arrived at them. Her growing collection of charms dangled off her. Anyone at home who went to a shrine brought one back to add to it. Slowly Farzana began sleeping through the night. With a progress as slow as the ageing mountains moving out of the city, the Shaitan began to leave her.

On 27 July 2016 the consultants presented their plan to shrink the trash township to Mumbai's municipal commissioner, Ajoy Mehta. Through April and May they had walked the mountain slopes with municipal officials. They had collected samples and drawn up reports that laid the mountains bare, and the toxic halo that seeped in and settled into those who lived around them.[1] They had gone over the rules that bound the mountains, had considered the municipality's brief and had made a plan for a plant that would shrink the mountains and produce power for the city.

Some of the mountains rose to 120 feet, their report said. Their noxious halo had thickened, data that the consultants collected from the municipality's air-quality monitoring laboratory showed. Hydrogen sulphide, a poisonous flammable gas known for its rotten-egg smell, had more than tripled between 2010 and 2015, as had methane, feeding the ever-burning fires.[2] Carbon monoxide, which could cause headaches and dizziness, was five times higher. 'The health hazards associated with rag picking were confusion,' the report began by listing, laceration, indigestion and hazy vision, among other illnesses. As I read I thought of Farzana, fainting, crying, dizzy and calling out to the unseen spirit perched on the washboard.

The consultants proposed clearing out a section of the 326-acre township where, eventually, more than half of the 5,000 tonnes that garbage caravans delivered every day would get fed to the plant. At first the trash would be segregated, passing through a metal screen and then a magnetic screen to keep out larger bits of garbage. The rest would get spread on the incinerator floor, where hot air would blow from below, 'causing the waste to bubble and boil, much as a liquid, allowing intimate interaction between the waste and the fuel and facilitating drying and combustion,' the report stated. The heat would produce electricity, which would get supplied to the city – although, I noted, often less than the municipality's brief of 25 MW of power, enough to power thousands of homes.

The burning incinerator would spew smoke over the mountains and the communities around, and the consultants planned three rows of trees around the plant to absorb it. The trees, whose verdant pictures they stuck in the report, could reduce ammonia released from the plant by more than half and absorb most of the dust thrown up by the incinerator, the consultants said. The plant and its border of flowering trees would 'improve the aesthetic of Deonar', while saving more than 8 million tonnes of carbon dioxide and other greenhouse gases over two decades. Without it, Mumbai would need the Deonar township to double its size to accommodate the city's trash by 2021, they estimated.

The future they laid out was utopian, so close that it hovered in the room: as it shrank the mountains, and the trees soaked up its halo, the plant would create better jobs in the lanes. The diseases that the mountains may have given the pickers would fade away.

Soon after the presentation, officials and political leaders from the Shiv Sena, the party that controlled Mumbai's municipality, began meeting executives from India's largest power companies informally. The waste-to-energy plant they had planned at Deonar was to be among the world's largest, they said. The contract to make it would be given through an international bid. There was a lot of interest, they stated. Large foreign waste-to-power companies were keen on the project, officials suggested, as they coaxed power-company executives to bid for it. Being in Mumbai gave them a moral responsibility to make the plant that would clean the city and its air.

They would invite bidding in a few weeks. And then the mountains, their halo and their spirits would finally leave the city.

16

Indian Independence Day, 15 August 2016, was also the first birthday of Alamgir's son Faizan. Farzana had begun saving for it soon after her own birthday. As dusk fell, she and Farha stood on 90 Feet Road, as they did every year, and watched bikers whizz by waving flags. They collected the chocolates and sweets the bikers distributed, and soaked up the patriotic songs playing on loudspeakers installed in the street, then walked back through their lane to more such songs floating softly out of homes.

Farzana changed into a long white-lace kurta with dark-green piping on its edges. She put on a deep-red lipstick, powdered her face and pinned back some of her long, loose hair. In a photo studio nearby she held Faizan in her arms and posed against a leaf-green curtain, her fingers digging into his pudgy cheeks. The pressure to smile led only to two intent stares in the photographs. As the flash popped, Faizan burst into tears.

When Farzana woke up the next morning, the rain of the previous evening had abated, leaving an overcast sky. She put on bright-blue leggings, a parrot-green kurta and a black jacket, with a large white handkerchief around her hair. Carrying her gumboots, she left unnoticed while her parents lingered over half-filled tumblers of tea. Farzana stopped at Jehana's house to pick up her sister, and the two walked over to the mountains to work. It was a little before 10 a.m. and the sun travelled slowly across the sky behind grey clouds. It was a mottled day.

After the fires, the municipality had created a new trash hill towards the creek, across from the *jhinga* or prawn loop, officially called Loop One. Pickers called it the new Loop One: trucks were increasingly sent to empty on it, and pickers followed them to the rising slopes. It had quickly developed a reputation for being slippery and precarious, but they had stayed on, hoping its craggy slopes would smoothen as the trash settled on them.

That morning, with the clouds threatening to erupt, Farzana and Jehana thought the New Loop One was their best chance of finding trash before the weather made it impossible. As they walked up the slope, they saw yellow-and-orange bulldozers and forklifts buzzing fitfully against the grey skies. Trucks had already been there. Pickers were at work, several of them in black jackets like her own, Farzana noticed.

They watched trucks come in through the gate, pass the municipal office and grind slowly up the slushy slope towards them. As the trucks got to the clearing, pickers fell on them, working quickly. Farzana put on her earphones and reached for the pick of the trash before the bulldozers moved in and began pushing it down the slope. As the bulldozers reversed to flatten the clearing, she retreated, moving to the rhythm of the music and the machines. It was always songs of infidelity from Hindi films that she hardly ever saw, she told me later. Absorbed in this intricate dance, Farzana barely looked up to hear the skies rumble. More than an hour went by in the mucky, frantic scrambles to fill her bag with plastic bottles. Farzana barely felt time pass by.

A truck drove up, and Farzana dived into the scramble to sift through its contents – wire, mushy paper, lurid-coloured cloth and vegetable peel – to pick out her squashed plastic bottles. Tangled clumps fell into her bag. She would sort through it at home, Farzana thought, as she reached out for more. Jehana worked close by. Emptied, the truck was driving downhill when it got stuck in the muddy track. It revved up noisily, trying to move ahead. Farzana looked up quickly, watched it struggling and returned to fill her bag. The truck stayed stuck.

In a little while she looked up and saw a bulldozer on the slope down below.[1] It was moving backwards and uphill, towards the clearing. Farzana saw it get closer. Pickers rummaged around her. She waved lazily at the driver and went back to filling her bag.

Then she heard the bulldozer again and looked up. It had stopped and then restarted and was moving back up the hill, towards her. She saw some pickers scatter away from its path. She took a step forward too and nearly tripped and fell into the slimy trash around her. Surprised, she looked down and saw a wire entangled around her ankle. She banged her foot on the clearing to free it, but the wire only pulled tighter into her. She twisted her foot round in the air. The wire stayed stuck. The bulldozer moved closer. She sat on the clearing and struggled to untwist the wire from her foot. It would not come off, and the bulldozer was now moving up towards her again.

She stood carefully, and waved towards the driver to indicate that she was behind him. The wire pulled her back awkwardly and she nearly fell again. Farzana picked up stones and threw them at the driver to say she was there. They didn't reach him. She yelled out at him to stop moving back, but he kept backing up slowly towards her.

It was nearly at the clearing, and Farzana was still rooted to the spot. She screamed and craned her neck, trying to catch the eye of the driver inside the cabin. She was close enough to see that he had earphones on. He was probably listening to music and her voice could not reach him, she thought. She waved at him frantically. The bulldozer moved closer. She saw him wearing sunglasses. He could not see her, she thought.

That was when Farzana tripped and fell on the slushy mountain clearing. Hyder Ali believed it was when the Shaitan gripped her and pulled her down. The bulldozer drove over her left thigh as she lay on the ground. Screaming and flailing, Farzana tried to pull herself up on her stomach from underneath the bulldozer. The bulldozer shovelled up a load of trash and moved forward. Farzana fell back in agony.

Some pickers were gesticulating and screaming wildly at the driver too. They were not sure which of the black jackets lay under the bulldozer, and called out different names. As the bulldozer drove downhill, pickers tried moving closer to see who had been crushed underneath it. The bulldozer dropped its load of trash downhill and began moving up again. The driver did not see the frantic waving around him.

He drove back slowly, rolling over Farzana. This time the bulldozer went all the way up the left side of her body, nearly to her chest. Jehana and some of the other pickers were shouting, trying to catch the driver's attention. Catching sight of the commotion, he stopped the bulldozer. A skinny young man with a straggly moustache

jumped out of the cabin and walked back to find a bloodied mess under his tyre. Farzana's bloated face emerged
just in front of it. Most of the rest of her was underneath.
Her eyes had nearly popped out of her face and stared
at him, startled. Blood trickled out of her ears and nose.
The driver turned and ran away. Some pickers chased him
downhill. Fear kept him ahead of them. In a few minutes
they gave up and turned back to check on Farzana.

Jehana, and others, huddled around her. They stared
quietly at the swollen head and crushed body, spattered in
bits of flesh, blood and muddy trash. The relentless pursuit
of garbage had suddenly halted. Pickers were not sure
what to do. Jehana heard the people around her saying that
this was Jehangir's sister. She heard them call out to him.
Someone had seen him buying trash nearby, a little earlier.

Watching municipal officials come out of their offfice,
hearing the commotion, Jehana too called out to Jehangir.
When Jehangir heard Jehana's voice calling out to him,
he thought Ramzan, their youngest brother, had missed
school again and was up to no good on the mountains. He
followed Jehana's voice uphill, thinking of how he would
drag Ramzan back home and give him a thrashing to make
sure he didn't dare venture back. Instead, he saw a small
crowd milling around his older sister. He looked under the
halted bulldozer and saw the battered remains of a person.
Green-and-blue clothes peeked out brightly under a black
jacket. As he got closer, he saw flesh hang loose, a bone
protruding, a swollen face streaked with blood. Blood
soaked the mountain trash around. In her right hand, she
clutched a half-filled bag of plastic bottles. Jehangir realised it was Farzana that they were calling him to see.

Jehangir got into the driver's seat and drove the bulldozer

off her. Scavenging birds swooped down, forming shadows over Farzana's ripped-open body. Her insides spilled out onto the mountain. A milky-white calf bone jutted out of her leg. Blood trickled down from her ears and bulging eyes. Jehana stared, not knowing what to do.

Pickers suggested that Jehangir take Farzana to the municipal hospital Shatabdi (properly known as Pandit Madan Mohan Malviya Shatabdi Hospital), not far from the mountains. He hailed a garbage truck that had just emptied. Friends helped him pick up the broken Farzana carefully in his arms. He laid her down on the back seat, in the driver's cabin, and directed the truck through the mountains' slushy tracks towards the highway. When Sahani arrived at the clearing, just after they had left, she could still see Farzana's outline pressed into the trash.

One of Jehangir's friends, who had come with him in the cabin, turned back to see Farzana. *Uska haath dekh Jehangir, bhai*, he said, staring at the blood and the torn flesh spilling out of her left arm. *Look at her arm, Jehangir, brother.*

Usko dekho, Jehangir replied wryly. *Look at all of her.*

At Shatabdi, Jehangir wheeled Farzana on a stretcher through the back door that opened across the Emergency Department. He pushed his way through the sick, waiting restlessly outside. The doctors that he managed to stop drew back at the sight of Farzana. They told Jehangir they did not think she would make it, that there was not much they could do for her. Their hospital was not equipped to deal with such grievous injuries. They asked him to take Farzana to Sion Hospital (known as Lokmanya Tilak General Hospital), one of the city's largest and busiest public hospitals.

Jehangir demanded an ambulance to move Farzana

there, so that treatment could begin. Doctors called for one and bandaged Farzana loosely for the ride. As Jehangir waited outside for his parents, for the ambulance to arrive and for the money they would need for her treatment, Farzana's life hung by a thread.

When Jehana came home and told him what had happened, Hyder Ali knew the Shaitan had struck. He had haunted Farzana for months, Hyder Ali said, trapped her and tripped her at that moment when she had faced the bulldozer. *Vo uska nuksaan karne ke liye hi aaya tha,* he said. *He came to harm her and now he has.* Hurriedly he scraped together some money from friends and neighbours. When they arrived at Shatabdi, the ambulance that would transfer Farzana to Sion Hospital had still not arrived. Together, Farzana's family and their neighbours hounded the doctors and staff.

When it finally came, they inched slowly along the highway. Afternoon traffic was piled up in the light rain. Farzana had heard the doctors. *Bhai mein bachoongi nahi,* she told Jehangir. *I won't survive.* Her breathing was laboured. Don't worry, her brother repeated. Don't worry.

At Sion Hospital he pushed her stretcher through the frenzied Emergency Department. Doctors drew a curtain around Farzana's body to make a small examination room. They put an oxygen mask on her; the long and painful breaths she drew to get even the tiniest bits of air suggested the bulldozer had punctured her lungs, which were filling with air.

Her left arm and leg were filled with broken bones and open wounds. Her left calf bone stuck out of her leg. Lumps of dark clotted flesh spilled out of her left thigh. Her right calf was wounded too, the doctors wrote in their examination report. Farzana's left arm and leg were both broken in several places. Scans revealed that her liver and intestines were injured. Internal bleeding had led to some blood accumulating in her abdomen. Her back and pelvis were fractured. There was hardly a bone in place in Farzana's body, their report suggested.

Doctors moved a torch near Farzana's eyes. When they brought it close to her, Farzana could follow it with her right eye, but not with her left. It was her distended face, with a contusion and bruises, that had worried doctors at Shatabdi most. They thought her brain might be swollen or injured. She was so badly wounded it was hard to know where to begin fixing her, but, at Sion, doctors started by inserting a tube between her ribs to suck out the leaked air and by ordering brain scans.

There isn't much hope, the doctor said to the crowd of mud-splashed family and pickers waiting outside the examination room, but they would try their best to treat her. The next three days would be crucial. If the swelling in Farzana's brain reduced, they could begin treating the rest of her injuries.

Jehangir's glass business and private garbage-clearing had nearly ground to a halt since the fires, but he went home and emptied his savings, which he had deposited for the surgery. Then he left for the Shivaji Nagar police station to file a complaint about Farzana's accident.

Farzana's sisters and brothers crowded around her, crying. They bent low to hear her repeat: I won't live long. She whispered that she was sorry for all the troubles she had caused them. Yasmeen and Sahani told Farzana they would pray for her. *Tu theek ho jayegi*, Sahani said softly into Farzana's ear, teary and unsure. *You'll get better.*

The corridor outside the intensive-care unit was filling with hundreds of pickers in their muddy clothes and oversized gumboots, which left trails on the hospital floors. Some were neighbours and friends, others were not sure who was inside. It could have been any of them – the people whose lives existed in the flash between the trucks emptying and the bulldozers moving in to shovel the trash away. Farzana's was the kind of accident they tried to push out of their minds while they worked. It brought back memories of a lifetime spent under the trucks ferreting out garbage, jumping onto moving vehicles, dodging bulldozers as they picked trash and stepping aside just as forklifts moved in to scoop them up with the trash. They had held tightly to tipping trucks and turned away from bulldozers just as they got too close. Some had crushed fingers, others limps that came from failing to escape as truck tyres approached. As they waited to hear about Farzana, they shared stories of their narrow escapes and unspoken nightmares.

Doctors began blood transfusions and intravenous medication and waited for Farzana to respond. That evening a police officer arrived to take Farzana's statement. Doctors had recorded most of her injuries as being grievous, in the medical report they submitted to be attached to the police complaint. The officer spoke to Jehangir, Jehana and Shakimun instead of Farzana and recorded their statements. Other officers had visited the mountain clearing and spoken to pickers who had seen the bulldozer roll over Farzana. They filed a complaint against the driver for causing grievous injury by accident and rash and negligent driving. If he was convicted, it would lead to a maximum of a couple of years in prison and his driver's licence being revoked.

Police got the number plate of the bulldozer from the entry registers at the mountain gate where it had entered that morning. The driver's name was Mohammed Hashim Khan. Pickers who had seen him that morning described him as a slim young man with an intent stare. By coincidence, he lived in the same sprawling complex of buildings that the police station had recently moved to, occupying a white multi-storeyed building at the entrance of the complex. The lift did not work and there was no place to eat close by, but it was a relief from the constant smell and the knee-deep murky monsoon waters that had periodically filled the squat old police station near the mountains.

Officers walked through the tightly packed complex of one-room tenements to Hashim Khan's apartment. The complex, which took up a vast tract between the mountain communities and the highway, was a step up from living on a street. People constantly arrived from the flimsy settlements that filled Mumbai's pavements and rail tracks, claiming their first concrete homes, their first address. Hashim's older brother opened the door and told them that Nanhe, or 'the little one' as they called him at home, had not returned from work that day. Police parties searched for him through the night. The next morning he walked into the police station alone.

An officer recorded Hashim Khan's statement. He said he had come from his village to live with his brother and sister-in-law five years ago. He was twenty-six and had worked as a bulldozer driver for several years on the mountains. He had started work at his usual time of 7 a.m. that day and had been shovelling trash on the mountain slopes all morning. A little after noon a truck had emptied out garbage at a clearing near him, he said. While going down the mountain slope, the truck had become stuck in the tracks, which were muddied by rain. Khan was driving his bulldozer back to help clear the way so that the truck could move.

He had been struggling to shovel away the mud and trash for a while before he saw rag-pickers waving and yelling in his rear-view mirror. He stopped and got out as soon as he heard the commotion and found a girl under his bulldozer. She had headphones on, which had drowned out the sound of his bulldozer getting closer, he said. He thought the pickers had waved at her too, to warn her, but she had stayed in place, not responding to them or his approaching bulldozer. He ran back to his cabin and drove the bulldozer forward, off her body.

He had been so frightened of the pickers that he ran away from there until he was near the mountain gate. He sat outside the municipal office under the old banyan tree that marked the end of the vanished *cuchra*-train track that had settled their township, turning the swamp into the mountains. He watched the usual hum inside the small, single-storey municipal office. No one was looking for him. He caught his breath and then walked home. He had come to report the incident on his own, Hashim Khan told the police officer. They arrested him.

On the mountains, work ground to a halt. Some pickers joined the vigil at the hospital, while fear and anger paralysed others. Guards patrolled zealously to keep away those who still came to work. Older pickers spoke to staff at the non-profit that gave them identity cards. Rage – which had been simmering for years while they stayed invisible to the city that relied on them to clean up after it – had boiled over with Farzana's accident. The pickers planned protests and met municipal officials. Any of them could have been crushed like Farzana, like the garbage they picked. They pressed officials to punish the driver, to compensate Farzana's family and to protect them while they worked on the mountains.

The accident took place on municipal land. Farzana should never have been there at all. Municipal officials knew that Jehangir, who had filed the police complaint, had appropriated one tip of their mountains. He was more liable for punishment than compensation. It was a painful reminder to the pickers that they lived in an unofficial world of shadows – less people than intruders. Farzana had been part of an invisible army who stalked the mountains, preyed on by its spirits, poisoned by the gases that filled the air. Unseen and unheard, she had hunted its castaway treasures and had been crushed with the mountain's trash.

The municipality's staff at the mountains had seen Farzana squashed under the bulldozer. I heard her accident made for a note in their daily registers. However, months after requesting this note, officials had not provided it. No one, other than Nanhe, 'the little one', was responsible for what happened to her.

Hashim Khan was presented in court the day after he had come to the police station. His brother posted bail and Hashim returned home. Pickers heard that his brother, Azad, did house calls as an electrician. He had borrowed money to post Rs 20,000 as bail. Hashim put out word for new jobs to pay them back, while the police built a case against him in court.

Meanwhile Farzana's family prayed and waited through the longest three days of their lives. Hyder Ali sat in the filigreed white corridors of Makhdoom Shah Baba's shrine, praying. He brought back a rose, which he placed under Farzana's pillow in the intensive-care unit. Jehana kept her company by her bedside, while the others waited anxiously outside. Nurses used eye drops to shrink Farzana's staring eyes.

Pickers waited in the chaotic and teeming corridors of Sion Hospital every day to know Farzana's fate. Yasmin was often in the crowd. Every time the doors to the air-conditioned intensive-care unit swung open and doctors came out, to a gush of cool air, she felt a gnawing pit in her stomach. Each time she could not help thinking that the doctors had come out to say that Farzana had gone.

17

After the three days were up, doctors told her family that Farzana's head injury was healing, and her brain scans were clear. They would begin the long and arduous task of putting her body together again. Hyder Ali believed it was the intercession of Makhdoom Shah Baba, tugging his daughter back to the land of the living.

Days turned into a haze, as the surgery went on. Farzana drifted in and out of consciousness. Her painful cries ebbed only when her swollen eyes, shrinking gradually back into their sockets, closed in a sedative-induced sleep. Then she awoke too soon, cold in her metal hospital bed, howling in pain.

At times Farzana seemed to drift back to their world, asking for friends, or for something cold to drink. At other times, hearing her scream, Jehana felt that Farzana spoke from the world of the spirits, which had pulled at her limbs and had dragged her down under the bulldozer. Looking at Farzana's broken body, Jehana wondered if she had already slipped into some kind of underworld where she was unreachable. It was as if the world of the living and the world of the dead battled within Farzana. Jehana kept her covered in a blanket.

Farzana remembered waking up in long, green corridors outside operating theatres, waiting for them to be free. She waited for hours, alone, afraid and crying. Attendants arrived later and sent her back to the ward: there were too many surgeries lined up at the theatre. She returned to wait outside operating theatres for days before making it in. Farzana woke up from surgery to find herself increasingly bandaged. Her chest was held in a brace. So was her left leg, to draw her calf bone back in. She could barely move.

To keep the surgery going, Jehangir dipped into his savings, carefully accumulated over the years from his trash business, from his own mountain clearing and from Javed Qureshi's patronage. When it all fell short, he sold the motorbike that had helped to give him a glow of success in their lanes. He was sinking fast, but all Jehangir could think of was Farzana. It was something I had seen many times throughout my years of walking the lanes around the mountains. With nothing else to fall back on but the fickleness of mountain luck, love in the shadow of the mountain acquired an intense, burnished glow. Through the precarious turns of their lives, it was often the only constant. When Jehangir's money began running out, Hyder Ali walked up to Farzana's hospital bed and took off the earrings she wore, as gently as he could, and sold them. *Jab ladki hi nahi bachegi to sona leke kya karenge?* he asked me later. *If she doesn't make it, what good is the gold?*

At the mountains the pickers kept away, or were kept away by guards. They protested everywhere they could, trying to get help for Farzana and to make themselves visible. They heard that a local corporator owned the bull-dozer that had run over Farzana. They protested outside his office. He was not there to meet them. Later they learned that he didn't own bulldozers after all. Still they kept up their protests, finding new spots for them. They had spent decades trying to stay invisible to the municipality, the police, the city, to the trucks and bulldozers. But something had changed with the fires, the tightening security and Farzana's accident. Now they fought to return to the world of the visible. Fought for someone to see them. Someone to avoid them, if they got too close. And someone to be held responsible for running them over.

At the municipal office, officials were consumed in their own battles. In the plant's schedule, made to match Justice Oka's deadline, September 2016 was the month for pre-bid meetings.[1] They would confer with interested companies and take in their suggestions, before inviting first bids in late October, nearly two months away. Consultants had suggested that only companies with years of experience building large waste-to-energy plants be allowed to apply. But if Deonar's was to be India's largest waste-to-energy plant, no one had made anything like it before. Throughout August and September rumours circulated that municipal officials had met companies from China, South Korea and Brazil. They would partner with Indian companies, it was said.

In meetings, though, these company officials voiced worries that Tatva's troubles could return to torpedo their plant. They could be stranded without garbage to incinerate, without the land lease, without the funds to construct the plant or the municipality's support, just as Tatva had been. The spectre of the failed project, and continuing arbitration with the municipality, haunted the proposal, dampening interest. Back at the mountains, the pickers' frustration was growing. They looked for the bulldozer owner, whom they later found and brought to Hyder Ali. Farzana should not have been on the mountains at all, he said. The bulldozer was nearly as big as his room. Why had she not moved away as it approached? Was she crazy? They had heard that she was.

Sahani heard that bulldozer owners had told municipal officials they would not work on the mountains, if people came under their bulldozers and they were asked to pay compensation. They knew their bulldozers would have to keep moving in order for garbage caravans to keep arriving from the city, and the contents to be pressed down onto the hills as it always had been. This shouldn't be our problem, Sahani heard that bulldozer owners had said to municipal officials. Officials informally said the bulldozer owner had paid the Shaikhs some money for Farzana's treatment, but Hyder Ali denied this.

Hyder Ali decided that Jehana would stay with Farzana at the hospital while the others would return to work, so they could look for money for Farzana's treatment. He mostly stayed at home. He cried too much when he saw his daughter's broken body and Jehana would have to send him away.

After several surgeries, Farzana was moved out of intensive care to the hospital's E Ward, lost in a haze of pain and semi-consciousness. More than thirty women patients, and the smell of their sickness, filled the ward. Jehana walked through it, looking at patients she drily called *bhayanak*, terrifying. They were all recovering from accidents or burns.

But no one cried like Farzana did, when the doctors came on their morning rounds to change her bandages and dress her wounds, every few days. Jehana turned away as they unwrapped the long gauze bandages to reveal Farzana's raw, pink body, barely held together. The doctors checked to see if her wounds were drying up, sprinkled powders, rubbed ointments and wrapped on new bandages. *Poora kamra sar pe utha leti thi*, Jehana often recalled, with a wry smile, about dressing days. *She had the eyes and ears of the whole room.*

When they left, Farzana often fell into a deep, exhausted sleep, while Jehana got medicines or test results. She chatted with the relatives of other patients, who asked why Farzana was so bandaged up. At night when Jehana was sleepy, Farzana was awake, crying in pain. Bony and austere, Jehana had the firm air of being the oldest of nine and the mother of six. On the slopes she had often been able to make the intrepid, unstoppable Farzana follow her terse instructions. But in the hospital she could only watch Farzana mumble and shriek in the darkened ward. She could not bring Farzana back to her senses, as she always had.

Later, Jehana would say that she thought the spirits had finally left Farzana as she lay under the bulldozer. But in those unending nights, Jehana thought it could only be the Shaitan flailing within. As the lights went off in their ward, Jehana felt a fog rolling over Farzana. When she closed her eyes to sleep, Farzana found herself in front of the bulldozer on the cloudy, grey mountains that morning. She called out to the driver to stop moving back. She was behind him, she shouted.

Farzana called out to their mother, and to God, to get her away from the approaching bulldozer. Sweat soaked her body as she saw it move closer. She called out to someone called Riyaaz. Jehana thought Farzana could see someone who was invisible to her own eyes, and wondered if it was the spirits within her who spoke, and who saw through her sleepless eyes. Her mouth felt dry. Jehana got her plastic packets of fruit juice. Farzana sucked the cool juice hungrily, struggled to curl up her long limbs and sleep without tugging at staples or wounds. If she turned the wrong way, or too quickly, the pain could make her howl for hours. Jehana, who slept on a sheet that she laid out on the floor, cried softly, waiting for sleep to come over Farzana, usually as dawn broke.

One afternoon Sahani, the sister after Jehana, arrived. She and Jehana chatted while Farzana slept. Jehana asked if Sahani knew who Riyaaz was. Sahani reminded her that there had been a boy in their lanes, around her own age, called Riyaaz Shaikh. He had left school to come to work on the mountains when his father's hand was injured and he could not work any more. They had not seen Riyaaz for years.

When Sahani left, Jehana found Farzana awake. She didn't remember calling out to Riyaaz or the bulldozer driver in her sleep. But Farzana reminded Jehana that they had known Riyaaz in the years before she came to work on the slopes all day. He too came to pick trash in the afternoons and usually stayed on after the others left.

On a stormy August morning in 2009 the sisters had seen a small crowd, on a hilltop, as they made their way up the slopes. They watched pickers standing in nearly knee-deep mud and soaked in rain. Jehana and Farzana had walked up and seen them huddled around Riyaaz, lying pressed into the trash, his face and body flattened. Thick tyre marks ran over him. One of the oversized bulldozers that the municipality used in the monsoon season must have rolled over him, the pickers figured. They had taken him to Rajawadi Hospital, but he arrived there cold and long dead. He had probably been lying amidst the trash throughout most of the rain-soaked night.

Farzana heard that his mother, Shakila, had walked the soggy slopes all morning looking for him. Maybe Riyaaz had stayed the night there because evening had come before he had found enough trash, she thought. Maybe he had tired of looking, not wanted to return with an empty trash bag, waited for trucks filled with valuable trash from hotels to arrive and slept on the slopes. She asked pickers if they had seen her son sleeping in the trash. He was in brown trousers that might have faded into the muddy slopes. She had gone to the hospital when she heard that someone in brown trousers had been taken there. Riyaaz's death certificate had said his was an accidental death. That grey morning swam in Farzana's eyes. She saw Riyaaz's flattened, tyre-marked face when she tried to sleep, she told Jehana.

Shakila's husband had sat by his son's grave all day for months, while she had walked, adrift, in Banjara Galli. She had seemed like half a person since I had met her in 2013, gaunt as a ghost, tears never far away, never leaving the lane except to take our loans to run a corner shop. There had been weddings in her village, her mother had fallen ill and died, but Shakila had not left. *Usko yahaan chod ke kaise jaoon?* she would tell me. *How can I leave him here? Mujhe dhoodne aaya to? What if he comes looking for me?* she would ask, even a decade later. Riyaaz wouldn't leave Farzana, either.

Jehana kept up her tired vigil as Farzana drifted painfully between the worlds of the living and the dead. As dusk fell every evening a friend of Alamgir came into their ward, the shimmery puff in his hair just a little paler than the golden sun, deepening outside. The crowd of pickers had thinned out, but he still came. Jehana often sent him to get painkillers, or asked him to help prop up Farzana on pillows. The sides of his head were buzzed, to make his puff seem higher and win him a few extra inches of height. He came in, taking long hurried strides as if to make up for something: his lack of height, and for being away all day.

He became Farzana's shadow. His arms moved as if they were her own bandaged, immobile ones, feeding her dinner, massaging her head and her swollen feet until she slept. He fiddled gently with her bandages so they didn't tug painfully at her and make her cry. He moved as if he was her still-broken legs, bringing water to drink, or a blanket. He perched himself next to Farzana on the bed. Jehana could not hear what he spoke, softly, into her ears. But sometimes she saw it bring a weak smile to Farzana's face.

Jehana had first seen the boy in the crowd of pickers in the early days when their lanes had poured into the hospital's corridors. Most people she knew from their lanes were there, and Jehana had barely noticed him, passing by while looking for Jehangir or Alamgir. At first when Farzana was moved to the ward, Alamgir's friend began coming in to see her with him, and then by himself.

Every evening, as the sun faded and the lights came on, Farzana tossed restlessly in her bed. The boy arrived, muddy from work, his puff of hair wobbling and nearly falling to make gold streaks on his face, and sat at Farzana's bedside. Jehana saw them bicker and talk. She was not sure he should have been there. But he offered to bring any medicines she had run out of, or juice from the cafeteria. Jehana began to leave him to watch over Farzana while she took short breaks away from her bedside.

She walked in the corridor outside, watching the night attendants walk by hurriedly, holding bedsheets and woollen nightcaps. For the first time in the day she thought about her children, wondering if they had got dinner. Trying to scratch a meal together for them had taken up her evenings for years. Now she barely thought about it. Jehana had tried to get her husband to work. But the card games, and the gossip, alcohol and drugs that went with them around the mountains' rim, had filled his mind with stories of suspicion and conspiracy, making him lash out at Jehana. In his mind, she was always with someone else. He chased trucks desultorily and earned enough only for his stash. He searched carefully for the jewel-coloured bottles of alcohol that were steeped in the trash and stayed late on clearings, emptying their sour, leftover dregs.

He and his friends, their hair slicked back with gel, their eyes lined with kohl and with emaciated bodies, had reoccupied the abandoned sheds made of dried leaves that Farzana and her friends had once built for their parties on the mountains. Sometimes, when I walked the hills, I saw their glossy, stiff hair and their rows of glassy eyes staring vacantly at me from within the dark sheds. Every time I turned and saw them in the distance, glazed in the sun, a chill ran down my spine. Their minds and bodies had been shrivelled by their intoxication, which fuelled suspicion, uncontrolled fits of rage and violence. They poured it all out on their women.

Jehana had tried picking trash to keep the house going, but her husband's rage had often pulled her back. Tears ran down ran her eyes as she thought of long evenings planning dinner around an empty stove, with him circling outside to ensure she didn't step past the threshold. Eventually the children would ask her for a few rupees to buy a bag of chips or biscuits. She would tell them to get it from Hyder Ali's house.

Jehana's days with Farzana had been painful and sleepless, but they had taken her away from the constant anxiety and failure to produce meals at home. Farzana's struggles had lulled her own, given Jehana something to think of, other than her own troubles. She thought of Farzana's endless nights of crying and moaning, as she stood in the corridor. Nadeem, meaning 'companion', was among the names she had taken to saying in her nightly mumblings, Jehana realised. It was Nadeem – the little man elongated by a gold puff, who had visited to care for Farzana – who had become her shadow, who had made his limbs into hers.

He offered to bring the dinner that Shakimun cooked every evening. Even looking at it made Farzana nauseous. Jehana insisted that she eat, and the two sisters squabbled over Farzana's barely touched dinner. Nadeem stepped in to broker a truce. He made little morsels and fed her. Farzana, whose stomach had churned at the sight of food for weeks, began finding it bland. Suddenly she wanted something spicy. One evening he arrived with dinner from his own home. He had got his mother to make a *saalan*, a deep and rich lamb curry, with rice.

Farzana tried fighting, feebly, when he was late. He sat with her all night, watched her cry, helped her turn over and spoke softly until she slept. Jehana and he watched Farzana scream in pain at the smallest movement. When she finally fell asleep, a little before sunrise, Nadeem left for work. As dawn broke, he rode garbage trucks as they began their rounds of the lightening city, filling them with its detritus and emptying it on the mountains.

18

Farzana returned home, late in September 2016, to the ebbing rains. Warm, dry winds would soon bluster against the scorching sun of Mumbai's returning summer, blowing up dust, making a haze on them. The winds could reignite with the heat and mountain gases and set them ablaze again. In the dusty haze, pickers saw military personnel on the mountain slopes. They stood on newly settled watchtowers to police the hilly township of trash and surveyed its edges with binoculars.

Farzana had returned into its shadow, barely held together. Carefully, Jehangir and Alamgir had carried her in their arms through the slender, long lane and put her down on the floor at home. Doctors had finished her surgery, Hyder Ali had run out of money to treat her in the hospital, but Farzana had hardly healed. Yasmeen and Rakila learned to change her dressings at home, to avoid the arduous and expensive journeys back to the hospital. Farzana still cried out, until the neighbours arrived. Shakimun sat hunched over her, chasing out boys who strayed in to collect cricket balls and footballs from games in their lane and who gawked at Farzana's still-disfigured limbs.

Through September and October municipal officials had presented potential bidders with their plans to mend the mountains and shrink their halo. They had elicited suggestions from companies and had offered to tweak their plans accordingly. But the troubles with Tatva, and its continuing court cases, loomed over the meetings. Who would want take on the township, with its fires, its shadowy army of pickers who stalked the slopes, its messy past? Could the township ever change? they worried.

As the dates to begin bidding came closer, so the spectre of the fires came to meet them. Days earlier, the municipality had hired the Maharashtra State Security Force (MSSF) – a commando force that was trained by police and could be hired to guard installations, companies and wealthy people – to secure the mountains.

Hyder Ali stood by the mountain wall watching the new guards wearing army fatigues, baseball caps and dark glasses, looking bigger than anyone he had seen guarding the mountains previously. He squinted against the afternoon sun to crack their patrolling schedule. When did they take breaks for lunch? When did they walk to the far end of the mountains' long periphery, so that he could get in? When did their shift end? Someone always seemed to be there. The new guards were to rid the mountains of old ghosts, of fires, of encroachers and prepare them for new suitors.

Hyder Ali returned home late one evening from following the new guards' unstopping patrols and saw Farzana standing. The stick they had found for her, so that she could stand or take a few halting steps with its support, lay abandoned on the floor. She leaned against Nadeem instead. Hyder Ali had heard people speaking about Farzana, in his walks to the mountains. Would she be scarred for ever? Could she ever get mended? Most of all, they asked, who would marry her? Could she have children? They had heard that all her bones were broken. They heard she had come back from the dead. Was this how her life would be? Hyder Ali had evaded Nadeem for months. Everything about him meeting Farzana was inappropriate. If being seized by spirits, crushed by a bulldozer and being left for dead were not enough, being visited by an unrelated man, at night, would strangle Farzana's marriage prospects entirely. And yet Nadeem was bringing her to life again.

That night Hyder Ali decided he had to find out about Nadeem. He called to Alamgir, sprawled on the floor near the sleeping Farzana. Alamgir came out, wearing a stiff, sleepy air, followed by Nadeem, who left for home. Alamgir told Hyder Ali that Nadeem was from Padma Nagar, the last of the communities that hugged the mountains, settled on a swamp of lotuses. His father had been a mason, who had earned well as the city inched its way towards Deonar. For a time he had built a life away from the trash, even in the mountains' shadow. He enrolled Nadeem and his brothers at a private English school nearby. At several city hospitals he sought treatment for his daughter, the youngest of the children, who was born with a heart defect. As she grew older they discovered she could neither hear nor speak. He began retrieving Nadeem and his brothers from the mountains, after they had missed school. With his disappointments mounting, he transferred them to the municipal school. All three boys quickly dropped out. Alamgir had seen them on the mountains ever since.

Nadeem's father had died in April 2016, after battling cancer. Days later, with debts to clear from the treatment, Nadeem began working as a garbage-truck cleaner, often on the trucks Alamgir drove. They sped through the empty streets as dawn lightened the city. With the early-morning breeze blowing over them, they hardly noticed the stench that their gradually filling truck emitted. They did the rounds of the central suburb of Kurla, filling the truck with the sooty remains from one of the city's longest stretches of spare-parts stores and car garages. The outer edges of cheap rubber soles from the city's shoe-makers, and fish food from the aquarium market, emptied into their truck. They watched a mall rise over the stunted skyline and tall buildings stretching in from the far end of a swamp, to make a gleaming new financial district. They drove on to Saki Naka and then Powai, where low-slung lakeside homes were giving way to condominiums, call centres, technology start-ups and softly lit coffee shops. Nadeem kept things aside from the trash for himself and Alamgir to sell. As Alamgir drove on, Nadeem leaned over to watch. Somewhere between filling up with trash from the old Kurla and Powai districts and bringing it to the Deonar mountains, the two became friends.

Alamgir had begun keeping his headlights on during the day, to get to the distant edges of the hazy, curving township. He kept the horn pressed down, so that approaching trucks could see them through the fog. The fires had upended life on the mountains. Fresh trash fell on the old and charred. Hidden treasures surfaced from under the burnt layers. Around then Nadeem had seen for the first time a tall, slender girl pulling bottles, glass and metal wires from his emptying truck. She was beautiful, unstoppable in the melee – and she paid him no attention at all. Friends told him it could only be Farzana: Jehangir and Alamgir's younger sister. Hadn't Nadeem seen her before?

Jehangir was Javed Qureshi's man, rising on the hills with his restless energy and lispy chatter. Nadeem needed to learn driving from Alamgir, if he was going to follow his route to a garbage-truck driving job. Neither of the brothers could be messed with. Farzana was trouble. And yet, on days when he didn't see them around, Nadeem watched her edge into the garbage scrambles and turn into a blur.

One afternoon, when Nadeem was returning to the city, his emptied truck winding slowly down a slope, he spotted Farzana standing below, with Farha. Could he help? Nadeem stopped near them to ask. Farzana recognised him as Alamgir's long-haired friend, always with brightly coloured mesh vests peeking out of half-open shirts. As Farzana and Farha got in the back seat, to sell their trash at *katas* near the municipal office, the conversation froze. They watched the trash hills pass by outside. Nadeem deposited them and left.

After that day, Nadeem thought he saw Farzana watching him at garbage clearings. She spoke to her friends one afternoon and giggled. She seemed to be pointing to his long, poker-straight hair, which gave him a slightly electrocuted air. Nadeem's heart sank. A few days later, when his truck arrived at the clearing, his hair was buzzed at the sides and the puff had appeared atop it. Farzana nodded tightly in approval, turned and burrowed herself into the trash shower erupting from his truck.

A truck cleaner approached Farzana on a clearing. His friend, Nadeem, liked her. Did she like him too? *Sochoongi*, she replied, returning to fill his truck into her bag. *I'll think about it*. She began staying buried in the trash scrambles around Nadeem. She used the proceeds to buy Chinese Bhel, crispy fried noodles mixed with sliced cabbage, hot sauce and Indian spices. It was a blend of two Eastern cultures that left Farzana and Farha orange-tongued and teary-eyed. In the middle of getting their fix, Farha often nudged Farzana: Nadeem was standing behind them, across the street. Farzana felt his eyes on her.

She heard his calls ring, wherever she was. When they got home she dug out of Farha's bag the phone they had collected on the mountain and had repaired, checked for Nadeem's calls and hid it again, sorting the day's trash, hoping that Jehangir or Alamgir had not seen. Sometimes, when Farha pushed the ringing phone in front of her, Farzana spoke airily for a bit, then hung up. A few weeks after Nadeem had asked, Farzana took his call to say she liked him too.

The mountains seethed, smoke still floated through their township. Drones hovered over the slopes and television crews walked them. The mountains began closing in on them. Farzana waited at clearings, but Nadeem's truck often got sent to the Mulund mountains. On other days he looked for her at clearings when she had already been sent home by the guards. They fought over their increasingly averted meetings. Farzana kept trying to make it through the fires, smoke and security. Fevers raged in her, and Shakimun thought the Shaitans possessed her. Talismans filled her arms. But nothing could keep Farzana home.

In the evenings Nadeem began following Alamgir to his *kata* to help organise the trash, weigh it and pay the pickers, except that the fires had slowed business and there wasn't much to do. They locked up early and moved to Alamgir's house to chat. Farzana hung around, usually ignoring them, occasionally turning to tell them that their news about the guards, friends who had been beaten up or others who had paid to get in and work nights was wrong. What did truck drivers know about pickers?

When they did make it to the trash clearings together, Farzana and Nadeem walked furtively, sealed in the smoke. The blazing sun parched Farzana's mouth, the smouldering mountains scalded the soles of her feet, peeling the skin from them. Smoke made her cough and her throat and chest itch. Nadeem began bringing bottles of water for her.

One afternoon, when Nadeem arrived, Farzana was waiting for him with a small transparent plastic pouch. Nadeem looked up at the smile that lit her face, then quizzically at the bag, which held his gift – a grain of uncooked rice. *Dhyan se dekh*, she said. *Look at it carefully. Zyada*, she repeated. *More.* She had had their names written on it at the Haji Ali shrine: Nadeem and Farzana, united for ever on a grain of rice.

With Farzana's eighteenth birthday, rains had cleared the fires and smoke, the hills began filling with rain and rising again. Adulthood had arrived, and Farzana spoke to Nadeem in the glow of the phone, after everyone slept, asking him to meet her parents, speak about marriage; they were looking for someone for her. She had hung up green bangles at Mira Datar's shrine. She would be married to someone else if he did not come and see them soon. Nadeem came home, but avoided her parents, avoided Jehangir. He waited for his driving licence, for the job that would come with it, and which he hoped would impress her brothers. Farzana slept fitfully and worked before dawn.

Alamgir's wife, Yasmeen was already suspicious. *Naak to uski pakode jaisi hai,* Yasmeen told Farzana one afternoon, asking indirectly about the short man who was always at their house. *His nose looks like batter dropped into hot oil to make a pakoda.* Yasmeen had not had any luck asking Alamgir, who only said that Nadeem was new on the truck and needed to learn driving. Did Nadeem like her? Yasmeen asked Farzana, eliciting no reply. *Naata hai vo*, she scrunched her nose. *He's too short for you.* Farzana was the tallest of the six sisters, and Yasmeen thought she could do better than Nadeem.

One morning Nadeem had come to the mountains in his truck, his water bottle rolling under his feet. Farzana waited for him. When she was done picking from his truck, Nadeem handed her water. It dribbled down her long neck as she drank thirstily, chatting and giggling at the same time, barely pausing to breathe. When he returned from his round in the city, late in the afternoon, he didn't see Farzana or the usual crowd collect around his truck. A picker told him that the others had taken to hospital someone who had been crushed by a bulldozer and left in the clearing for dead. They would be back soon. The victim was unlikely to survive for long.

The mountains were filled with stories. Nadeem had heard about children getting eaten by mountain dogs while their mothers whirled within the garbage scrambles. He knew that gang rivalries led to stabbings on quiet mountain peaks. A gangster had hidden, rolled up in a discarded carpet, for days to avoid the police. Cocooned within, he had been reformed, and when he emerged he had become a cleric at a mosque close by. It was hard to say which of the tales that filled the mountain air were true and which were not.

Then Nadeem heard it was Farzana who had come under the bulldozer. He left the truck midway through his shift and hung around in hospital corridors for days, unable to see her. Their friends had slowly returned to work, but Nadeem waited outside the swinging doors until Alamgir told him that Farzana had called out for him. Even as doctors gave their dire prognosis, Nadeem heard, she had mumbled his name. For weeks Nadeem spent nights at the hospital and days on the truck, keeping his household running and his head in a daze. As the days wore on, both his mother and Hyder Ali waited for Nadeem to return to his own house in the evenings. But he kept returning to the hospital corridors, the ward and then to Hyder Ali's home.

That night, when Hyder Ali realised it was Nadeem that Farzana had worked through the fires for, suffered smoke-induced fevers and coughs for and called out in hospital for, he asked Alamgir to summon the young man. He asked Nadeem: why did he come every day? He knew how mangled Farzana's body had been. How scarred she still was. Nadeem told Hyder Ali that he hadn't stuck through the long nights at hospital only to leave Farzana now. He wanted to marry her. Tears welled in Hyder Ali's eyes.

For weeks his friends had told Nadeem that Farzana could be deformed for life. It wasn't the only problem; his older brother had told him to keep away from mountain girls. They started love affairs on the slopes. *Bhai, tu door hi reh,* he warned. *Stay away, brother.* But Nadeem had given his word to Farzana, and then to Hyder Ali. Jehangir, too, had wanted a match that would take his sister away from the mountains. But, he knew, word travelled fast in the marriage market. Who would marry Farzana as she was?

Besides, she would not budge. *Usse nahi karoongi to mar jaoongi* was all she would say about it. *If I don't marry him, I will die.*

The plans began to progress. Nadeem told Hyder Ali that he would bring his mother to approve of Farzana. Then he would have to bring his uncles over, from the village. As the elders of a family, albeit one that had never lived together, they would have to endorse the match. Hyder Ali charged Alamgir with taking Farzana's marriage proposal to Nadeem's mother. Enduring, unchanging rituals would replace the promises made on the shifting, rising trash peaks, amid the wafting smoke.

The municipality prepared to advertise for a match for its intractable mountains. Interest in the pre-bid meetings had stayed tepid. A municipal engineer told me they had often been sent for seminars on what makes a model tender, how to write it so it would work well, so that it would elicit bids. They had tweaked this one. But finding the balance between what worked for the municipality and what would attract an eligible suitor was hard. The company that built the plant would pay a large deposit, which it would get back only after five years, to ensure it kept the plant in good running order. An Indian partner was to operate the plant, but such a big plant had never been run in India. Companies worried that the city's terms were too hard to meet.

Potential bidders were concerned also about the messy fallout with Tatva, the allegations that the municipality had not met the terms it had agreed on, and the still ongoing arbitration. Then there was the mountains' army of pickers, which, despite so many efforts to evict them, had never left. *Itkya varshaat amhi poorna bhint bandhu shaklo nahi, It is true that we have never really been able to build a wall around the mountains*, a municipal engineer involved in planning the plant had told me. But without the wall to mark it as theirs, and with the army of mountain denizens who broke through the wall every time it was made, how could a new company settle on the slopes? potential bidders worried. On 8 November 2016 the municipality advertised for bids to make the waste-to-energy plant at the Deonar mountains. Sanjay Mukherjee, Mumbai's additional municipal commissioner, was upbeat, telling reporters that 'this will be one of the largest plants in the world'.[1]

The Hindu festival season ended days later, leaving the winds on the mountains drier and fiercer. They would soon wither the plants, turning the mountains brown and squeezing out any rain left in them, deflating them. As winds travelled through the slopes they could hit gases emanating from the slowly putrefying mountains, fire-crackers or trash boiled by the sun and erupt in fires, even while the bids were open. Guard patrols remained tight. Hyder Ali watched pickers make their way slowly up the slopes, guards gather around, batter them with sticks and turn them back. He hoarded and relayed these worrying stories to friends who dropped by at home in the evenings. They recounted their own anecdotes. A chill ran down their lanes.

Rag-pickers from the far ends of the city came before daybreak and worked in the deep, unpatrolled mountain recesses. Days later, guards discovered them and the pickers scouted for new places to trawl for trash in. The secret spots shrank. Hyder Ali heard of more friends working nights, returning home before the guards arrived in the morning. The guards began patrolling at night too. On his bench outside, Hyder Ali pulled his knees up, resting his chin on them. He stared at the silvery-grey remnants of a fire that Sahani and Yasmeen had made with scavenged wood scraps to cook meals on. The family's life lay suspended between Farzana's illness and the fading mountain luck, and he had not bought cooking oil for the stove inside in weeks. The soap operas that had wafted out of the television all day had silenced, after he stopped paying the cable bills. Shakimun's tailoring machine and the blender had sputtered out too. Sahani brought a mortar and pestle and ground chutneys to eat with chapatis they cooked on the silver-ringed fires. Earlier, Hyder Ali had showed me house-tax bills – the municipality's acknowledgement that he lived here and had to pay taxes on it. He had been getting them for three years, but had not paid any. *Bhar doonga. Ayenge hatane to bhar doonga*, he had told me. *I will pay if they come to evict me.*

The municipality planned that the bids were to be submitted by January 2017. Work would only begin after April. The plant would then take nearly three years to build, making Justice Oka's June 2017 deadline almost futile. But by making a little progress, officials hoped to keep the mountains going for just a little longer.

19

Nadeem's mother, Shaheen, had waited for weeks for the arrival of the marriage proposal. She knew that Nadeem had stayed out for nights on end because a friend's sister was in hospital after an accident. When he asked her to cook for the girl, who didn't like hospital food, Shaheen's neighbour had asked if she knew she was cooking for her prospective daughter-in-law. Shaheen watched Nadeem fix his hair endlessly in the small mirror stuck on the wall and figured it was for the girl in hospital.

When Alamgir finally appeared, Shaheen told him that their house was unlike Hyder Ali's. Theirs had been the first plinth of brick and stone in a lane of trash-made homes, marking them as one of the more prosperous families in their settlement. Their house rose over the rainwater that flowed down the mountains through their lane. It had risen in fits and starts above this foundation: when Shaheen had been a bride, it had only side walls, and monsoon winds and rain blew through the house. Alone at home, she had sat at the front opening with a stick, to keep the Shaitans out, she would tell me later. Nadeem's father had slowly built a front and back wall and then a higher floor. But unlike Farzana's flimsy house, which Shaheen had heard of, this one was solid – all brick. Farzana would be marrying up.

It was agreed that Shaheen would come to inspect Farzana a few weeks later. Nadeem's uncles, here for the ceremonies, would come after the first anniversary of Nadeem's father's death, to approve of the match too. After Hyder Ali heard this, he paced Banjara Galli all afternoon, fretting about the tests Farzana would have to pass. It was for Nadeem that Farzana dragged herself out of bed, tried pulling her leg painfully forward to walk. It was with him that she would have the life others thought she could never have. If only she could make it through the bridal inspection. But how could she? he worried.

A few weeks earlier Hyder Ali had watched fairy lights getting strung up in their lane, glinting past his house towards the mountains. They ended at Parveen Shaikh's house. For years the bespectacled, petite and dour Parveen had taken pride in saving up from picking trash to push both her sons through high school. She had checked their pockets every evening, to make sure gangs didn't lure them away with money or drugs. *Khaane se zyaada to maine fikar khayi hai*, she would often tell Shakimun. *I ate worry more than food when my boys were growing up*. Shakimun was never sure how to respond; apart from the youngest, Ramzan, her sons had never seen the inside of a school.

Parveen's elder son, Ismail, collected payments for a cellphone company, while her younger son worked as a tailor and passed on scraps for her to sell. A few days earlier, when Parveen was cooking dinner, Ismail had walked in with a bride, a girl from work he had secretly married. Parveen's dreams of finding a pliant girl from their village had crumbled, but faced with a bride at home, she planned a wedding ceremony and reception, and had lights fixed in the lane.

Farzana had grown up with Ismail; he was only a few months older than her. She decided that she had to go to the reception. Besides, she wanted to see the bride who had overturned Parveen's carefully nurtured plans. Everyone in Banjara Galli was talking about her. Farzana said she would go early, before her parents, and return soon. The reception hall was at the lane's entrance. Hyder Ali could not bring himself to say no.

Farzana picked out a long blue skirt and top, sewn with gold threadwork, to wear. Sahani helped her dress up. As she fixed her hair in the mirror, Farzana thought her throat bulged out awkwardly, making her face look frozen and distorted. She wrapped her blue dupatta with gold tassels tightly around her face to cover her neck, and powdered her face to brighten it. When she came out, Hyder Ali saw for the first time in months a skinny, drawn shadow of the old Farzana.

As she walked slowly down the lane to the wedding hall, with Farha, he settled down with a tumbler of tea on the bench jutting out of the house. He heard Farzana crying. It was all he ever heard these days, Hyder Ali thought. But her crying only got louder. He put his tumbler aside and craned to look down the lane. He saw Farzana limping slowly back with her arm around Farha. Tears smeared her whitened face, crumbling the glowing excitement that she had left with. Sahani helped her into the house, sat her on the floor and tried fiddling with her dress.

They had only walked halfway down the lane, Farha explained, when a long metallic thread from the scallops embroidered on Farzana's skirt had caught on one of the sutures that held her calf together. Farha bent down and tried to get it unstuck, but tugging at it threatened to reopen the wound. Farzana could only feel her leg throbbing. The lane spun in circles around her.

Farha cried with Farzana. Her palms got clammy and slipped on her sister's skin. She stood up, wrapped Farzana's arm around her shoulder and brought her home, hobbling. Farzana's screaming filled the house as Sahani and Farha tried disentangling her skirt from her calf. Hyder Ali cried helplessly outside. He heard them ask her to stay still so that they could unfix the gold thread.

Then the room fell silent. She must have got out of the dress, he thought, relieved. The silence stretched on. She must be asleep, Hyder Ali thought, sipping his by now tepid tea again.

Then Farzana stepped out in a baby-pink salwar kameez. She had fixed her hair and her face again and was ready to leave. She had missed the wedding already, but would not miss the reception for anything, she told him. It really was the old Farzana, Hyder Ali thought, as he watched her walk down Banjara Galli again.

Nadeem came over in the evenings. Farzana took slow steps forward with her hand on his shoulder. Was she taller than him? Yasmeen asked Farzana. Is that why her hand sat so comfortably on his shoulder? He was bending for her, Farzana said, bending a bit herself. She stopped in the middle of their walks, within the house, most evenings, turning to ask Nadeem what he would give her as a wedding gift. She would have to wait to know, he said. The wedding suddenly shimmered ahead. Farzana had to get to it.

She joined Khula Aasman, a free football class for girls in their lanes, to try and fix her limp. Mehrun and some of the other girls all tried to finish cooking, filling up with water and their embroidery by the afternoon so they could play, in a small open space. Farzana was sure to make any team that she was in lose. The others begged her to sit on the side and watch them play. But Farzana wore her baby-blue T-shirt with 'Khula Aasman' – 'open sky' – emblazoned on it and was there before the game began, twice a week, waiting to be picked. Doctors had advised her to get some exercise, she told them. She loved coming back home exhausted, having walked, having tried to run.

She tried walking down the lane to her sisters' houses, and then further, to friends' places. That would heal her limp before Shaheen came, Farzana figured. One afternoon as she was walking down 90 Feet Road to a friend's house, she looked down to straighten her knee. When she looked up, a bulldozer was rolling slowly towards her. She watched it approach. Its growing rumble rang in her ears. She stood in place. It came closer. Tears streamed down her face. There was nowhere to go, Farzana thought. It was coming at her, as it did in her dreams.

A neighbour had seen Farzana standing in front of a retreating bulldozer, crying. It was pressing down molten concrete to fix the road cratered by the rain, reversing. The neighbour walked her home. Farzana sobbed through much of the afternoon. *Vahi cheez thi*, she told Nadeem that evening, as they walked in the house. *It was the same thing*. He kept her walking.

When he left, she massaged her knee to reduce the pain and swelling. Wanting to be married – looking like she did, walking like she did – did she want too much? Farzana fretted. But Nadeem came every evening. They bantered: Nadeem softly, Farzana more loudly, his soft voice making her brighter. He egged her to stand, to walk, to move.

Farzana had no memory of being possessed and had never been sure about the spirits – or anything that held her back. But with Shaheen's visit coming up, she let Hyder Ali and Yasmeen fiddle with her amulets and have new prayers read into them, to ward away any leftover spirits that they thought trembled in her hand and dragged her leg. Farzana worried about what she would wear and how best to sit and sip tea without her hand quivering. She got Sahani to buy lime-green glass bangles to match the rose-pink salwar kameez embroidered with small, lifelike rosebuds and roses, their bright-green stems and leaves in place. She would wear it the day Shaheen came, hoping that Nadeem's mother would see Farzana not as she was, but as she could be.

The municipal ads for building the plant were in the papers, and officials hoped nervously that bidders would look past the sprawling mountains, and their troubled history, and see only the possibility of the plant. They had tweaked clauses in the tender conditions to give potential bidders the comfort that the plant could make money, that Tatva's troubles would not haunt them. They waited for bids to come in.

When officials had presented their plans to the court committee, some members had worried that they were too ambitious. The plant might not make money, even after the concession to run the plant expired after twenty years, some thought. Could officials begin with a smaller plant? Besides, the incinerator would have to be fed dry waste. But only unsorted tangles came out of homes to fill the garbage trucks, and the wealthy homes that produced the most valuable trash often didn't even have rubbish bins, their owners being unsure what happened to their possessions after they were done with them. Everything from food to shoes, to razor blades, used batteries, syringes, tablet strips and nappies came to the mountains mashed together. Less than 10 per cent of Mumbai's waste was segregated, surveys showed.

In old newspapers I had read of incinerators being installed in the city and in the Deonar township since the seventies, and of one that even pre-dated the mountains.[1] But even as the incinerators had floundered, pickers had separated all that arrived on the mountains in trucks, turning *cuchra*, or trash, into *bhangaar* – scrap, raw material for something else, someone else. *Phugawalas* had trawled for plastic, *chumbakwalas* for metal, *chindiwalas* for cloth scraps. They had brought it to their lanes, sorted and resold it to be remade.

Officials increased their campaign to get household trash segregated. The municipality asked building managers to separate and compost the biodegradable waste in their compound and send only dry waste in trucks that left for Deonar, Mulund or Kanjurmarg. They could get fined or lose their building licences if they didn't. Consultants had planned for screens and magnetic segregators at the mountains to separate the trash, instead of pickers, so that they could feed the right kind of items to the plant. The mountains' invisible army would be replaced, but there would be better jobs for them at the plant, or in their cleaned-up lanes, the consultants' report stated. They waited for bids to build the plant.

Sahani didn't know how to tell her sister that the more Farzana tried to walk, the further her leg dragged behind. On an early December evening I had trailed Sahani up the shaky metal stairs to the loft where Farzana lay awake on the bed. She wore a blue salwar kameez, with her head demurely covered. Sahani threw away the quilt and lifted up her loose-fitting salwar to show me the pink wounds that began a little above Farzana's ankle, travelled up her leg and ended at her buttocks, which were caved in from being stitched up over the missing flesh. Long stitch marks ran the length of her arms too. Sahani jabbed at Farzana's swollen knees and ankles. *Kaun isse shaadi karega aise*, she asked, agonising over the test that lay ahead. *Who would want to marry her like this?*

The next day Shaheen, who had a plump softness that might have come from never having worked on the mountains, never having scrambled for garbage, walked up to meet Farzana. The two spoke little, but felt they knew each other. Nadeem had told his mother that Farzana could not carry heavy things or squat to wash clothes. *Mil ke ghar chalaenge*, she told Farzana. *We'll run the house together.* She came down and gave Hyder Ali her assent to the marriage. *Nahi to bachon ka dil tootta hai*, she would tell me later. *I would have broken their hearts if I didn't.* She told him that Nadeem's uncles would come to give their final approval when they visited for the first anniversary of his father's death in April 2017.

Hyder Ali came down, thinking about how he could stall the wedding without cancelling it. Shaheen had told him that this was the first wedding in her family since her own. Much of their large and extended family would come. Hyder Ali could barely even pay for his half of the wedding. There was no one he could ask for money any longer. He could not even ask Jehangir, who had borne the brunt of the hospital expenses.

Hyder Ali fixed Farzana's wedding for June 2017, nearly eight months away. He desperately needed money, but work on the mountains was still erratic. Guards had not let the pickers work since they began finding money in the trash a few weeks ago. Hyder Ali heard that someone had found a gunny bag full of notes. As word spread, the police arrived, took it away and told the pickers most city notes were worthless. The prime minister had banned high-currency notes in order to prevent terrorists from printing fakes that undermined India's rising economy. Notes stashed secretly in the city for years began to arrive at the mountains. They had suddenly turned into rubbish. Pickers sold them for less than the printed amount, before guards and policemen blocked their entry into the mountains. Why was it that when money arrived at their township, packed in bags, it was useless? Hyder Ali thought.

Pradhan Mantri hamare liye i-card bhej rahe hain, he told Badre Alam as the two chatted at home one evening. *The prime minister is sending us identity cards.* Hyder Ali would work at the mountains only when the cards, which let him walk their slopes officially, came. The guards would not be able to drive them away if he had the prime minister's card on him, he thought. It was how he had understood the new solid-waste rules that volunteers had told him about – the ones that said pickers were to be included in managing the city's waste.

When Badre Alam dropped by, the cousins chatted about reviving the embroidery workshop before Farzana's wedding. Hyder Ali softly let on that, despite his resolutions, he had gone to work on the mountains yesterday. Options on the mountains were running out; they had asked our loan officer for a new loan, but we had stopped lending in these lanes, after seeing the pickers lurching from one failed business to another. They used the money to get through a few weeks of home expenses instead, making it hard to pay instalments back. Often they took higher-interest loans that came with more coercive repayment tactics in order to repay ours, sliding further into debt. They mounted until some people disappeared, as Moharram Ali and Nagesh had. While some had gone from hand-carts to shops and had grown their embroidery workshops, others, such as Hyder Ali, had returned to the mountains.[2] Watching them lurch from loan to loan, we had stopped lending around the mountains and then in Mumbai, lending money in rural areas instead, where we could bolster the loans with training to ensure the businesses worked.

Hyder Ali had collected 22 lbs of squashed plastic, he told Badre Alam, looking towards the black bags in a corner of the room. Badre Alam threw him a befuddled look. Hyder Ali just threw his hands up. What was he to do? Farzana's wedding was not so far off.

Ten-year-old Ramzan, the youngest of the children, walked in. *Isko kabhi nahi bhejoonga*, Hyder Ali told me. *I'll never send him to the mountains.* His eyes shone as he spoke of how Ramzan was the only one of his children who woke up on his own, made his tea and left for school by 7.30 a.m. Ramzan's school tie and bag hung on a wall hook, along with a back-brace for Farzana. Ramzan responded by saying that he loved going to the mountains. Hyder Ali stared in mock horror. *Bagule marne jata hoon*, Ramzan reassured his father. *I go there to kill storks*, using the Urdu equivalent of 'shooting the breeze'.

As the year came to a close, the strange harvest of currency notes had left the mountains and trash had refilled them. The grey market for the old notes shrank, as new pink-and-orange notes arrived on the market. Pickers gave up on waiting for their official identity cards. Security eased and they returned to picking trash. Officials waited nervously for fires and prepared to quell them. The deadline for the plant tenders was 5 January 2017. Not a single bid came in.

20

Late on a breezy January evening Yasmin returned to her house after a medical trial. She paid rent with the money she brought with her and moved back into the room that she had vacated before she left. The children returned, bringing back bits of their home that had been stored at *katas* and other people's places during their mother's absence. Mehrun resettled the family, folding everyone's clothes into the metal cupboard and lining up dishes along the kitchen counter while Yasmin dozed off.

A long line of people blocked Banjara Galli's entrance when I got there the next afternoon. I ran into a borrower in the queue, who told me everyone wanted a consultation at the free health clinic that had opened across the slim entrance. I looked up to see a bicycle on a background of green and red, the symbol of the Samajwadi or Socialist Party, painted on a board perched atop the clinic. Elections for Mumbai's municipality, said to be India's or Asia's wealthiest, were weeks away, the borrower reminded me – and had I heard that Yasmin had returned? Mumbai's election machine was moving through their lanes, glinting amid them. But its promises barely reached Yasmin's house, which was dark in the mountains' shade, teetering at the edge. Inside Mehrun, who was always home, was graduating from the cusp of teenage straight into adulthood.

The faintly sweet smell of rice that she was steaming filled the room when I dropped in. Some of the women had not made it through the medical tests, Yasmin, wearing a sunflower-yellow salwar kameez with pink-and-gold flowers scalloped at the edges, told Sharib, Mehrun and me. They had to be sent home. But she felt nothing after she took the drug, a contraceptive, Yasmin beamed. In a few weeks she would return so that doctors could check if the medicine had any side-effects, earning her another month's rent and expenses.

The kitchen counter darkened and Mehrun turned to see her brother Sameer, two years older, standing at the door, blocking it. The sun streamed around him, framing his edges with a gold rim. Coated in a patina of dried mountain mud, he looked like a sepia-tinted photograph, except for the blood trickling down his legs. Mehrun served Sharib, the older of the brothers, who looked up with a sour expression, which was not aimed at her.

He was walking to work in the morning, Sharib told them, when he heard screaming. He turned to see guards raining their sticks down on a picker whose long body curled up tightly under their blows. As their sticks swung back up in the air, the picker uncurled to breathe, and the guards kicked his stomach, curling him up in pain again. Pickers stood around and along the slope, watching. As Sharib, breathless, drew near, the guards stopped and the dusty figure uncoiled beneath them. It was Sameer.

Sharib had pleaded with the guards to let Sameer go. He would never come back, Sharib promised, retrieving his brother. The two had walked down the slope until Sameer veered off, limping towards the market to scour the overflowing dustbins that the garbage trucks hardly reached. He returned home, trickling blood, which Yasmin asked him to wash off before Friday prayers and Arabic class. Whenever she returned with money from the trials, Yasmin resumed pushing her children out of the mountains' shadow. Sameer ate the rice that Mehrun served, then messed through the clothes that she had laid out in the cupboard, nearly missing prayers, until he found a dark, mismatched set and left with Sharib.

Mehrun tidied the cupboard and settled to fill a long saree border with gold flowers, when Hera arrived, followed by her mother-in-law and sister-in-law, who was wearing a red salwar kameez. She topped it with a red-and-green dupatta with a bicycle motif, as if the board above the clinic had draped itself around her shoulders. Mother and daughter had spent the morning walking through their lanes, campaigning for the Samajwadi Party.

The Party's traditional voting base was among Muslim and Yadav communities (the Yadavs being a pastoral Hindu community often listed among India's backward castes) in Uttar Pradesh, where it ran the government. Its roots had spread in the mountains' shadows as pickers came to fill them, and these lanes formed the Party's only stronghold in Mumbai. The city's major parties – the Bharatiya Janata Party (BJP) and Shiv Sena, who had controlled the city and its wealth for almost two decades – mostly stayed away. Instead they mounted furious campaigns in the city; after years as a junior partner, the BJP had taken control of the central and state government and had now set its sights on one of India's largest and richest cities. Devendra Fadnavis, Maharashtra's young chief minister, smiled out of campaign hoardings across Mumbai. Among the promises splashed on them was one to make electricity from waste.

The tender dates had passed without any bids coming in for the project at Deonar, but the promise floated there, unwavering.

The Samajwadi Party's councillors had opposed the plant, saying it would sicken the lungs of their constituents, already weakened by years of inhaling the city's detritus, without giving them the jobs that the pickers had waited for. With the municipality controlled by Shiv Sena and the BJP, who represented the city that sent the waste to the unseen mountains, the plans were approved. The plant would come to the mountains, if only someone would bid for it.

The city arrived in Yasmin's house – partly through official means, but more often through unofficial routes, couched in stiff officialese. While the women chatted that afternoon, gang debt collectors waited at the door to collect payments for the power they had illegally connected to homes in their lanes. Mehrun asked them to come back in a little while. She would borrow something to pay them.

Within days Yasmin had nearly run out of the money she had brought back from the trial and returned for another one. An angry red rash began growing across Sharib's back. It stretched and reddened in the sun as he constructed a house near Ashra's school. Watching it grow, the boss had sent him home. At the house Sharib lay on the floor in pain, turning onto one side and then another.

In charge of the house, Mehrun planned their days around bringing back the free municipal water supply. She would have to walk down their long lane to 90 Feet Road, slip into the loud, slippery gaggle for the municipal water tanker, then make sure she ran into someone to help her bring the water cans. She could also buy it from a neighbour who had surreptitiously connected his pipe to the water supply. But he asked a fee that she could not pay.

Through the afternoons she stayed buried in fixing flowers on women's sleeves, worrying that her brothers would ask her what was for lunch when she had nothing. Yasmin returned, sooner than expected: she had tested anaemic and been rejected from the trial. She had begged them to take her anyway, as she needed the money, but returned only with her travel expenses. It began getting to the early winter dusk before Mehrun could buy supplies and light up the stove to cook. During the long, quiet afternoons that I spent watching her embroider beads, I saw her hazel eyes get larger, her face thinner. The gold flowers that she stitched floated in her eyes and in her empty stomach.

The only topic that made her seem like the twelve-year-old she was comprised her collection of discarded dolls, lost in the many moves in and out of the same house. I asked if she had ever wondered how the dolls had landed at the mountains. *Vo log ub jaate hain na*, she said. *Those people must have got bored, right. Theek hai. Tabhi to hamein mila. It's okay. That is how we got them.* It was also how the city arrived at their house.

As their lanes filled with party flags, Yasmin searched for work in the election industry. A friend had taken her along to a campaign rally in the city, where she heard their state representative say that he had brought water to the lanes around the mountains. She knew it hadn't reached their house, but Yasmin clapped on cue. Later she heard that the rate for filling crowds at rallies had gone up to Rs 800 (a little more than $10) – far more than on her first visit. If she went to a few rallies she would not need to go for a medical trial for a month, Yasmin thought. But the well-paid rally attendances were in great demand and she could not get any more.

She used the last of her notes for ointment to shrink Sharib's rash, and handed Mehrun embroidery instead of money. I arrived late in the afternoon, bringing a packet of biscuits as I often did those days, suggesting that we eat and chat as they work. *Bhook nahi hai*, Mehrun told me flatly, turning back to work. *I am not hungry*. I asked to see what she had made and Mehrun stood up, stretching a gold saree border, longer than her, which could probably buy them dinner.

Explaining why she left Mehrun to fill the intricate borders and sleeves, Yasmin would tell me how the medical trials had weakened her. She knew that people in her lane talked about her long absences, with Mehrun locked in the house; about her odd hours and her irregular, mysterious earnings. She knew that they thought it was why Moharram Ali had left her.

Yasmin wanted to enrol Sameer in a drug de-addiction programme. She suspected his foggy mind, slow, halting speech and fitful head rolls were clouded by more than just the *gutkha*, or chewing tobacco, that had stained his teeth. But Sameer pulled out money when she could not find it anywhere else. She put off his treatment until after she had got Mehrun out of their lanes. Stuck in the mountains' shadow, Mehrun had stayed out of school, scrounging for meals, struggling for water, getting quieter and more translucent by the day, even as creditors hung closer. Yasmin wanted her out.

One afternoon Yasmin decided to go to Mehrun's school to explore if her daughter could return for class or to get a leaving certificate, so that she could enrol her elsewhere, far away from the mountains. Both covered their heads with dupattas that they held tightly at their chests, wore their slippers and turned to close the house door behind them. Yasmin began to giggle, seeming childlike. *Aadmi ghus sakta hai*, she pointed out. *A man could get through it*: the bottom plank of the door had come off, leaving a hole. Mehrun placed the plank loosely in place, so that a potential intruder would think it was a closed door, and the two walked out of their lane.

The newly built orange-and-green school building was across a public park and had a large foyer with pictures of national leaders, most of whom Mehrun could not recognise. They walked up the stairs, painted with signs in Marathi and Urdu asking the children not to litter. There was a poster showing pictures of children breaking stones in a quarry, with slogans encouraging them to go to school rather than work. But Mehrun's guess was as good as Yasmin's: she could not read it, although she had studied in Urdu until middle school. At every landing the mountains streamed in through the geometrical grilles in the wall. At every landing the reluctant Mehrun asked to go home. Yasmin kept her going.

As they reached the fourth floor, Mehrun looked breathless and relieved. It was Friday and school had closed for the day. They walked back down, with Mehrun telling Yasmin this was the first time she had come back to her school since she left more than a year ago. She had told her friends and teachers then that she was moving to a private English school. She would only speak English the next time they met, they had teased her. Since then her friends had moved on to the next class and had learned more Urdu and more English. *Main unse kya kahoongi?* Mehrun asked. *What will I say if I run into them?*

Outside, they joined the lane jammed with the hand-carts and shoppers they had seen from high up. A Friday sermon began to crackle over a loudspeaker as the two walked through the clouds of flies filling the lane. If you do your *namaz*, your prayers, before you sleep, then you will never sleep alone. He will be with you, a voice called, rising above the din of shoppers as they walked back home.

Weeks later Shiv Sena had nosed ahead of the BJP in the municipal elections, but didn't secure enough seats to elect its own mayor; again the two parties would have to work together to realise the city's rising aspirations. As expected, the Samajwadi Party had won in the shadow of the mountains made by the leftovers of those aspirations, but hardly made a dent in the rest of the city. The city and its mountains would stay in different worlds.

21

In the neatly gridded schedule in the project report the municipal consultants had made, March 2017 was filled with blue blobs to show when the company it had selected would finalise the design for the plant. By the time the court deadline came, in June, the blobs in the voluminous report's table would turn green and orange, indicating the beginning of construction for the project that would finally burn away the city's trash. The colours moved forward like a rising wave on the long, gridded schedule, but the plant stayed stuck. More than two months before the deadline to make the plant, stop dumping waste at the Deonar township and to mend it, the municipality was back in court, asking for an extension of four more years.[1]

Raj Sharma, the activist, had filed his own petition, stating that hardly anything Justice Oka had asked for – the boundary wall, the cameras or the prevention of building debris being dumped – had happened. For months he had photographed people getting through the broken wall and seen increasing construction debris. There were no lights.[2] As security tightened further around the mountains' border with the lanes, other court committee members had heard that pickers made rafts from the rubber and plastic they foraged, then sailed into the township through the creek. The committee had asked for barbed wire or a wall to be installed along the mangroves that ran into the creek. It had not been installed yet, either.[3] Sharma opposed the extension of the deadline. The court set a date to hear both petitions, just weeks before the 30 June deadline to stop dumping garbage at Deonar.

When hearings began in Room 13, nearly one and a half years after he had handed down the construction ban and set the deadline, Justice Oka was joined by the newly appointed Justice Vibha Kankanwadi on the two-judge bench. I watched from the back of Room 13, moving slowly towards the front, as I could barely hear. I had hardly been to a court before, but as Justice Oka took centre-stage in the room, as designated for him, it felt like at long last the mountains would move.

Petitions filed in the public interest, such as Sharma's, came before Oka's ornate, elevated chair, forming a moving tableau of Mumbai's aches and wounds, of dreams that clashed as they rose. The concerns were varied: the city's cramped jails; the sound of the millions-strong orchestra that played day and night at festivals; residents cooking meats that their neighbours' gods prohibited them from even smelling; the smoke that wafted from unseen garbage mountains into its rising towers. I watched Oka make room for endless dreams in a city with little space.

Petitioners, lawyers and an assortment of government functionaries squeezed past one another to recount these often years-long troubles to Oka. The only comfort in the courtroom's crush came from the air conditioning, which had been installed when Justice Chandrachud had adjudicated on the Deonar mountains' fate, more than a decade ago. A deep thud sounded as Deonar's case papers, accumulated over years, and in which the mountains' invisible army appeared only as fire-starters, landed on Oka's desk.

Why would Mumbai's garbage be emptied on the hills for four more years, Oka asked, when the waste rules gave only two more years to fix the garbage dumping grounds around the country? Anil Sakhare, the municipality's long-standing lawyer on the case, said it was making progress on meeting Oka's goals and the waste rules. It was Sharma who had the obstructionist attitude.

The diminutive Sharma stood behind his lawyers in his oversized shirt and high-waist trousers and nudged his lawyer to point out that he had asked to visit the mountains. When the municipality had not set a visit up, he had gone by himself, photographed them and written a report for the court, detailing all the ways in which Oka's orders had not touched the mountains. Justice Oka asked the municipality to allow Sharma and his lawyers to see its mountain registers, and set the next hearing for 29 June, one day before the deadline for dumping at Deonar to end.

As Sharma stepped out into the colonnaded corridor that ran alongside the courtroom, a municipal engineer pulled him aside, into a sun-filled courtyard off the corridor, and chatted affably. The waste-to-energy plant they had planned for Deonar would take off this time, he told Sharma, making no mention of the lack of bidders or that the date for eliciting bids had been extended. Mumbai's waste could produce enough power, he said. It would just have to be dried several times, to reduce its wetness, before incinerating it. He bought Sharma tea from one of the vendors who walked around the busy court, steaming kettle in hand and with little glasses stuffed in their trouser pockets.

Ham idhar hi paida hue, idhar hi bade hue. We were born

here and lived here our whole lives, the engineer said animatedly. *Hamko pata hai idhar kya chalega. We know what will work in Mumbai.* He didn't look at what was happening anywhere else, he said. Swallowing the last dregs of his tea, he expanded on how the project would transform the city and the Deonar township. *Pune model, Pune model,* he said, imitating the people who had asked him to look at the awards the neighbouring city had won for managing its waste. They had no idea how big and complex Mumbai was, he continued. They needed Sharma's help getting their project off the ground – these court cases only soaked up their energy and delayed the plant. Sharma nodded.

A few days later Sharma and his lawyers would go over the municipal reports, from which they calculated that more construction debris than garbage had been dumped on the mountains over the last few months.[4] He wondered why garbage traders were in jail for dumping debris illegally on the mountains when the municipality was dumping excess amounts itself. Municipal officials said the debris was well within permissible limits and would quell fires when dropped on the mountains.

At the next court hearing, both legal teams waited nervously as Justice Oka grilled the lawyers representing the state in the preceding case. The newspapers had been full of the death of Manjula Shetye, a thirty-eight-year-old female prisoner at Mumbai's Arthur Road Jail, who had been serving a life sentence for murdering her sister-in-law in 1996. Her fellow inmates alleged that she was beaten brutally and left to die by jail staff, after she asked for eggs and bread that they were supposed to get for breakfast.

Oka looked down through his glasses, selected pages from the case papers, then looked up and read out the orders he had given on improving the city's jails, just months ago. Had they done it? Lawyers said that – much like at Deonar – a committee had been formed to improve prison infrastructure and reduce the overcrowding in jails, on Oka's instructions. It would submit a report in a few months. Oka interrupted, his voice rising. He didn't think progress would be made, even months later. For a few moments the lawyers and petitioners in the court-room looked up from their own case papers to take in his anger. Cases could stretch on in court, but in the city such delays could lead to abrupt, dark turns – the mountain fires, Shetye's death. Behind the cases, the courses of the lives they obscured sometimes turned suddenly, ended or darkened for ever, through accidents, fires and violence.

The Deonar lawyers moved in for their hearing. Oka instructed Sharma's lawyer to suggest the names of waste-management experts who could visit the mountains and report back to the court, then he extended the deadline for closing the dumping grounds until the next hearing, a few weeks later.

A few days after the hearing, Sharma began calling waste experts that he had met as he had traversed Mumbai's waste world for years. He asked them to visit the trash township at the court's direction. But no one wanted to testify against the municipality. The city's secrets were hidden in the mountains, it seemed, and no one wanted to uncover them.

As the city attempted to tighten its grip on the waste, it kept spilling from underneath it. No one seemed to know how much waste there was: one report estimated that the city generated around 9,000 tonnes of garbage every day, concluding that as Mumbaikars continued to move out to suburban utopias, their waste would follow them, growing only by 1 per cent a year for the next twenty years.[5] Deonar could almost absorb this, and it fitted the municipality's contention in court that the township could keep going for longer.

But another study, commissioned slightly earlier, which had formed a part of the thick tender documents for the waste-to-energy plant, estimated that the city generated 11,000 tonnes of garbage, and almost 2,500 tonnes of construction waste, every day.[6]

Together, the reports commissioned by the municipality suggested there was not so much trash that the Deonar township had to close, or for construction in the city to be suspended, but there was just enough for the plant to make a profit. Mumbai's garbage mysteriously swelled and deflated to fit its precarious plans to manage its waste.

A scandal had also erupted over a garbage-truck contractor who had sued the municipality for not paying his bills. The municipality's own investigation revealed that some of the garbage he ferried, and billed for, never existed.[7] Mud was mixed in with waste to add to the weight of the garbage. He was paid for the increased weight and passed a portion of the payment to municipal officials. It seemed that officials had colluded with him to make inflated claims for garbage, and get overpaid, for several years. The Lohiya report, investigating the fires in January, also found that the weigh-bridges at the township were fixed to show 15 per cent overweighing of garbage, so that contractors could be overpaid.[8] The artificially inflated garbage brought with it money for equipment that was not needed, fees for transporting and handling garbage that did not exist, and pay for contractors who were not needed.

Cameras and automated weighing machines were placed at the weigh-bridges where garbage trucks brought in their load, to ensure it was garbage that emptied from trucks and not mud, and to keep out buses and rickshaws. Payment registers started to be carefully monitored. But the problems seemed endless. 'Can you ever repair a house while you are living in it?' an ageing and retired municipal engineer who had managed the Deonar township and the city's waste for years asked me, when I met him to discuss the intractable situation at the mountains. 'As long as waste keeps coming to Deonar, how will we fix it? And our waste won't stop coming.'

22

In April 2017 Nadeem's uncles had come to see Farzana. The day before, Hyder Ali had called Nadeem in a panic, asking how to explain Farzana's scars and her limp to them. Nadeem had told him not to say anything. Tell them only that you sent a proposal through Alamgir, he had said, and Hyder Ali had felt his nerves calm as Nadeem navigated the way forward. He spoke to Nadeem's uncles now about their families, their villages and the journey that both families had made to settle in the shadow of the mountains.

Farzana had come into the room and sat before them with her gaze lowered. She wore a peach and gold kurta, its long sleeves hiding her wounds. Her sisters had covered her head with a dupatta and stuck in a hair-pin, to make sure it did not slip. Hyder Ali told the uncles that she had stayed home, had learned Arabic and knew some verses from the Koran.

Nadeem's uncles approved the match, asking only to anticipate the wedding, so that they could attend. It was set for 21 May 2017, six days before the first fast of Ramzan. Hyder Ali knew that he could not delay Farzana's wedding any longer for lack of money. Most of Shaheen's family from Nasik, and her husband's family from further away in Akola, would cram into SUVs and drive up for the wedding, she told Hyder Ali. He tried to dissuade her from inviting some of them. She called back, only to tell him that the number in their party had gone up.

Hyder Ali had hired the wedding hall at the entrance to their lane, and the next few weeks went by in a frenzied scramble to collect money for the growing wedding party. Jehangir, Alamgir, Badre Alam and he borrowed from friends and worked nights on the mountains. Hyder Ali asked Yasmin, who said she had no money to lend. But she had friends with political connections. She took him to meet their state representative, who asked an assistant to hand over some money and a dress for Farzana's trousseau. Hyder Ali wasn't sure how these contributions added together in those last few days, but they did.

On the wedding day Sahani and Jehana helped Farzana into a red dress embroidered with gold flowers that Shaheen had sent. They draped a red dupatta over her head and topped it with a blanket of milky tuberoses and scarlet roses. The flowers framed her face and felt cool and velvety against her palm when she touched them. The heavy costume, topped with gold jewellery and the flowers, kept Farzana's movement so limited that no quiver or limp showed. She kept her head bowed and unsmiling, as Jehana had asked her to, making Farzana a demure, fragrant and glowing bride. In the wedding hall Nadeem sat in a separate room, wearing his own flower blanket over a white-and-powder-blue salwar kameez. A crescent moon was strung across his forehead, a flower veil hanging below it.

Banjara Galli had emptied into the hall that night. Yasmin came with the children, Ashra wearing the dress and skirt that Moharram Ali had got her at the market last Ramzan. They ran into neighbours and old friends from the mountains. And yet Nadeem's relatives more than matched them. Together they packed the rooms, the greatest sign of a successful wedding. Tables filled with flame-coloured meat curries began emptying too quickly.

All evening the men pushed and edged towards Nadeem, and the women towards Farzana. They paused to pose for pictures, in which Farzana's face was turned down at the floor and her new gold handbag up at the camera. After signing the marriage contract, Nadeem took off his veil, and he and Farzana met guests together. Nadeem's gold-flecked puff of hair was teased even higher to make him look taller, but his bride still inched over him. Later both would insist it was because of her heels, Farzana pointing to her shoulder to show where she reached up to on Nadeem – the height for good brides.

Guests crowded around Farzana's trousseau. Shakimun had laid out clothes, oversized cooking dishes and sandals, along with gold studs that Hyder Ali had got to replace the ones he had taken out of Farzana's ears while she lay unconscious in hospital – all on a cot that was Jehana's gift. Friends wanted to tell Shakimun to add their gifts, but it was hard to speak to her. *Meri maa poori shaam roi*, Farzana recalled. *My mother cried all evening.* Five of Shakimun's children had married already, but letting go of Farzana was a wrench.

Two days later Farzana and Nadeem dressed in wedding clothes again and left for their day-long honeymoon in the city, accompanied by Nadeem's cousin, his wife and their children. They went to Haji Ali, the white marble mausoleum that rose from the sea, where Farzana had got the rice grain engraved with their names. They walked along the slim, rocky pathway with waves lashing its sides, Farzana making sure to walk behind Nadeem, as she had seen brides do. Groups of beggars lined the pathway, chanting softly, asking for money. Little stubs of limbs hung below their elbows or knees. Farzana drew back, turning away, as they edged closer. They could have been her, she felt. She could have been them.

Nadeem and Farzana entered through separate entrances, gave flowers and a brocade sheet to be laid over the tomb to the *mujawars*, the keepers of the tomb, who waved and then tapped peacock feathers on their heads to bless them. Then they walked out through the sun-filled courtyard onto the wind-blown rocks jutting from the waves, where Farzana sat and felt the spray of the sea on her face. Nadeem got his brother to photograph him, leaning into the waves. Later they would go to a photo studio, where Farzana sat on a cardboard sliver of crescent moon with Nadeem's baby nephew on her lap. Nadeem stood behind, amid the stars in the backdrop, holding the moon's strings for her.

Weeks later, on a sun-baked afternoon, Nadeem walked Farzana back to Hyder Ali's home. It was one of the last days of Ramzan; the rains had set in, but that afternoon the air was warm, heavy and humid. Banjara Galli wore a languid air. Most people had retreated into their homes to escape the heat, their energy dissipated by hunger.

Hyder Ali, Shakimun and I chatted at Yasmin's house. I had come to meet Farzana and Nadeem, having missed the wedding. Confounded by his explanation of the Shaitan gripping his daughter, I asked him why he thought it had gripped Farzana right as the bulldozer approached. *Vo khoobsurat thi na, usne fasaya* was Hyder Ali's only reply. *She was so beautiful.* Even the Shaitan desired her. *He entrapped her.*

As Nadeem and Farzana walked in, I was surprised to see her in a burqa. Shaheen had given it to her after she got married, Farzana told me. She unbuttoned it, revealing freshly made maroon henna patterns on her palms, with Nadeem's name written in English. Neighbours had dropped in with *mehendi* cones the day before, to prepare for Eid, Farzana said, curling her palm shyly into a fist.

Hyder Ali basked in the glow of the wedding; his estimate of guests ranged from 500 to 2,000. He could hardly afford any gifts for Farzana himself, and yet she had received thirty sets of clothes, he said. Nadeem's driving licence would come through any day, Shakimun piped in: he would graduate from cleaner to driver.

Their lives buoyed in the rising tide of destiny, Hyder Ali had an explanation, and it rhymed with Nadeem: *naseeb*, or fate. He fiddled with the cracked plastic phone screen in his hand. A man's deep voice rose, filling the room with a slow-paced song inspired by Koranic verses, Hyder Ali told me. Onscreen, the singer's callow, thinly moustached face gave way to shots that panned through a row of dead bodies wrapped in white shrouds being lowered slowly into graves. He was singing about *naseeb*, Hyder Ali explained, even as Farzana looked away. How it steered lives.

Upar vala pahunchata hai apne naseeb tak. God takes us where our destiny is. It was not me or her, Hyder Ali pointed at his wife. *Naseeb ne use Nadeem se milaya, shaadi karai*, he said, enjoying the rhyme. *Fate, or* naseeb, *had brought Farzana to Nadeem, her companion.* It was Farzana's fate that helped him pull off such a big wedding with so little money, and escape the life that he and Shakimun had worried she would have. It was her fate that had led the wedding party to be so big that the food ran dangerously low.

He fiddled with his phone. Onscreen, the camera panned across darkened graveyards and freshly dug graves, keeping Hyder Ali on the subject of fate and destiny. Everyone has to go back into the earth, whether the person was from a bungalow or from a place like theirs, he said, explaining the verses. Only a few yards of cloth would go with them – this was fate. All the stuff that filled up the mountains would stay, he said, waving his bony hand at the hills that rose behind Yasmin's house. Only the mountains would remain, rising constantly.

A few weeks earlier I had visited a sprawling beach outside New York City, still strewn with the belongings of people long gone. I had heard that Dead Horse Bay, as the beach was known, had absorbed much of the city's trash during the fifties. Half buried in the sand were switchboards, cups, dishes and other things made of Bakelite, an early form of plastic that could be moulded easily. It didn't break, didn't conduct electricity or heat and could be made cheaply into products, allowing people to possess their desires in forms that ranged from rotary telephones to lidded serving dishes. Unbroken but later unfashionable, these objects had been discarded for new things, and found their way to the beach. I pulled out a pair of sand-filled stockings, of the kind that had given women a shimmery sheen as they had begun working at offices around that time. The landfill had been emptied out and moved elsewhere, but the stockings were still there, strangling weeds on the beach, their stretchy nylon filament lasting more than half a century.

I had often asked municipal engineers in Mumbai: of all the trash that had emptied there, over the century, what would remain? Only animal bones and gold bits, they told me. Much of the older trash was food that would have rotted to make the soil fertile. Since I began seeing trucks emptying, they had delivered plastic takeaway containers, large cloth and plastic sacks that once contained grains, foil and plastic boxes for milk and juice, stretchy tubes to squeeze out toothpaste or sandalwood-scented creams. They had dumped metallic strips packed with tablets that the pickers consumed, home-use syringes to control diabetes that jabbed the pickers, and other things that would never turn into soil. Would these top layers of Deonar's hills fester, unchanging for ever, over the older, enriched soil? I wondered. Mumbai's age of dizzying growth left its own immortal trail.

In New York I had also visited the Fresh Kills garbage township, where the city's trash had later been sent, after Jamaica Bay. It was a garbage city so vast that there were traffic lights to direct trash caravans through its towering garbage hills. At the entrance of the township I saw crushed bits of bathroom washbasins and pots. They had been left to dry in the sun and would later be immersed in the ocean bed so that oysters could breed on their surfaces, I was told. The name Fresh Kills came from the Dutch word for the fresh streams of water that had once flowed through here, and our guide from New York City's parks department told me that streams would run through the slowly detoxifying hills again, and that one day fish would be reintroduced in them. Later I read about a tree that had mysteriously grown on the hills, which had only a thin topping of soil over its decomposing trash.[1] Could Deonar's hills too yield trees, house fish and birth oysters? I wondered.

For now I imagined the old, degradable trash becoming enriched soil, and the thick, new layers of unmeldable trash that emptied constantly making ever more of the hills. Only the pickers took this new trash away to be remade into new items. But these days guards asked for Rs 100 to let them pick through the mountains. Hyder Ali didn't earn much more than that in a day. So he mostly stayed home and watched videos, like the ones he had shown us. *Aur hain. Aur achhe*, he said, and sifted through the videos stored in his phone. *I have more. Nicer ones.* He continued, narrating their message to us. *Vo bata rahe hain, kaise sab cheez jama karo par naseeb yahi hai ki jana akele hai. They tell you all about how you can accumulate everything, but destiny makes us leave the world alone.*

Nadeem shifted awkwardly. He had to get back for an afternoon shift on the truck, he said. He would take Farzana back with him. Shakimun wheedled him to let Farzana stay, promising that she would get Alamgir to drop her back later, but Nadeem motioned at Farzana to leave. As Hyder Ali and Shakimun walked them to the end of the lane, Yasmin stayed behind to plan for Alvida Jumma, or the last Friday of Ramzan, the next day. The crescent moon that brought in Eid was likely to be spotted the next night, bringing in the luckiest day of the year.

23

At the next court date, in July 2017, Deonar's case did not come up until nearly lunchtime. Raj Sharma watched the crowd in the courtroom ebb and flow and thought his hearing would be quick. He had already spoken to a waste expert to arrange a visit and report on whether court orders had reached the mountains. When the Deonar case number was finally called, Justice Oka asked the lawyers if they had thought of an expert. The municipality's lawyer said there was no need for one; the township fell in the purview of the committee that Oka had set up, and included scientists. Why would the court look outside for help in monitoring the mountains?

Sharma's lawyer said the chairman of the court-appointed committee had resigned a few months ago, after doctors had told him the mountains' halo could damage his already-weak health. The committee had remained headless ever since, and had not met often. The municipal lawyer interrupted, claiming the opposite: another member headed the committee while it looked for a replacement, and it had met. Oka and Kankanwadi, who was also on the bench, watched, with bemusement, as their committee died and came alive in the sparring between the two lawyers, while the mountains and their halo hung in the balance.

*

The judges resumed their attempts to shrink the halo that had quivered but hardly moved from over the mountains and their denizens. Oka asked the court committee, and especially the two scientists, to visit the mountains and report on what progress had been made. Municipal officials began calling committee members to set up a date for the mountain visit. But the day before, one of the scientists had pulled out. The others watched a presentation on the waste-to-energy plant that officials still hoped to attract bidders for, months after they had first invited them. The group then left to inspect the hills, their stomachs churning with the deeply cratered road and the heady smell. They could not make it to the far end, but watched garbage hills rise on either side, grey with monsoon water and Mumbai's discarded detritus. A broken electricity pole joined one craggy hill edge to another. There were bits of bricks, cement and concrete left over from the pre-monsoon repairs. Security guards had kept the pickers away, giving the dogs and swooping birds their fill of the garbage that fell out of trucks that afternoon. The mountains looked like an isolated archaeological find, filled with the city's dated desires, ringed by rising new buildings of glass and steel.

A few weeks after their visit, Justice Oka's courtroom hit the news headlines in the city where ambitions burned and clashed, where things trembled on the edge of change, seemed to move, but often didn't.

In court Sharma had often watched proceedings on a petition that asked for national regulations on silent zones – where the city's roar would be reduced to a whisper – to be met. Oka had ordered that any place within 100 yards of a court, hospital or educational institution should be a silent zone.[1] Enforcing his order, in a city where everything and everyone was jammed too close to something else, would gag the festivals, marches, whistles, horns, processions, protests and music that floated incessantly through Mumbai, keeping it always on edge.

Weeks later, new national guidelines let state governments mark their own silent zones, and the government quickly sidestepped Oka's order. Oversized drums from Mumbai's rambunctious festival season would roll into the city soon, and loudspeakers would fill the streets. But Oka persisted. The state's lawyers accused him of bias and asked for his recusal. The chief justice replaced him on the noise-pollution cases. Oka's picture quickly began appearing on the television news and in newspaper sketches, with accounts of how the state had dislodged a judge who was trying to clear the miasma of conflicting interests and move the city ahead. Lawyers' associations organised packed protest meetings in support of one of the toughest judges they had faced, and Oka had to be brought back on to the case. But his victory was a pyrrhic one. The state withdrew its opposition in the High Court, only to appeal days later in the Supreme Court, which scrapped his silent zones and restrained him from passing any further orders on the issue.[2]

Oka had spent fourteen years as a judge, and more than two decades as a lawyer before that. His father, Srinivas Oka, who had died earlier that year, was a lawyer in neighbouring Thane's district courts, and Oka had taken over his grandfather's and father's busy legal practice. He must have spent his career, I thought, seeing things, growth, justice, waste plants and even clean air move forward in the courts and nearly arrive in the city, only to turn and slip sideways at the last moment.

The waste rules asked for thin layers of soil or construction debris to top the garbage mountains, keeping them stable and preventing landslides. Officials had brought in more than the usual amounts of debris from the city to fill the potholed roads that wound through the township. They filled it into gentle waves to extend the township, so that fire engines could reach its far end. They topped the mountains with debris, to bury the fires burning within and keep the mountains and their halo invisible and the garbage caravans coming.

Fires and other such disasters were usually the way that garbage mountains became visible. A few months before the committee's Deonar visit, loose garbage had tumbled down in an avalanche at the Koshe trash mountain in Addis Ababa. The city's partly consumed belongings buried pickers and their sloping homes, while they hunted for things to resell. The authorities had struggled even to get ambulances and stretchers to the mountain crevices, and pickers had fashioned stretchers from trash to bring down the injured and dead. The landslide of used belongings had probably killed more than 100 people, although ultimately no one was sure how many people had lived and died on the slopes of Mount Koshe.[3]

At Manila's vertiginous Smokey Mountain, too, garbage had tumbled down in landslides for years, burying pickers. Tired of this, the city had razed it and made mixed-use apartments, which it conducted tourist tours of. Pickers had moved to the Promised Land mountain, where waste slopes had inched higher, and garbage landslides and quiet burials had continued. At Deonar the debris would augment the mountains' noxious halo, municipal engineers told me. When fed to the incinerator, it would not burn well to produce power. But it would trap fires within the mountains. As the rains retreated that year, fires had still erupted, although not as fierce as the ones last year.

Aware that mountain luck was draining fast, the pickers tried breaking away. But there was nowhere to go. The mountains drew them back. Looking for work again, Jehangir met an agent who could get him a job filling the garbage trucks. At first he would get hired on the rolls of a private garbage-filler supplier. In a few years he would graduate to become a municipal employee, giving him an official identity card, a salary, work until he retired and a pension after that. It was one of the most vaunted jobs in these lanes.

But the municipality had asked suppliers to stop hiring garbage-fillers, being unable to afford their gushing pipeline onto its already-overfull rolls. It had already battled a court case by fillers who had worked for years, but had not made it on to the staff yet. The agent had filled Jehangir into an empty spot. While he waited for the municipal job, he had tried sidling into the space that the Khan brothers had vacated, more than a year ago. Javed Qureshi had been arrested for being a part of Atique and Rafique Khans' organised crime ring, making it hard for him to get bail. Jehangir tried collecting fees on a strip of 90 Feet Road near one the Khans had managed, until he began getting unknown calls asking if he had a fee-collection contract from the municipality for the strip. But the Khans' contract from the municipality, to collect parking fees for a part of 90 Feet Road, had expired years ago and Jehangir did not have one. He would get arrested just as they had been, the anonymous caller threatened. Alarmed, Jehangir yielded the spot and got out of trouble. His attempts at breaking away – both illegitimate and legitimate – now foiled, Jehangir returned to accumulating stuff on the mountains.

Farha often went over to see Farzana in the afternoons, after work. She usually found her sister watching movies on the television, its noise washing over her, untouched by the increasingly desperate hunt for trash that filled Farha's own days. She talked to Farzana about how she hardly saw Jehangir these days. *Is baar kuch bada soch raha hoon, dekhna* was all he would say. *I am thinking of something big this time. You watch.* Farzana hardly made it back to the family home, either. Nadeem was usually working and could not accompany her, and she was not to step out of the doorstep by herself, he had warned her, or she could end up at the mountains, pulled into their dangers again.

Only Nadeem could afford for Farzana to stay home, Farha thought. Jehana and Sahani, their older sisters, both worked on the mountains, struggling to produce food for their families. Often Farha saw Farzana in her rose-pink salwar kameez with tiny rosebuds and green stems, the one that she had worn on the evening Shaheen had visited their home and given her approval for the wedding. Farzana covered her head demurely with a dupatta and draped it around her neck, obscuring it from view. It was how middle-class women, away from the mountains' shadow, lived, Farha thought. Farzana, whom she had seen aglow in the mountain sun, afloat in its breeze, had become cocooned within the candy-pink walls of Nadeem's home. The mountains had drained out of her, Farha figured.

Sometimes Farzana's dupatta slipped, and Farha got a glimpse of her swollen neck. It made her face seem bloated too, her eyes staring. She looked a bit like she did when they had got dressed for Parveen's son's wedding. Her neck had seemed swollen then too, Farha recalled. Sometimes it ballooned on one side, pushing her face to the other side. At other times it looked swollen all around and her face seemed shrunken and yet at others her neck seemed smooth behind her flimsy dupatta.

Shaheen, too, had noticed Farzana's growing neck with alarm. She planned to ask Nadeem to take Farzana to the doctor. But these days she saw Nadeem only at night, or not at all. He worked ten hours a day ferrying city trash to the mountains in Deonar or Mulund. When Farha returned to Nadeem's house, weeks later, she saw uneven bumps rising around Farzana's neck again. Farha wondered if the wounds from her sister's accident on the slopes were reappearing from within her, bubbling under the surface of her skin.

The rains retreated, and the season of fires had returned to the township. Smoke rose from the mountains for days, filling the lanes, while fire engines doused the flames to keep them from drifting into the city. But the pickers still woke up hours before dawn, walking through the dark and empty maze of lanes of Rafiq Nagar, with its shuttered shop fronts and gambling recesses, and rose gently uphill. Half asleep, they slipped through the cracks they had hacked in the wall and walked up the trash slopes in the dark, trailing trucks, sifting for plastic bottles, gadgets and wires, torches in hand.

The lights that Judge Oka had asked for had not been installed on the slopes yet; cameras flickered. Pickers hid in dark crevices if the guards passed by, or picked until the patrols began as day broke. The first rays of the dawn guided them home, trash-filled bags in hand. As the sun rose over them, some of the women sat together and sorted through the bags, which they emptied in the lane outside their homes. They flicked away the mud and trash, making heaps of varying thicknesses of plastic and some glass all around them. They would have to sell it at *katas* further away; the long stretch of deep and roomy *katas* that curved around the wall, and had once been filled with trash by Atique and Rafique Khan, was now bolted shut.

The Khan brothers' cameras had lined these streets, and their grip had been fierce. But the women remembered with fondness their rule over life in these lanes. *Koi police ka matter rahega to vohi dekhte the na, nahi to hamari kaun sunega?* one woman said, flicking items away from a muddy tangle. *They are the ones who helped us with police matters. Otherwise, who would listen to us?* The brothers had lived close by and had lent them money when they needed it, bought their trash, employed their children and supplied cable television to their homes for years.

It was a girl, Farzana, who was to blame for the constantly patrolling security guards and the continually rebuilt wall, and not the Khans, they told me. *Main thi na us din*, one of them said. *I was there that day*. It had rained, she continued. The slopes were slippery. Farzana's foot got entangled in something, so she was stuck. The bulldozer went over her slightly, the picker recalled. *Zara sa*, she repeated. *Slightly.* She touched her index finger to her thumb to show how slightly the bulldozer had gone over Farzana.

Ab to vo theek bhi ho gayi. Farzana was married and walking around. *She is fine now.* The mountains should not get shut down because of her. The women didn't seem to know of the court cases swirling over their township. Another woman piped up, saying that she had worked there since childhood, that even her mother had picked trash. *Ham kidhar jayenge? Where else would we go?* It wasn't as if they were going to ask the municipality for anything, she said.

Moharram Ali, whom I had come to meet, dropped by with some friends and sat down to chat, not letting on that he knew Farzana or her father, from his days in Banjara Galli. He was new in the lanes of Rafiq Nagar, but these were old friends from his years of night shifts on the mountains and he seemed to know the women too. He joined in, with the group trading stories of cuts and wounds that the mountains had given them. A broken tube light had once lodged itself in his calf, Moharram Ali chortled, lifting his trousers to show them. He had hobbled home, bleeding. Later he got fifteen stitches. Did they remember? He looked at the group expectantly. They didn't. The men lifted their trousers and pulled up their shirt sleeves to reveal their own calves and arms, filled with scars, mountain memories that they laughed over. They exchanged notes on guard-patrol schedules. Best to work before the sun arose and the guards arrived.

I had found Moharram Ali only after months of walking these lanes looking for him. Yasmin had told me she wasn't sure where he lived. He didn't take her calls, and phoned her only occasionally to tell her that he did not work on the mountains. He did construction work. He told her he travelled to Pune, Navi Mumbai and other towns further away, building homes. He was away for days, he said. Then, she told me, a friend had seen him emerge from one of Rafiq Nagar's lanes, slim as a crack in a wall, their openings obscured by shops, houses and a thicket of hand-carts. He had melted into the crowd of shoppers and pickers before they could get to him. When she called to ask if it had been him, Moharram Ali told her he was working on the mountains only between construction jobs and would not be here for long. He was going back to the village. But the mountain lanes were filled with Muslims and others from the lowest rungs of the Hindu caste ladder with no land in the village, nothing to go back to.[4] Like Moharram Ali, who as a teenager had sat in a train for hours, they had made the long journey away from having nothing.

When I found him, Moharram Ali seemed gaunt, but full of his old charm. He told me, too, that he was hardly here. He spent months in his village, performing the rituals he had learned from his father. Villagers came to tell him of ailments that they believed only he could cure, he told me, beaming. A friend had come late at night and taken Moharram Ali to his cow, which had howled all evening with labour pains. Moharram Ali said he had chanted his prayers and, in less than an hour, it delivered a calf. Most of all, he performed the powerful *tohna* ritual, he told me. As he recited prayers, a sharp smell of mustard rose and filled up rooms, he said. In a few minutes the smell abated and, with it, their troubles vanished too. It seemed to resolve most problems, except his own. Debts from his sister's wedding and from the city had accumulated, and he had sold the land he bought in the village, with the gold chain he had found on the mountains. His sister had committed suicide – Moharram Ali believed that her husband had murdered her and had filed a police case, only putting him deeper in debt. He returned to the mountains, trawling for treasures already taken by city pickers. There was nowhere to go but here.

Sometimes, Moharram Ali told me, when the guards spotted his tall frame in the dark, they hurled their sticks at him. The sticks gathered speed as they travelled through the air and hit his calves or the back of his knees, flattening him with pain. If only Farzana had not brought this upon them, he thought.

At the other end of the mountains' long, looping and fragmented wall, in Padma Nagar, Farzana stayed curled in front of the television, her neck spilling into her face, her eyes glazed, bile rising in her throat. Shaheen waited for Nadeem to get an afternoon off and asked him to take Farzana to the nearby Shatabdi Hospital, where Jehangir had first taken her after she was crushed by the bulldozer.

They waited for more than an hour in its heaving corridors to see a doctor – Farzana warm and itchy in her burqa, Nadeem in a hurry to make his work shift on the truck. The doctor prescribed tests and the two left, realising on their walk back that they had forgotten to ask about her neck. A few days later Nadeem and Farzana reluctantly returned to the hospital. Pulling out the test results, the doctor told them that Farzana was pregnant.

The medical file that Farzana took home said she had no previous illnesses. Farzana had told the doctor in the overcrowded examination room that she had nothing to report. She believed that the mountains had retreated from her bones. There was nothing to say.

24

The High Court hearings began again early in 2018. It was now more than two decades since the first petitions asking to close the mountains were filed, and a decade since Justice Oka had started hearing the case. It was nearly 120 years since the swamp at Deonar began filling up. In that time the municipality's attempts to shrink the mountains had sunk into their soft, towering slopes, which were mirrored in the growing mound of papers on Oka's desk on an early January morning. A fog had arisen in the court that seemed to match the mountains' immovable halo.

Oka looked at the case papers and asked the state government's lawyers if they had provided the two plots that had been promised to the municipality, so that they could establish a new trash township to replace Deonar. The state's lawyer shook his head to say yes, the municipality's lawyer shook his head to say no.

The municipality's lawyer said that the city had paid the state an advance, but could not accept the land it was offered in Navi Mumbai, more than a decade ago. People had lived there for decades and resisted being moved out. Oka looked down and asked the state's lawyers to turn to paragraph three on a page of their submissions. He asked how the city could even begin dumping garbage at the plot when more people lived there than when it was first offered, years ago. Tribal people were settled there. They had blocked officials from even surveying the land.

The state's lawyer said that only five of the thirty-eight acres of grounds had people living on them. It could fence off these bits and give the rest to the municipality for dumping and processing waste. 'But the encroached pockets are all over the site,' Oka noted, pointing to more lines in the middle of the thick written submissions. He asked the state's lawyers to look into resettling the residents or finding new dumping grounds by the next hearing, a few weeks later.

At the next hearing, on 11 February, the municipal lawyer spoke of the gas pipeline that ran the length of the grounds. Waste heaps could not cover the pipeline, rules said. Could the pipeline be rerouted around the plot? the lawyers discussed.

Oka moved on to another plot that the state government had offered the municipality, near the soon-to-be-closed site at Mulund, within the city. Some municipal maps already showed it as garbage dumping grounds. But when officials went to survey it, some years before, the central government's salt commissioner's officers had blocked them. The land was filled with saltpans, they said; they owned it. The state government had been fighting for it, in court, for years. Unless they lost the case, salt-commission officials would not hand over the land to the state government, which had already promised it to the municipality.

On 15 March the Supreme Court allowed fresh construction in the city to restart, a little less than two years after Oka had banned it.[1] Without striking down his ban, it allowed a six-month construction window to 'explore the possibility of safe method of permitting certain constructions', bringing instant relief to the city's developers. Sharma and the monitoring committee, which still remained headless, were charged with 'preventing dispersal of particles through the air', by ensuring that Mumbai's debris-filled caravans emptied at quarries far outside the city, and not at the Deonar township. The last chairperson had left because the mountain air could sap his lungs, the court was reminded. 'Anyone will have this problem. They will have to visit,' Oka smiled, and asked for the names of possible chairpersons for the committee.

Then he turned back to the nearly two-decades-long search for grounds to replace the Deonar township. 'Why this insistence on encroached land?' he asked Ramchandra Apte, the state's lawyer. Apte responded by saying that the government would clear the encroachments at the Karvale grounds, buy the tracts it did not own and hand it all over to the municipality, soon. Oka pointed to a line saying that there were seventy-nine houses on the land. 'From your experience, Mr Apte, how many lawsuits do you think that will lead to?' Oka asked. Lawsuits from evicted residents would drag on for years, adding to the fog in court and to the paper hills, holding up the transfer of the grounds and stretching out the Deonar townships' life, he suggested.

Days later the familiar sight of the Deonar hills throwing up flames and smoke against the dark sky lit up television screens. It was the second fire in two weeks. More than a dozen fire engines sprayed water through the night and day. After all the debris that the municipality had topped the mountains with, it had reduced but not quelled the fires, which still swirled within the decaying trash. Dr Anurag Garg, a member of the court committee and professor of environmental engineering at Mumbai's Indian Institute of Technology, had asked for foam instead of water to be sprayed on Deonar's mountain fires. Water sprayed on fires would seep through the hills, absorbing trash and flowing into the creek, polluting it, he said. Foam contractors had not yet been found, either, thus keeping the water splashed on the fires flowing through the mountains into the creek.[2]

On 29 June monsoon rainstorms lashed the city. Lawyers dashed through the court's open courtyard, using case files as cover. The lawns of the Oval Maidan, a nearby recreation ground, glowed through the glass doors that lined the far end of the courtroom.

A tall, silver-haired petitioner, dressed in spotless, bone-dry white, came forward, beginning, 'Sir, we worship an invisible God and destroy visible nature.' The Ganpati festival, celebrating the arrival of the god Ganpati on Earth, would return to the city in a couple of months, bringing with it immense idols of the elephant-headed god, adorned and luminous. Ten days of feting later, they were given over to the sea, as a lesson in material detachment.

But the gods, which were said to bring good luck, were growing in number each year, clogging the sea, slowly dismembering and dissolving, leaching plaster of Paris into it. The shiny chemical paint that induced a fleeting happy haze in the city made long, shimmering toxic streaks in the water. Every year, as the gods went in, dead fish and turtles washed ashore on Mumbai's beaches. The government had made photographing the soaking, mutilated gods illegal. Now Bhagwanji Raiyani – whose first name meant God, and who was a rationalist and one of the city's best-known public-interest litigants – had filed a contempt petition against the state government for not complying with national idol-immersion norms.

The norms had been created at the court's direction a decade ago, after Raiyani filed a case. Winning the case had not helped. Court orders had not touched the gods, just as they had not reached the trash township. Raiyani, who had filed more than 100 public-interest litigations, was back in court with his contempt petition, much as Dr Rane had returned a decade ago, to bring the court's orders to the trash township. Oka pressed on, asking the state government to explain its plans for ensuring the state followed immersion guidelines that year. He gave the state's lawyer two weeks to respond and turned to direct the usually voluble and expansive Raiyani, with whom he had sparred for years: 'The petitioner will be heard, but only on compliance.' The court then turned back to the question of Deonar.

Over the decades Deonar's case had seemed nearly resolved several times. I had felt it while watching Oka at work, setting deadlines, checking if they were met, pushing to meet them. Each time I had felt as though the mountains trembled on the edge of movement. The municipality had needed only a few more weeks, and then a few more months, and each delay had stretched the mountains' life precariously on. The mountains had stayed. I heard that Oka presided over a similar case to find a new home for the High Court, allotting land in a distant suburb, and then near the new financial district. But the court had stayed where it was too.[3]

By the next hearing, on 11 July, the rain clouds had emptied out onto Mumbai for weeks and had flooded the city. A lawyer, his damp coat slung over his shoulders, swept through the courtroom to get to Oka's bench. He asked to fix Mumbai's Debt Recovery Tribunal, one of several courts set up nationwide, in 1993, to help lenders recover their dues from bankrupt companies. 'Sir, it is like a swimming pool. I was there this morning. There was water up to my knees. Can they deny it?' The tribunal's sole judge was still in Kolkata, at the far end of the country, since he had not been given a place to stay, the lawyer went on. The judge had paid for his own hotel room when he last came for a hearing, the lawyer said, pulling out crumpled hotel bills from his voluminous coat pockets.

The government did want the court to function, the central government's lawyer defended. It had even put out advertisements for a new judge to replace the one stuck in Kolkata, but no one had applied. 'Why would anyone apply?' Oka asked, smiling. He set deadlines for renovating the tribunal's office and courtroom.[4] But it was the endless years of missed deadlines that had led to Mumbai's courtrooms pooling with water and to judges remaining in Kolkata, the gods stuck painfully between Heaven and Earth, and which had swelled and lengthened the distant mountains at Deonar.

Elsewhere, on the spreading edges of Delhi, some trash peaks had risen so high that they nearly touched the power lines looping into the city. When pickers, immersed in the search for trash, brushed against these wires, they died of electrocution. Days before the courtroom in Mumbai had flooded, garbage had tumbled down in a landslide in Delhi, killing a picker and bringing the capital's trash mountains into the view of the Supreme Court, which asked Delhi's municipality to shrink and fix them.[5]

At the next Deonar hearing on 25 July, Oka began by reading the response the state government had filed that morning. He read and looked up, surprised. It said that the land at Mulund was rented out to a private salt-maker, who harvested salt there and had sued the salt commissioner, also in Mumbai's High Court. This case too had gone on in the same rambling court building for more than a decade, unknown to Oka. He asked Apte what the chances were of the municipality getting the land. 'Bleak? Very bleak?'

As Oka had pushed on in court, the distant hamlet at Karvale in Navi Mumbai, which had been allotted for the replacement of the Deonar township years ago, had withered to a stub. Some months later, when I visited, it was a green expanse filled only with streams, the empty husks of homes and the shadow of the Haji Malang shrine, which towered on a hill above. When Farzana had drifted between their world and the netherworld at Sion Hospital, Afsana had gone to visit the shrine of Haji Malang, said to be the saint of common people. She brought back a bracelet, which she tied to Farzana's wrist. It had tugged her back into the world of the living, Afsana believed.

Just before Farzana's wedding, Farzana, Afsana and her in-laws had walked up the last stretches of the rocky cliff to the shrine. They thanked the saint for Farzana's improbable life. The sisters had sat at the edge of the cliff, soaking in the breeze, the last fragments of Farzana's single life and the unending spread of green that lay ahead, with slim streams shining through it. They didn't know then that their putrid mountains and their spirits could come to fill a patch of it one day.

While Farzana conducted her pilgrimage, in the hamlet

below the shrine residents were meeting their representatives, who promised to keep their homes in place. They thought of filing a court case, but their representatives did not think there was any need. The city's endless trash caravans would not make the bumpy two-hour journey to deposit trash here. Besides, they could hardly afford to pay for a lawyer, perhaps for years; and even getting to the court from here would be hard. But as Oka piled pressure on the municipality, the representatives had returned empty-handed. By the time I visited, in the autumn of that year, police had evicted the residents into boiling tin-sheet homes that lined the edges of the plot instead.

A little more than a year later I was listening to Oka give a talk to law students.[6] He said that he had no memory of why he switched to study law, nearly four decades ago. At first he got cases only from litigants who could not afford better lawyers – cases with no hope of winning. 'When you connect with such litigants, you learn what life is about. After becoming a judge I realised ... the real challenge before our legal system is not of docket [legal case file] explosion but of docket exclusion.' While the unending pile of pending cases clogging up Indian courts had often been spoken about, Oka suggested, the bigger problem was that people like Farzana and those in Karvale stayed invisible in the courts.

As the rains ebbed and Mumbai's warm winter settled in the city, the question of whether its trash would arrive at Farzana's mountain community or at the hamlet in Karvale's green valley remained. Municipal lawyers had asked for more time. At a hearing during the Christmas break, municipal lawyers announced that the city would need at least three more years to reroute the trash caravans away from Deonar. It had extended the deadline for bids for the waste-to-energy plant at Deonar seven times, but no bids had come. One of the reasons no company had bid to make the plant, a presentation by Tata Consulting Engineers had shown, was that they wanted Deonar's township without its towering mountains of garbage. Moving them would be too expensive and arduous, making the plant unviable. The municipality had scrapped the plan and decided to make three smaller waste-to-energy plants at Deonar instead. The first of these would only be ready in 2023. The court extended the Deonar township's life until Justice Oka could hear the case again, after the holidays, in the new year.

25

Throughout the summer of 2018 Farzana's stomach had swollen. Perched on her ballooning throat, her face grew too. Fevers came and went. Most mornings, after Nadeem left for work, she spread a bedcover in front of the television and watched until sleep drifted over and shut her eyelids. Music from Hindi action movies from the eighties washed over her. Sidekicks died, lovers reunited and credits rolled. Farzana woke up, switched channels and stayed in place.

Shaheen had asked Nadeem to show Farzana's neck to the doctors when they went to Shatabdi Hospital. But somehow Farzana was always too exhausted when she arrived in the room packed with pregnant women, and Nadeem had to return for his shifts. Twice they were halfway home when they thought of her distended neck, carefully covered under her dupatta and billowing black burqa.

At home, Farzana's movements shrank as her belly and neck grew. Her neck had stiffened, making her face look stuffy and sour. Her arms itched, filled with long, pink scars from the stitches that covered her carefully held-together bones. The next time she sat across from the doctor, Farzana unwrapped her burqa and dupatta to show her swollen neck. She pulled up her sleeve to show the doctor her arm. *Bulldozer chad gaya tha*, Farzana explained softly. *A bulldozer ran over me.*

The doctor looked up, surprised. She asked Farzana to bring her case papers from the treatment at Sion Hospital. At the next visit she rifled through the thick file that Nadeem had asked Hyder Ali to send over. A heavily pregnant woman stood behind Farzana, waiting for her to vacate the shiny examination stool. Others in the queue outside poked their heads into the room. The doctor shut the file and told Farzana to go back to Sion Hospital. Farzana was relieved to have avoided the inspection of her old wounds. She returned to her spot in front of the television, absent-mindedly scratching her arms.

To bring Farzana home for childbirth, Hyder Ali would have to take gifts for Nadeem's family. He tried working on the mountains in order to save up for the gifts. But, running into Yasmin in their lane one afternoon, he told her how life on them was not as it had been. Security guards crushed his trash bags under their vehicles, or asked for so much money that there was nothing left after a morning's work. Farha had found a gold chain while scouring for trash a few weeks ago, but Hyder Ali didn't say anything about it to Yasmin, and Farha later told me it was fake. It's all that came to the mountains these days, she shrugged.

As the mountain treasures shrank, Moharram Ali had travelled further out in search of jobs, returning home empty-handed, to an empty house. His new wife had left him, tired of waiting for his get-rich plans to work. He called Yasmin and asked her and the children if he could move back in. *Phir chala gaya to?* she asked Hyder Ali.

What if he leaves again? Meri usse koi ummeed nahi rahi, she said softly, almost to herself. *I have no hope in him left.*

The summer wore on and Nadeem stayed busy, travelling in the garbage caravans through the nights and during the day. Farha began accompanying Farzana on hospital visits. On their way they walked along the outer edge of the mountains' long, carious wall. From the outside, they watched people climb through cracks onto the slopes where they had spent so much of their lives, observing cricket games, evading the buffaloes wandering up the parched hills and chasing garbage trucks. Farha now worked alone on the mountains.

They passed by the parking strip that Jehangir had relinquished. At the same time Jehangir seemed consumed by a new business, Farha told Farzana. All she knew was that this time it was not in trash. He had told them he was going to do something different – something that would take him away from the mountains. He spoke constantly to his business partner, who sounded like a woman, or to his men. Around the mountains Jehangir, and others, nipped at the edges of the gang bosses' sprawling fiefdom of illegalities.

As Farzana's time for childbirth drew close, Hyder Ali worked desultorily and waited for Nadeem to bring her over to his house. On 8 July Shaheen called to say the baby was on its way, and late that night Farzana gave birth to a baby girl. Waking up in a haze of sleep and pain, she saw her sisters huddled over the baby, exclaiming how she looked just like Nadeem. Shaheen draped a quilt over the baby that she had made from patched-together cloth scraps collected from the mountains, and then relented, letting Farzana go to Hyder Ali's house from the hospital.

Shakimun ripped up white cloth, filled it with cumin and turmeric and tied it into two small bundles, attaching one to the baby's wrist and the other to Farzana's. These would trap spirits within them, forming a shield around Farzana and the baby in these early months when they could fall prey to illnesses, sadnesses or spirit possessions that could hold them in their grip for ever.

They stayed wrapped together, mother and daughter. Farzana babbled to her baby all day and late into the night. She spoke endlessly until *Guddi*, meaning 'little doll', became *Buddhi*, meaning 'old woman'. *Tune suna, Guddi? Tera kuch bhi nahi hai. Kuch bhi? Sab there Abba se aaya,* she whispered, wiggling the baby's nose or cheeks until she cried. *Did you hear, Guddi? Nothing you have belongs to you. Nothing at all. It all came from your father.* Farzana picked up and swung the baby in her arms to calm her.

Weeks later, when Farzana went home, Shaheen had stitched more quilts from mountain scraps to wrap the baby in. She laid out the largest cloth she had and covered it with scraps in a deep shade that was called chocolatey in Marathi and Mumbai Hindi, but that could be maroon, brown, plum or dark purple; emerald green, like the grass that grew on the mountains after the rains; and a pink so intense it could be purple. She edged the quilt with a slim border of baby-pink. But Shaheen was alarmed to see Farzana. Her neck was so swollen that her face was frozen in place and she had to look from the corner of her eye to see sideways.

Days later, Farha called Farzana and asked her to switch on the news. *Bhai hai. Brother's on.* Jehangir's face, covered with a scarf, flashed on the television news, with a voiceover giving his name and age. Police had busted a kidnapping ring of five, including Jehangir, and had released a child that the gang had held for ransom.

With a succession of businesses floundering and his mountain clearings flattened, Jehangir had made one last ambitious plan to break away from the mountains. A friend from their lane had introduced him to a woman whose brother-in-law was a wealthy businessman in the city. Police would later allege that she wanted to kidnap his son for ransom, giving Jehangir and his friend a portion of the money.[1]

On the evening in question, it was claimed, she led the target to Jehangir and his friend, who covered his face with a scarf, bundling him into a rickshaw. The boy cried the whole way to the garage in a mountain lane, where they planned to keep him until they got the money, feeding him cough syrup with a cold drink. When they unwrapped the scarf from his face, they discovered it was their target's thirteen-year-old older brother. This could get them even more money, Jehangir thought. He rehearsed the ransom call. But before they could make it, police stormed the *kata*, released the boy and arrested Jehangir and his gang of conspirators.

Sanjay Nagar's lanes were abuzz with news of Jehangir's arrest. Pickers saw his covered face in the newspapers, on television and in messages travelling through phones in their lanes. Hyder Ali did not have the money to hire a lawyer or post bail. I tried calling him, but cellphones in these lanes flickered with mountain luck: pickers topped them up only after a good trash haul, and so Hyder Ali's phone usually stayed dead. I ran into him, outside his house, one afternoon. Hyder Ali noticed me look him up and down, and said he was not there. I asked him about Jehangir's arrest. *Ham hote to zaroor bataate*, he said. *If I was here, I would tell you.* An hour or so later, when I was still there, he walked me out of Banjara Galli. *Hamein kuch pata nahi tha*, he said, his voice turning hoarse with shame. *I didn't know anything.* We walked out of Banjara Galli in silence.

Days later, Shakimun and Hyder Ali arrived at Shaheen's house holding a cradle, with coloured ribbons wrapped all round the metal frame. He had saved up to buy it and placed it against the wall where Farzana had spent her days slumped during her pregnancy. She had vacated the spot now, walking around, ferrying things for the baby, piling soiled clothes for her sister-in-law to wash, folding washed clothes, cradling the baby to sleep while talking to her the whole time. *Guddi, tu samjhi na? Teri naak kiske jaisi hai? Teri aankh kiske jaisi hai? Doll, you understand, right? Who does your nose look like? Whose are your eyes like?*

A few weeks after Jehangir's arrest I accompanied Farzana, her throat spilling into her face, to Nair Hospital to see Dr Satish Dharap, who headed the team of surgeons who had operated on her two years ago. He looked at her yellowing case papers, asking how she was and going over her treatment, and the metal rods in her bones.

She nodded, unwrapping her burqa to show her neck while holding onto the baby. As he gently pressed and prodded the bumps around it, Farzana winced in pain. She did get fevers, and it was painful, she said in reply to his questions. They would have to extract the fluid within and test it, he told me. It could be cancer, or perhaps tuberculosis.

Farzana returned a few days later for the procedure, with Farha holding the baby while doctors took her sister into a procedure room. A little later the nurse called Farha in; with her neck wrapped in blood and gauze, stained with yellow ointment, Farzana sobbed softly, helplessly, drooling onto her cheek and the rubber sheet that covered her metal cot. With her burqa gone, Farzana's legs and hands coiled tightly into spindly V-shapes. Her pink lace kurta, lined with satin, puffed around her, glinting in the late-afternoon light.

Farha watched and then slid the baby into her arms. Farzana's tears rolled onto her daughter's soft, nearly bald head. *Buddi, teri aankh kiske jaisi hai?* she whispered, breaking into a weak smile even as tears rolled down her cheeks. *Old woman, you know who your eyes belong to?* She babbled softly, holding the baby close, feeding her even as she cried.

Slowly Farzana spread her palm to grip the bed and lifted herself up. She put on her burqa, lifted the baby and set off for home with Farha. They waited at the bus stop across the street from the hospital, watching the late-afternoon light turn dusky and then dark. It was an immersion day during the Ganpati festival, and pot-bellied idols in giddily happy colours moved slowly through cars, buses and drilling machines that dug into Mumbai's slim roads, turning them to dust in preparation for Mumbai's metro transit lines. The baby howled. Thumping from the outsize drums rose over the buzz of drills and horns and was intermittently drowned out by them. Traffic stopped for construction, then construction stopped for traffic, both moving fitfully in a jagged dance to Mumbai's accidental orchestra. Farzana stepped onto the street, baby in her arms, to look out for buses that would take her home. She saw them waiting stationary in the distance, then move slowly towards her before turning away.

Nadeem called. Why had Farzana not reached home yet? She was still near the hospital? How could the bus take so long to arrive? Had she really gone to the hospital? It was nearly midnight by the time Farzana got home. The next day Nadeem, sulking from the previous night, dropped her at Hyder Ali's house with instructions to stay away from the mountains, their men and their hazards. Farzana slept for days, enclosing the baby within her arms. She had tried allaying Nadeem's fears and had stayed away from the mountains that loomed above, for the most part.

One afternoon Shakimun sat at the mountains' edge and watched Farzana walk by with the baby. *Kaam kaise karein? How do I work?* she asked me. Her son was in jail, her daughter sick. *Fikar khaye jaa rahi hai,* she said, inhaling deeply from her *bidi,* or unfiltered cigarette. *Worry is eating away at us.* She thought of sending Hyder Ali back to the healer on 90 Feet Road as she watched the sun turn pink and inch into the hills.

When Farzana returned to the hospital, alone except for the baby, to hear her test results, the doctor told her she had tuberculosis. He told her he would prescribe daily medication; stopping the medication might mean the infection turned deadly and wouldn't respond to the medicines, even if she restarted them. Farzana interrupted impatiently to say that she would go to a doctor near her house and begin treatment there.

She knew tuberculosis haunted the pickers. She had watched it whittle down Badre Alam, Hyder Ali's cousin who had lived in their loft for months, until he left for his village. They had not heard from him for more than two months and Hyder Ali feared he had died, until Badre Alam had reappeared, a week or so ago, his cheeks filled, his face shining. A healer's rituals and his wife's care had cured him, he said. But Farzana knew that not everyone returned, as he had. Some of her childhood friends had come to work on the mountains after tuberculosis had wasted their parents away, only to be consumed in their turn by the insatiable appetite of the peaks.

A few days later Farzana bundled up the baby, collected a bag filled with clothes and towels and went with Alamgir to Arthur Road Jail to meet Jehangir. At every previous visit Jehangir had instructed his brother, *Farzana ka khayal rakhna. Look after Farzana.* Alamgir teased him, asking if he had any other brothers and sisters? *Hain ...* Jehangir trailed off. *I do.* When Alamgir broke in, *Par tu usko hi sabse zyada chahta hai? But you love her the most?*, Jehangir would only say, *Bhejna usko. Send her to meet me.*

Farzana was ushered into a room with a glass screen. Jehangir walked in and sat on the other side. *Kaisa hai, bhai?* Farzana asked softly into the phone on her side. *How are you, brother?* Jehangir nodded, looking at the baby. Farzana picked her up and held her against the glass screen. *Teri beti hai? Your daughter?* Farzana nodded to say yes. *Achhi hai,* he replied. *She's lovely.* The siblings looked at each other. They had both so nearly left the mountains and their shadow, but the slopes had lingered within them both, holding them in their grip, keeping them back. The guards came in to tell Farzana to leave. *Tu theek hai na?* Jehangir asked. *You are okay, right?* She nodded.

A few days later someone from Nair Hospital called me, asking if Farzana had her medicine regularly and for her bank-account details, so they could transfer the government subsidy for TB patients. I went over to her house to ask her and found her playing with the baby, whom they had named Ayesha, the wise one. She had stopped the medication a while ago. It made me dizzy, Farzana said. It brought a darkness in front of her eyes. Sahani later told me that Nadeem had not bought any more.

Farzana's fevers raged and abated, her neck swelled and seemed to shrink. But she was immersed in the baby, who was getting taller, plumper and gave gummy smiles. *Guddi, Guddi, tujhe pata hai na, teri hasee teri nahi hai? Doll, you know that smile is not yours, right?* Farzana tickled her nose, making Ayesha break into peals of laughter. In Farzana's babbling, Ayesha grew from a baby to an old woman, but nothing would ever belong to her. It would all come from her father, from the mountains that rose behind them and, endlessly, in caravans, from the city.

Tujhe pata hai na, teri naak bhi teri nahi hai? You know, right, even your nose is not yours? Buddhi, Buddhi, tera kuch bhi tera nahi hai, theek hai? Old woman, old woman, nothing you have belongs to you, all right?

Postscript

In the first week of 2019 I walked up the court's grand stone staircase to the second floor. Justice Oka's cases and his courtroom had been reassigned. The Deonar case had moved with him.

As I arrived at the dark landing I saw a marble plaque engraved with the words of Bal Gangadhar Tilak, a freedom fighter who had been convicted of sedition against the British state in 1908,[1] in the courtroom that lay behind it. 'There are higher powers that rule the destiny of men and nations and it may be the will of providence that the cause which I represent may prosper more by my suffering than by my remaining free,' he had said after the judge, Justice Dinshaw Davar, had ruled against him.

By a quirk of fate, in 1897 Justice Davar, then a lawyer, had defended Tilak against sedition charges while the plague raged through Bombay and neighbouring Pune, where Tilak lived.[2] As the anger over the invasion of British troops into homes, lives and bodies grew, Tilak had written a veiled attack on the British plague campaign in his newspaper *Kesari*. Government lawyers had accused him of bringing tensions to a boil and of inciting the murder of W. C. Rand, the chairperson of Pune's plague committee, and Tilak was sentenced to eighteen months in jail, which only inflamed the anger in both cities. A few weeks later *cuchra* trains had begun ferrying Bombay's trash to the swampy dumping grounds at Deonar. The plague abated, prosperity returned and the city's bounty was consumed, discarded, ferried and eventually dumped in the distant marsh that began rising, unseen, in the city.

In the mountains' 120th year, the attempts to deal with Mumbai's waste township, to shrink the toxic halo that spread over the city and the illnesses it created, floundered on in a room further down the corridor. I turned the corner into Oka's new courtroom, so outsize and empty. His voice came like a distant, echoing muffle, discussing a criminal case: 'Where did they find the body?'

Then the familiar thud of the Deonar files fell onto his desk. Had the officials who had avoided telling him of all the court cases around the proposed Mulund dumping grounds been punished yet? Oka asked. When would the land to make a modern, new township of trash get handed over? Most importantly, how soon could Deonar's township of trash close? It nearly had, the municipality's lawyers told him, sensing Oka's familiar indignation. The garbage caravans now mostly went to the modern trash hills at Kanjurmarg. I had seen these hills rising across the creek when I stood on the trash peaks at the outer edge of the Deonar township. Trash hills had been rising there for five years and would be taken apart next year, as compost.

On 9 April 2019 Oka passed an order: this would be the last year for the township of trash.[3] No new garbage could be dumped there after 31 December 2019. The old hills would slowly begin flattening or would turn to power or compost. The next day Oka was transferred to become the chief justice of the High Court in the neighbouring state of Karnataka.

I continued to visit the mountains and the lanes around them, waiting for the garbage caravans to stop arriving at Deonar's hills, for the contract for the waste plants to be given out, for new trash townships to begin. The caravans had dwindled but not stopped. It was all about to happen, municipal engineers told me.

At the mountains I ran into Jehana. Had she heard about the townships' final closure? In return, she asked if I had heard about Asif. Surely I knew him, she said; and I nodded, although I was in fact unsure whether I had met him. Asif went to school and worked on the mountains in the afternoons, pickers told me. He was fourteen. A little over a week ago he had been chased by a guard patrol. His friends had slipped away towards their homes, but Asif had kept running, straight ahead towards the creek. The guards stayed behind, following him. Then he had vanished from sight.

When his friends returned to Rafiq Nagar, Afsana, his mother, had asked where he was. Asif must be coming, they told her. Maybe the guards had detained him or he was hiding until they left. When dusk fell, she went looking for him, staying out all night. She asked at a guard post, but they had not seen him. The next day Afsana complained at the police station. She accompanied police officers to the slopes, but they could not find Asif. The guards and police looked for him for days, but they had not found him. Did he escape on a raft? they asked. He didn't, she said. Soon after that, Asif began appearing in his mother's dreams. He smiled, he spoke to her, saying he was close by. She had to find him, Afsana told me, when I went to meet her.

Every morning Afsana left for the mountains with the day-shift pickers. She looked in the thorny bushes, leafless in the summer heat. She walked to older clearings where trash no longer emptied, and waded chest-deep into the plastic-filled mangroves. She returned after the night-shift pickers began working, having seen no sign of him.

Afsana borrowed money, hired a boat and floated around the edges of the township to see if Asif had got stuck in the soft mud at the creek's edge, entangled in the plastic or the tree roots that swam in the water, or been washed further away with the effluent that gushed into the creek.

Pickers had begun to say that he must have jumped into the creek to avoid the guards. But he would have washed ashore by now, Afsana replied. He might have got kidnapped by organ-traffickers so that they could harvest his kidney, people said, as rumours floated around the mountains. But Asif still appeared in Afsana's dreams. She felt he was close. She had to find him. For months she left every morning, with his photograph, and returned only after dark. She showed me the picture of Asif in a beige salwar suit: his baby face, his still-pudgy cheeks, his unrelenting smile.

In my years of walking the mountains I had seen children's sandals with sunflowers blooming on them; shimmering, half-empty bottles of perfume that felt like gifts that people had tired of. I wondered what part they had played in the lives of their owners – whether they had made the relationships far from the mountains deeper, and the people who received the gifts more precious. I saw Afsana walk the mountains with Asif's photo. He came in her dreams. He stayed close to her. She had to find him.

On another visit I met Atique Khan, the younger of the Khan brothers, released on bail after three years in jail.

He had nothing to do with the mountains or the fires, he told me. His acolytes had misused his name. The wall had always been broken, fires occurred often. *Ham jhukte nahi na, to hame mohra banaya gaya*, he said, speaking of himself and his brother, Rafique. *We don't bend to anyone, so we were made into pawns.*

Farzana was pregnant again. Sometimes when her dupatta slid, her swollen neck emerged. At other times it stayed hidden, or perhaps had even deflated. Her doctors had seen it at prenatal check-ups: they told her to take a test for tuberculosis. She returned to hospital solely to deliver a baby boy.

I saw Jehangir only in court, where his children arrived in make-up and puffy clothes, as if visiting him was a festive occasion. *Maine phone to kiya hi nahi tha to phirauti kaise hua?* he would tell me, always looking for loopholes to get through. *I had not made the phone call, so how can they charge me with asking for a ransom?*

When I walked through Banjara Galli I sometimes heard my name and turned sharply to see a golden head hanging sideways, grinning at me. Standing in the lane, blocking the sun, Sameer, Yasmin's younger son, dropped his head down to his shoulder to greet me in a characteristic gesture. He had kept working in the area's overfull dustbins, pulling much-needed money out of their depths. Moharram Ali had finally disappeared for good. Yasmin had fallen at the railway station on the way to a medical trial, losing her front teeth and any remnants of her youth. Then she developed tuberculosis, barring her from the medical trials; and so did Hera. Mehrun had stayed out of school and got engaged in November 2020, at seventeen.

One afternoon I turned a corner into the lane to find the fragrance of jasmine filling it. Salma stood in a huddle, collecting the blossoms from a woman who was giving them out to be strung into garlands that she would sell. We walked up to Salma's house, with me matching her slow, shuffling walk. Every winter bumps appeared in her eyes, she told me. Everything got hazy. How was Aslam? I asked. *Vo to do hafte pehle off ho gaya*, she said softly. *He went off two weeks ago*, using the Mumbai expression for having died. For years tuberculosis, alcohol and other mountain addictions had swirled through Aslam, never completely draining from him until they consumed him.

Vitabai had taken on several cleaning jobs in the city, getting loans from bosses to treat her children's illnesses, to get a grandchild operated on after he fell off the roof, and to fix the house when it collapsed. She had to keep working, keep repaying, keep taking more. It kept her movement frenetic, her eyes dancing, as they were when I first met her, although I watched her arms sag, her rolling walk slow.

I often ended my walks at Hyder Ali's house, where he told me of his plans to raise money and post Jehangir's bail, hosting me with mountain finds. Once he tried getting me to sit on a pillowy-soft, black leather couch that I imagined had come from the house of a wealthy young couple. I sat down on the ground across from him, as always. He told me he was planning to sell the house to hire a lawyer for Jehangir. Where would they all live? I asked, thinking about the cast of generations that floated in and out of the house. At that moment Jehana's sixteen-year-old daughter, Muskaan, walked in, bent and halting. She curled up and lay down on the floor beside me. *Dekhenge*, he replied. *We'll see*. Muskaan was recovering from tuberculosis,

Hyder Ali told me. I remembered her – tall, feline and glowing – from Farzana's wedding photographs.

The next time I visited, Muskaan slept on the floor, where the couch had been. Where did it go? I asked. Hyder Ali laughed. Bedbugs from it had infested the house and had bitten everyone, and he had had to throw it out. He asked for tea in a porcelain teaset once; another time for water from a crystal glass – the person delivering it for him stepping over Muskaan on the floor, never fully awake or asleep.

The following time I went, tea and water came in steel tumblers. The front section of the house had collapsed in the rain, delaying Hyder Ali's plans to sell it. Had I heard, he asked, that Muskaan died three days ago? She had lost even the energy to get to his house by then, and lay in Jehana's house at the mountains' edge, too drained to flick away the flies that buzzed on her. The late-afternoon sun streamed in, drying her mouth. Jehana was getting Muskaan some water to drink and, when she turned back, Muskaan was gone, Jehana told me.

With work erratic, Hyder Ali had gone to his village. He returned with instructions: everyone needed to remember his grandfather's name. In December 2019 the Indian government passed the Citizenship Amendment Act that made it legal for Muslims who could not provide paperwork and proof of citizenship to be held in detention camps or deported. Outside Farzana's lane I saw a banner: *Vo kehte hain, Hindustan chod dein ham. Batao, bhoot ke dar se makaan chod dein ham? They want us to leave India. Tell us, should we abandon our home because it is haunted by a ghost?*

At Hyder Ali's home, the front of the house had gone back up, the plan to sell and post Jehangir's bail revived. In her home, Farzana repeated her great-grandfather's name.

No one was sure what the information was that they needed to tell officials when they came asking – information that would turn them into legal citizens – since they were not sure they had the right papers for it. They learned what they could and prepared for an interrogation that might, in a single movement, make them illegal occupants in their country.

As the months passed, Sharma worried that the court hearings to ensure the closure of the township had not yet begun. The case was never listed again for hearing at the Supreme Court. The six-month window for fresh construction in the city carried on without end.

In December 2019 hearings restarted in the Bombay High Court, with Justice S. C. Dharmadhikari now presiding over Deonar's fate. It was not the job of the court to set deadlines, he said. The municipality was working on closing the township of trash. Projects such as the waste plant do take time, he stated, as he stretched on the life of the township in orders passed on 19 December 2019.[4] On 6 November 2020 the municipality passed a plan to make a waste-to-energy plant that would consume 600 tonnes of waste at the Deonar township – a little less than half of what arrived every day by then.[5] It would take three years to arrive, they thought.

In February 2021, the Indian government announced a $40 billlion plan to reduce the country's worsening air pollution by shrinking its garbage mountains or 'legacy waste' and managing its construction debris.

The case for negligent driving and causing injury to Farzana, by accident, against Hashim Khan (known as Nanhe) never came up for hearing. He remains on bail.

Notes

Chapter 1

1   The townships' area varied from 270 to 326 acres in various official documents. After the fires the municipality was said to have dumped earth, extending the township further into the sea. Property ownership papers showed it to be 314 acres.
2   The height of the highest mountains was said to be 120 feet in the project report made by the municipality-appointed Tata Consulting Engineers. They had done drone surveys to arrive at these measures.
3   Throughout my research, I listened to stories of ghosts and spirits who haunted the mountainside, and while I did not endorse them myself, thinking them more likely to be the result of the teller's unlikely lives or the poisonous gases present on the mountain slopes, I understood that those who did had powerful emotional reasons for doing so.

Chapter 2

1   'Other Phenomena' section in the health officer's

account in the annual administration report of the municipal commissioner's report for 1896.

2 Gyan Prakash, *Mumbai Fables*, HarperCollins, 2011. Prakash goes on to record the exodus of residents from Bombay over the next few months, due to the plague and plague-removal measures making it a 'City of Dead'.

3 Myron Echenberg, *Plague Ports: The Global Urban Impact of Bubonic Plague 1894–1901*, NYU Press, 2007.

4 In his report, Bombay's municipal commissioner P. C. H. Snow stated, 'Dr Weir in trying to arrive at the probable causes of the epidemic lights on the theory of migration of people from plague stricken districts.'

5 'Bombay Plague Visitation', British Library; https://blogs.bl.uk/asian-and-african/2020/07/bombay-plague-visitation-1896-97.html.

6 Snow quotes Weir recommending quarantine 'or any other name by which inspection of traffic and restriction of communication may be called, stringent and careful examination of everyone entering Bombay and careful disinfection of every article, but the result to be expected from that measure is very uncertain'.

7 Municipal commissioner's report for 1896–7.

8 Health officer's account in the municipal commissioner's report. Parsi women surrounded a Hindu boy to prevent officers taking the boy to hospital.

9 'Escape from Ambulance. A pitiful case', in the municipal commissioner's report for 1896.

10 Snow in the municipal commissioner's report. 'Officers of the health department were charged with a brutal pleasure in dragging the sick from the

homes and in killing them, and it was stated that our Sovereign Lady The Queen had demanded 500 livers of the people of Bombay to appease the wrath aroused at the insult offered to her statue. Men have said to me "You think we are like mad dogs and you want to kill us, as if we were."'

11 From Snow's report. The room, in Khara Talao, that held fifty-seven people was 111 feet in length and 18½ feet in width, with no ventilation.

12 From Snow's report, in the section 'Desire to Wander in Delirium'.

13 From the municipal commissioner's report, which states that 'a number of influential citizens' wrote to him, on 14 October, a week after the plague measures had been imposed. They said that if the measures were enforced, a 'much larger number of inhabitants would fly from Bombay'.

14 Weir wrote of the night he and Snow met the police commissioner, with the crowds swirling outside. The police commissioner and the health officer 'were of the opinion that our sanitary staff would make common cause with the rioters, nor was it possible to ascertain in a time of such wild panic and excitement how far the fine discipline of the Bombay Police would avail'.

15 Executive engineer's account in the municipal commissioner's report for 1897–8.

16 Executive engineer's account in the municipal commissioner's report for 1899.

17 The bund was completed on 15 December 1901, according to the executive engineer's account in the municipal commissioner's report.

18 Executive engineer's account in the municipal
   commissioner's report.

19 *Times of India* Proquest Archive. Among the stories
   dating back to the early sixties is one about the
   residents of a *chawl*, or tenement, near Vitabai's house
   in central Bombay. The municipality had ripped out
   the door and window frames and the tiled roof, and
   withdrew the power and water supply, while some
   residents battled in court to stay on, rather than move
   to Deonar. The court eventually asked them to move.

20 Lisa Björkman, *Pipe Politics, Contested Waters:
   Embedded Infrastructures of Millennial Mumbai*, Duke
   University Press, 2015. Björkman shows how the
   slums around the mountains were planned and legally
   settled and yet demolished later. Stories from the
   Times of India archive chronicle the same.

21 https://www.livemint.com/Money/f0Rtetble3Chhd5
   P0AZ2KJ/Loan-approvals-depend-on-borrowers8217-
   address.html.

22 Shalini Nair, 'Gases Spook Comps in IT Park Built on
   Dump', *Times of India*, 2 April 2007. Also interview
   with Amiya Sahu, founder of the National Solid
   Waste Association of India, who tested and found
   gases from trash floating in the newly made corporate
   offices.

Chapter 3

1 Municipal Solid Wastes (Management and Handling)
  Rules (2000).

Chapter 4

1 From court orders passed by Justice D. Y. Chandrachud on 7 July 2009 in the Bombay High Court; https://bombayhighcourt.nic.in/generatenewauth. php?bhcpar=cGFoaDouL3dyaXRlcmVhZGRhdGEvZ GFoYS9vcmlnaW5hW5hbC8yMDA5LyZmbmFtZT1iDT05 QVzI2MDgwNzA3MDkucGRmJnNtZmxhZzz1OJn-JqdWRkYXRlPSZIcGxvYWRkDomc3Bhc3Nwa HJhc2U9MTAwMTIxMjIyNDI w.

2 From the petition filed by residents of Shanti Park/ Sorento against the Municipal Corporation of Greater Mumbai (MCGM) in 1996, obtained through the Right to Information Act from MCGM.

3 A study by the National Environmental Engineering Research Institute (NEERI) conducted in 1994 found Suspended Particulate Matter (SPM) to be 1,431 Mu/ gm^3 in twenty-four hours in the lanes around the mountains. The National Air Quality standards had set up to 200 Mu/gm^3 in twenty-four hours as the acceptable limit. This study was cited by residents of Shanti Park in their petition against the municipal corporation.

4 Petitioners quoted municipal findings in their court affidavit showing that the lead content in mountain air was two and a half times the permissible limits.

5 Petition by Shanti Park 'Sorento' Coop Housing Society Ltd and Others v. MCGM and others. They asked for police patrols, fire engines and water tankers to curb fires and a telephone number to complain on, when the smoke increased at night.

6 Details on Interstitial Lung Disease were given by Dr Kumar Doshi, a chest physician, in a letter to Dr

Rane that was included in Rane's contempt petition.
Dr Vikas Oswal, a well-known pulmonologist
who practises in the lanes around the mountains,
confirmed that he saw more Interstitial Lung Disease
in these lanes than elsewhere in the city, and that half
his patients arrived with respiratory diseases. Other
doctors confirmed this.

7 Men living near the illegal landfills in Campania
province in Italy had a 35.9 in 100,000 rate of dying
from liver cancer, compared to 14 in the rest of Italy.
Women had a 20.5 in 100,000 rate of dying from liver
cancer, compared to 6 in the rest of Italy. From a
study entitled 'Italian "Triangle of death" linked to
waste crisis' published in *The Lancet* in September
2004; https://www.thelancet.com/journals/lanonc/
article/PIIS147020450401561X/fulltext.

8 Rs 10,500 crore landfill fixing project, taken from
tender documents.

9 Among project and tender details for this project,
obtained through the Right to Information Act, were
letters to this effect.

10 Findings of high levels of formaldehyde were
communicated by NEERI to Dr Rane in March 2009,
according to court orders, while causes of death were
presented from a study quoted here: https://www.
downtoearth.org.in/news/gas-chembur-2658.

11 Dipanjali Majumdar and Anjali Srivastava, 'Volatile
Organic Compound Emissions from Municipal Solid
Waste Sites: A Case Study of Mumbai, India', NEERI,
2012.

12 Municipal Corporation of Greater Mumbai, *Human
Development Report*, Oxford University Press, 2009.

13 From court orders passed by Justice D. Y. Chandrachud on 8 May 2009 in the Bombay High Court;
https://bombayhighcourt.nic.in/generatenewauth.
php?bhcpar=cGFoaDouL3dyaXRlcmVhZGRhdGE
vZGFoYS9vcmlnaW5hW5hbC8yMDA5LyZmbmFtZT1D
To5QVzI2MDgwODAiMDkucGRmJnNtZmxhZz1O-
JnJqdWRkYYXRlPSZicGxvGxvYWRkdD0mc3Bhc3NwaH
Jhc2U9MTMwMTIxMTU0NjA5

Chapter 5

1 Orders of the Bombay High Court passed on 8 May
2009. Dr Rane visited, along with Phatak. They found
cattle, rag-pickers and insufficient guards to curb
them; and few lights fixed on high masts, most of
which did not work; https://bombayhighcourt.nic.in/
generatenewauth.php?bhcpar=cGFoaDouL3dyaXRlc
mVhZGRhdGEvZGFoYS9vcmlnaW5hW5hbC8yMDA5
LyZmbmFtZT1DTiDTo5QVzI2MDgwODAiMDkucGRm
JnNtZmxhZz1OJnJqdWRkYYXRlPSZicGxvGxvYWRkd
Domc3Bhc3NwaHJhc2U9MTAwMTIxMjIyNDIw.
2 Tatva means 'elements' in Hindi, and 'principled' in
Marathi.
3 Ajay Saxena Committee report on Public Private
Partnerships.

Chapter 6

1 From court orders passed in Tatva's plea for
arbitration in the Bombay High Court, 19 March 2015;
https://bombayhighcourt.nic.in/generatenewauth.
php?bhcpar=cGFoaDouL3dyaXRlcmVhZGRhdGEvZ

GF0YS9qdWRnZW1lbnRzLzIwMTUvJmZuYW1llPU9
TQVJCQVAyMjY4MTMucGRmJnNtZmxhZzıOJ
nJqdWRkYXRlPSZıcGxvYWRkdDoyNC8wMy8yM
DE1JnNwYXNzcGhyYXNlPTEwMDEyMTIzNDYz
OA.

2 From the police charge sheet against Atique and
Rafique Khan, filed in 2016. It includes photographs of
the broken wall at the far end of the township. Next
to it is a signboard saying 'Prohibited Zone'. Atique
told me that his brother's trucks came legitimately,
from the main gate.

3 Atique Khan told me that Rafique's trucks were
contracted by the municipality, brought only as much
debris as permitted and emptied it where asked. The
police charged Rafique with breaking the wall at the
far end and bringing in debris illegally.

4 From court orders passed in Tatva's plea for
arbitration in the Bombay High Court, 19 March 2015.

5 Maharashtra State Assembly proceedings on 3 April
2013.

6 From court orders passed in Tatva's plea for
arbitration in the Bombay High Court, 19 March 2015.

Chapter 7

1 S. K. Goel Committee report submitted in January
2015.

2 Documents showing the meeting at the municipal
commissioner's office showing concerns about the
plant may be found at: http://forestsclearance.nic.in/
DownloadPdfFile.aspx?FileName=0_0_51141237121II
AdminAppA-III.pdf&FilePath=../writereaddata/

Addinfo/. Details on the week-long fires may be found at: https://scroll.in/article/728135/why-are-fires-breaking-out-in-mumbais-garbage-dumping-grounds.

3 Termination of Tatva's contract. While this forms the subject of ongoing arbitration between the municipality and Tatva, it is referred to in several documents, including the Achrekar Committee report to probe the fires, ordered on 1 February 2016 by the municipal commissioner.

4 A study conducted by the non-profit organisation Pratham and the MIT's Poverty Action Lab found that teachers taught according to the curriculum, while students – often first-generation learners – lagged behind. Known as Teaching at the Right Level, or TaRL, it was conducted in Ashra's ward (among others) in Mumbai, and encouraged teachers to take some time teaching at the child's level. The scheme was eventually taken across the country and to several other countries.

Chapter 8

1 From the testimony of Rajan Anant Patil, junior supervisor. MCGM's Achrekar Committee report inquiring into the January 2016 fires.

2 Deepak Ahire in the Achrekar Committee report. Other municipal officers have said 8.30 a.m. The fire department's inquiry report states that it received a call at 12.58 p.m. and reached the grounds at 1.35 p.m.

3 From the inquiry report on the fires in January 2016, conducted by M. N. Dhonde, assistant divisional

fire officer. Report obtained through the Right to Information (RTI) Act. Tatva executives did not respond to several emails seeking comment.

4   Testimony of Deepak Ahire, Achrekar Committee report.

5   AQI measurement from SAFAR, the System for Air Quality and Weather Forecasting and Research.

6   Measured by the Maharashtra Pollution Control Board and quoted in the Lohiya Committee report (submitted on 11 April 2016).

7   Tatva bills from *Hindustan Times*, 11 February 2016.

8   From a story in *Mint* newspaper, 13 August 2019. It stated that Foxconn, the contact manufacturer of Apple phones, would invest $5 billion over five years in a factory that would be a replica of its second-largest plant in China. The plans had languished for years and were officially scrapped in 2020 when Chinese and Indian troops faced off in Ladakh.

Chapter 9

1   *Business Standard*, 14 February 2016.

2   Raj Kumar Sharma's petition, filed in January 2016.

3   RK Studios was named for Raj Kapoor, the actor, director and producer behind it.

4   From court orders passed in February 2016; https://bombayhighcourt.nic.in/generatenewauth.php?bhcpar=cGFoaDouL3dyaXRlcmVhZGRhdGEvZGFoYS9qdWRnZW1lbnRzLzIwMTYvJmZuZW1llPUNDQUkyMjY5NzEzLnBkZiZzbWZsYWc9WSZyananVkZGFoZTozMC8wMy8yMDE2JnVwbG9hZGRoPTEx

LzAzLzIwMTYmc3Bhc3NwaHJhc2U9MTAwMTI
xMjMyNjEw.

5. Court orders say that the new development formed
   only 18.7 per cent of all proposals for construction in
   the city, which was banned, compared to 81.3 per cent
   for the redevelopment of old buildings, which could
   continue (from 1 January 2014 to 30 September 2015).

6 Press Trust of India; the parents of a six-month-
   old baby said he had suffered from breathlessness
   since the fires began in January and died during
   those in March. The AQI was 319, which was 'very
   poor'. Authorities said the baby had had respiratory
   problems since birth.

7 From the statement of Dayanand Naik, junior
   supervisor at the Deonar Dumping Ground in the
   Achrekar Committee report. Others said that only
   four of the forty cameras were installed, and none of
   them worked.

Chapter 10

1 Letter from Tatva to BMC, on the wall at the far end
   of the township being broken.

2 Lohiya Committee report.

3 An inspection by the Pollution Control Board had
   found biomedical was arriving by cycle, in unmarked
   vehicles and only one of its four incinerators working
   as required. It also questioned whether permission for
   the plant should have been given in the middle of the
   packed lanes. The plant was closed for a day before
   compliances were met and it restarted, according to
   documents obtained through RTI.

4　From records kept by Praja, a non-profit organisation that conducts research on urban governance.
5　From the police charge sheet. (Atique Khan told me they gave up on the parking space when officials asked for such high bribes that they could not make a profit any longer.)

Chapter 11

1　Madan Yavalkar, Achrekar Committee report.
2　Bombay High Court orders passed on 1 October 2018. While the case had come up in a special court and then the High Court, these orders explain the police and Khan brothers' accounts of their role on the mountains, and denied bail. The Khans did get bail some months later; https://bombayhighcourt.nic.in/generatenewauth.php?bhcpar=cGFoaDouL3dyaXRlcmVhZGRhdGEvZGF0YS9jcmltltaW5hbC8yMDE4LyZmbmFtZToyQkEzMDIwMTcwMTEwMTgucGRmJnNtZmxhZzI0OJnJqdWRkYXRlPSZicGNGxvY1WRkdDoyMi8xMS8yMDE4JnNwYXNzcGhyYXNlTExMDEyMTE2NTAoNA.
3　I later read that Jehangir had given a statement in the Lohiya Committee report (submitted on 11 April 2016). He concurred with Javed Qureshi's statement, saying that younger pickers consumed drugs in order to keep working. They often burned wire to extract the copper, with the fires sometimes getting out of hand.

Chapter 12

1 From the well-known translation of the Koran by Abdullah Yusuf Ali.

2 In September 2019 the Bombay High Court ruled that city dwellers resettled in the two colonies in the halo of these refineries were to be resettled and paid compensation. The court relied on medical and environmental studies that showed air quality in the area had deteriorated as these refineries and factories around them had multiplied. One study measured benzene at 88.67 Mu/m^3 in these villages, increasing the cancer risk and health problems. An earlier study had shown benzene at the Deonar grounds to be 286 Mu/m^3.

Chapter 13

1 I found Beatrix Pfleiderer's book *Red Thread* (Aakar Books, 1994) helpful in reading on the history, legend and rituals at the shrine of Mira Datar in Gujarat.

2 From Draft Project Report and environmental clearance documents made by Tata Consulting Engineers.

3 From the Tata Consulting Engineers project report on environmental clearance; http://forestsclearance.nic.in/DownloadPdfFile.aspx?FileName=0_0_511412371211 AdminAppA-III.pdf&FilePath=../writereaddata/Addinfo/. A TCE spokesperson did not respond to an emailed questionnaire.

Chapter 14

1 Obtained through an RTI request.

Chapter 15

1 From the Tata Consulting Engineers project report on the waste-to-energy plant.
2 From the municipality's Air Quality Monitoring office, quoted in the project report. Air quality data for after 2015 was obtained through RTI requests.

Chapter 16

1 The account in this chapter was obtained from Farzana's medical treatment papers obtained from Sion Hospital with her consent, the police charge sheet, apart from interviews with family members, pickers, municipal officials, etc. The police charge sheet includes Farzana's medical report, Hashim's statement, and so on.

Chapter 17

1 From the Tata Consulting Engineers project report.

Chapter 18

1 https://indianexpress.com/article/cities/mumbai/deonar-tenders-floated-for-waste-to-energy-project-4365155/.

Chapter 19

1   Municipal commissioner's reports from 1897 show
    that there was a Garlick's incinerator in the city.
    It was sold as scrap when the *cuchra* trains began
    ferrying garbage to Deonar.

2   A randomised control trial by Abhijit Banerjee,
    Cynthia Kinnan, Esther Duflo and others at the MIT
    Poverty Action Lab had shown that micro-finance
    loans helped increase business investment, but
    increased profits only for those that were already the
    most profitable. Conducted in Hyderabad, the study
    found that loan-takers invested in growing their
    businesses, but those that were already profitable
    had grown the most. I too had found that the
    small profits they made were wiped out by sudden
    illnesses, weddings, deaths or village trips. Hyder
    Ali, Moharram Ali and others often stayed in this
    cycle of making small profits and then losing them to
    emergencies.

Chapter 21

1   Draft project report by Tata Consulting Engineers
    for the waste-to-energy plant at Deonar, (July) 2016.
    The accounts of the court proceedings come from
    my own notes. I attended hundreds of hours of court
    proceedings, moving slowly from the back to the
    front to hear. I later read, in Dr Rahela Khorakiwala's
    book *From the Colonial to the Contemporary: Images,
    Iconography, Memories and Performances of Law in
    India's High Courts* (Hart/Bloomsbury 2020), that this

was known as 'Auditory autism'. I later rechecked my notes with others present in the courtroom.

2 From R. K. Sharma's petition to the Bombay High Court.

3 From minutes of the Court Committee on 15 July 2017, obtained through RTI. Police officials said the mangroves formed a barrier for pickers to enter and regulations did not allow construction along the coast.

4 From inspection of Deonar garbage-arrival documents by R. K. Sharma's legal team and recorded in Justice Oka's orders.

5 Report by the All India Institute for Local Self-Government, presented in court.

6 Report by NEERI, part of a project report for the waste-to-energy plant at Deonar, May 2016.

7 Chore Committee report, in *Indian Express*, 12 July 2017.

8 Lohiya Committee report.

Chapter 22

1 William Bryant Logan, 'The Lessons of a Hideous Forest', *New York Times*, 20 July 2019.

Chapter 23

1 Bombay High Court orders passed on 24 August 2017.

2 Supreme Court orders passed on 4 September 2017.

3 https://en.wikipedia.org/wiki/2017_Koshe_landslide.

4 In their opening essay in *Muslims in Indian Cities: Trajectories of Marginalisation* (HarperCollins, 2012),

Laurent Gayer and Christophe Jaffrelot quote
National Sample Survey data showing that Muslims'
average monthly expenditure was just Rs 800,
equal only to that of Dalits and Adivasis. Dalits and
Muslims make up nearly all those who lived around
the mountains. Upper-caste Hindus spent Rs 1,469.
The data is from 2004–5.

Chapter 24

1 Orders passed in the Supreme Court on 15 March
2018.
2 From minutes of the Court Committee.
3 From Rahela Khorakiwala's *From the Colonial to the
Contemporary*. The case for finding new space to
build a High Court building was reported in the
newspapers.
4 High Court orders said the Debt Recovery Tribunal
was to be given appropriate space to work.
5 On 10 July 2019 the Supreme Court had passed an
order saying that 'mountains of garbage' nearly buried
the city and the civic administration needed to fix the
situation.
6 Talk to law students at the National Academy for
Legal Studies and Research, 6 July 2020.

Chapter 25

1 Special court proceedings, news reports and charge
sheet against Jehangir.

Postscript

1   Bombay High Court Archives; https://
    bombayhighcourt.nic.in/libweb/historicalcases/
    cases/1908%2810%29BLR848.pdf.

2   Judgement of first sedition trial in Bombay High
    Court; https://bombayhighcourt.nic.in/libweb/
    historicalcases/cases/ILR1898%2822%29BOM112.pdf.

3   Bombay High Court order, 9 April 2019; https://
    bombayhighcourt.nic.in/generatenewauth.php?bhc
    par=cGFoaDouL3dyaXRlcmVhZGRhdGEvZGFoY
    S9jaXZpbC8yMDE5LyZmbmFtZT1DQUkyMjY5NzE
    zMDkwNDE5LnBkZiZzbWZsYWc9TiZyanVkZGF
    oZTomdXBsb2FkZHQ9MDcvMDUvMjAxOSZzcG
    Fzc3BocmFzZT0xMDAxMjEyMzI2MTA=.

4   Orders passed by the Bombay High Court on 12
    December 2019 by Justices S. C. Dharmadhikari and
    R.I. Chagla, available on the court website.

5   *Times of India*, 5 November 2020; https://timesofindia.
    indiatimes.com/city/mumbai/mumbai-bmc-panel-
    greenlights-rs-1100-crore-deonar-waste-to-energy-
    plant-plan/articleshow/79053083.cms.

Acknowledgements

Mountain Tales could only be written because the residents of Banjara Galli welcomed me into their homes and lives. I remember returning there early in 2016, not offering loans, but simply to hear more about them. *Bolne se samajh mein nahi aayega, hum kaise jiye khaadi par,* Salma Shaikh had told me. *Speaking won't help people understand how we made our lives on the mountains. Video camera le ke aao. Bring a video camera.* She and others went on to walk me through the mountains, take me into their homes, the clinics they visited, the schools their children attended, their embroidery workshops and their *kata* shops, bringing alive their memories, their scrapes and their festering aches.

I am thankful to all those who chose to be written about. Other people, who barely featured or did not choose to, helped out too, including Shabbir Pathan, Miya Khan, Lilabai Pawar, Shakila Shaikh, Shiva Shaikh, Rauf Shaikh, Akhtar Hussain Mullah, Hussain Shaikh and countless others.

Geeta Anand read and shaped *Mountain Tales* every fortnight, even when it felt like a stormy, shapeless cloud that I was stuck in. Soon after moving to Berkeley, she told me it was Farzana who glowed through my messy drafts. Remotely she mediated between us, so that Farzana could say the things she could not bear to, and I could ask about them, hear them and write about them. For helping channel Farzana's story through my hands, and for her friendship, it will probably take me the Deonar townships' more than hundred-year-long lifetime to thank her.

My thanks to Taran Khan for walking me nearly every day through my failings and stumblings, in the face of a story that was inextricably stuck within me and had to be told. Manu Joseph kept showing me the light – at the end of writing tangles, apparent publishing dead-ends and mangled Mumbai metaphors. *Mountain Tales*'s hardest passes were traversed with Taran and Manu's unwavering support.

Cecily Gayford took this project and elevated my mind, and my writing, in ways I often wished were my own. Right from the start she saw that *Mountain Tales* was about Farzana, but also about a lot more. *Mountain Tales* is elevated and illuminated by her thoughtfulness, grace and polish.

Sophie Scard, my literary agent, kept guiding this project calmly through a worsening market. To her, Alison Lewis and Georgina Le Grice, my thanks for taking life in the trash-made homes of Banjara Galli to distant parts of the world, where castaway aspirations made other mountains and lives. I hope their work will help augment the project to shrink desire and its dark trail.

R. K. Sharma was often my intrepid co-traveller in the world of Deonar and waste. We frequently walked the mountains, visited waste plants, sat through court proceedings and drank endless glasses of tea while ruminating about the fate of the mountains. For sharing my obsession, I offer my immense gratitude to him. And I had turned to Dayanand Stalin when I figured that I needed data and documents to see the mountains, through their fog. For years Stalin helped me navigate the Right to Information application process, through which I collected thousands of pages of documents that brought alive the world of the mountains.

Around the Deonar mountains, Dr Khalid Shaikh and Dr Vikas Oswal, who run Vikas Nursing Home, provided research, context, contacts and support in innumerable ways through my reporting for this book.

K. P. Raghuvanshi and Rahul Asthana, both of whom had chaired the High Court committee on Deonar, provided their insights.

Jairaj Phatak, Ajit Kumar Jain, Bhalchandra Patil, Rajiv Jalota, M. R. Shah, Amiya Sahu and more than a dozen other retired and serving municipal officials who decided to remain unnamed provided context and detail on life at the mountains, on the challenges in managing them and giving them a new life. While the information came from them, the analysis was my own. Chandan Singh processed hundreds of RTI requests regarding the mountains with alacrity, patience and cheerfulness.

Jennifer Spencer and her team at Praja provided health and education data for the ward around the mountains, which gave much-needed context to the lack of development in the area. Jockin Arputham, who passed away during the writing of this book, not only held Vandana Foundation in his arms, but also provided great anecdotes on how the slums around the mountains were settled, demolished and resettled. His mentoring and stories are sorely missed. Rukhsana Shaikh, the area's corporator, helped provide assiduously collected research and insight on the biomedical waste plant, as well as on Deonar.

Vighnesh Kamath, from R. K. Sharma's legal team, provided documents and backed up my memories and notes from hundreds of hours of court proceedings. Rohit De and Rahela Khorakiwala helped me make sense of the court through their brilliant books and conversation.

Although Sukriti Issar had left Oxford to join the Sciences Po faculty by then, she supported my research at the Bodleian Library, helping me trace back the Deonar townships' history from 1927 – the officially quoted date – to records in 1899. Nilesh Wadnerkar at the Maharashtra State Assembly Library brought out proceedings and newspaper articles on Deonar.

Sarfaraz Arfu, editor of *Daily Hindustan* and a lyrical Mumbai watcher, read the manuscript and provided feedback. Dr A. D. Sawant patiently deconstructed the mountains' toxic halo and its impact on health. Anjali Bansal, Devina Parekh, Tanvi Kant, Shivaji Nimhan, Abdul Rauf Shaikh, Birju Mundada, Kishore Gayke and Prafulla Marpakwar provided invaluable help with research, while Kanika Sharma and Abhijeet Rane helped with legal processes.

The frail Sachin Tambe, who had collected loan instalments, kept walking with me through the skinny lanes around the mountains, helping me trace the pickers, their shifting homes and crumbling lives. Prashant Shinde at Vandana Foundation helped with sending, tracking and collecting my endless applications for documents.

Biaas Sanyal assisted with fact-checking my seemingly unending research. Ashlesha Athavale went through the Marathi documents. Both helped iron out my flaws.

Writing residencies helped transform all the interviews and research material that I had collected over the years into re-creating the world of the Deonar township on page. Two Logan Nonfiction fellowships helped me begin, and then nearly complete, *Mountain Tales*. Pilar Pilacia and her team at the Rockefeller Foundation's Bellagio Center provided the warmest cocoon for writing, along with brilliant company and views that were as far from Deonar as possible. Blue Mountain Center gave me a quietness and calm that I had almost never experienced as a Mumbaikar, allowing the world of Deonar to appear in slow motion in my mind and letting me capture it. I began writing this book at Sangam House. Notebooks emptied on to the computer, to the beat of Nrityagram's dancers, never letting me stop. My thanks also to Dora Maar House, where I was supposed to be when the pandemic hit and lockdowns shut travel opportunities, and I hope to work there later. Just as this book came from me being filled with the world of the Deonar township, it probably could not have been articulated without the distance of those residencies, for which I am deeply thankful.

Residencies also provided the precious company of writers who had written books more achingly beautiful than mine. Lisa Ko and Kiran Desai talked me through their experiences over long walks in Bellagio and Blue Mountain; canoeing and ferry rides; long meals and frantic emails. Suzannah Lessard, Adrian LeBlanc and Suzy Hansen provided invaluable advice on finding my voice in the first person, when all I wanted was to turn invisible. Risa Lavizzo Mourey helped me make sense of Farzana's dire medical records, even as I saw her heal, as did Parina Samra Bajaj. Abby Seiff, Melanie Smith and Justin Kaguto Go provided long-distance advice on writing, art, cities and looking at things a bit differently.

Marco Armiero at KTH, Stockholm, provided insights, anecdotes and learnings about the Italian waste crisis. Rajesh Parameswaran and Markley Boyer were my companions through the world of New York's landfills, its waste and even the art that emerged from it.

I am thankful also to Mandy Greenfield, Graeme Hall and the team at Profile for their careful editing, never letting me feel they were far from Mumbai. Shwetashree Majumdar generously helped to keep me out of scrapes.

Most of all, I would like to thank my parents and sister. My father ran the Foundation with me, while my mother and sister supported us – nudging me every day to feel our borrowers' troubles better. Throughout the writing of this book their love inflated me during my failings and deflations, squeezed out my inadequacies and poured out on to my computer when I stared, completely stuck.